MW01255123

Children of the Book

ALSO BY ILANA KURSHAN

If All the Seas Were Ink

Children of the Book

A Memoir of Reading Together

Ilana Kurshan

St. Martin's Press New York

First published in the United States by St. Martin's Press, an imprint of
St. Martin's Publishing Group

www.stmartins.com

Design by Meryl Sussman Levavi

The Library of Congress Cataloging-in-Publication Data is available
upon request.

ISBN 978-1-250-28826-4 (hardcover)
ISBN 978-1-250-28827-1 (ebook)

Our books may be purchased in bulk for promotional, educational, or
business use. Please contact your local bookseller or the Macmillan Corporate
and Premium Sales Department at 1-800-221-7945, extension 5442, or by
email at MacmillanSpecialMarkets@macmillan.com.

First Edition: 2025

1   3   5   7   9   10   8   6   4   2

CONTENTS

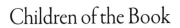

Children of the Book

INTRODUCTION

Paradise Lost

IT IS A RAINY AFTERNOON. IT'S TOO WET TO PLAY outside, but unlike the mother in *The Cat in the Hat*, I can't leave my children alone at home to stare out the window. Instead, they climb all over me as I sit on the floor of the living room, leaning against the bookshelves that line the wall from floor to ceiling. We keep all the heavy books on the bottom— *The Riverside Shakespeare*, the collected Tennyson, the leather-bound set of Bible commentaries. Now these books are strewn on the floor before me, a reminder of all I want to read and reread, and of the fear that now I never will.

My children are young. My son is three; his twin sisters are a year and a half. Over the next five years we will have two more children, and it will be a very long time before they'll be able to read any of the books my son is pulling off the shelf. Now he is reaching for an annotated edition of *Paradise Lost*—annotated by the volume's editors, but also by my own penciled scribbles from two decades earlier. I try to remember the person I was when I wrote those marginal notes, sitting uninterrupted in a university library with my forehead resting on my hand and a pencil between my teeth, oblivious to my surroundings. "The mind is its own place," Satan tells one of the other fallen angels in the opening pages of *Paradise Lost*. I wasn't really in the university library, but amid the rustling leaves of the garden where birds sang on every bough and dawn advanced with rosy steps, painting the sky.

Yet even this brief moment of paradise recollected comes at a cost, because somehow, I've missed that my son has dropped a volume of Bible commentary onto the toe of his sister, and she is in tears. The Bible and its commentaries are sacred books, and in Jewish tradition we do not put sacred books on the floor. I reach for it—it is the first volume, Genesis. I know how this book begins, of course—with the primordial chaos that preceded creation, with the earth still unformed and void. I know that the world will be created with the separation of light from darkness in the very first verses. But I cannot even open the book, because right now—in this moment, on this day, in this life—I cannot see beyond the chaos.

I retrieve the Bible commentary and set it gently back on the shelf, but the situation has deteriorated and now two children are crying. I look around. Where is the Cat in the Hat when I need him? I scan the bookcase, where he's been all along, of course, on a shelf I can reach without dislodging my children. "The sun did not shine, it was too wet to play," I begin reading in a low voice. The trick works. The kids settle down to listen.

As I read, I inhabit more than one role. I am the two children peering out the window forlornly with nothing to do. I am the Cat who arrives to entertain them, wreaking havoc on the home but then cleaning up my mess, leaving the children to sit there calmly as if nothing has happened. And I am also the mother walking up the driveway, happy to be back with my children in a house now so calm and quiet that we can hear the patter of the rain on the roof.

⚜

Before I became a mother, I was a reader. I carried a book around with me everywhere I went, often reading while walking. Generally, I didn't look around much. In high school, I once walked headlong into a brawl between two football players in the hallway; no one meant to hurt me, but somehow I got slammed into a row of lockers and my nose, bent out of shape, bled profusely.

My parents indulged my obsession, for better or worse. I remember a particular family vacation when I was in junior high school because of the worn L. M. Montgomery paperbacks I stuffed into my beach bag—by then I had finished the Anne of Green Gables series and was on to my next Canadian orphan, *Emily of New Moon*. The road signs said we were in Sanibel Island, Florida, but I rarely looked up from my book long enough to notice them; my mind was its own place, and I think of that trip as our family vacation to Prince Edward Island.

As a child, I did not enjoy activities that were incompatible with reading. I read while braiding my hair in the mornings, while eating lunch in the school cafeteria, and while sprawled on the floor of my room after returning home from my after-school job—at the library, of course. One afternoon in the windowless basement room of the library, where I was supposed to be sorting through recently donated books, I got caught reading a paperback copy of A. S. Byatt's *Possession*, a novel that begins in a library reading room. My boss invited me for a little talk in her office. She let me keep my job, but not the book.

Another afternoon, angry at my parents for insisting that I stop reading and help clean the house for Passover, I ran away from home—with *Huckleberry Finn*—and lost track of time, hiding in the bushes of our local synagogue until my panicked parents found me, just as the sun was sinking too low in the sky for me to find out whether Huck would turn Jim in after all.

My family spent every Saturday morning in synagogue. In our suburban American congregation, we sat in pews with a narrow shelf in front of each seat for storing a prayer book and a Bible. At some point in the service I would retreat to my father's office—he was the rabbi of our synagogue—and pull a volume off the bookcases that lined the walls. My father didn't keep any novels on his shelves, so instead I read about Jewish spirituality, the Jewish way in death and mourning, and why bad things happen to good people, pushing back his chair to huddle in the cavernous space beneath his large oak desk. My mother always knew where to find me when the service was over.

After synagogue on Saturdays, we would sit down to lunch together and speak about the section from the Torah—the Five Books of Moses—that had been chanted that morning. My parents had a vast library of both Jewish and secular books, and at bedtime they read them to us indiscriminately—*The Passover Parrot*, *The Steadfast Tin Soldier*, tales from the shtetl in Chelm. And yet my siblings and I knew that some texts were different from others, because they were sacred. If a prayer book or a volume of the Bible fell to the floor, we kissed it as we picked it up. The doorway to each room of our house was affixed with a mezuzah, its parchment scroll containing the same Hebrew words from the Bible that we recited each night before we fell asleep, and when we woke in the morning.

When I grew older and left my parents' home, I sought out professional environments where I would fit in as a reader and lover of texts. My employers included a publishing house, a literary agency, a Jewish feminist magazine, and a yeshiva for training rabbis. Though my roles shifted over the years, my work always involved books. Throughout the first two and a half decades of my life, I thought about time in terms of pages read. I savored my hours alone like a religious devotee, reading late into the night by a bedside lamp and falling asleep with my glasses still on.

How then would I ever share my life with another person? Clearly it would have to be someone who wanted to live inside books with me—to make my story his story, and his mine. But it took time and maturity, and it took getting it wrong. In my early twenties I moved to Israel following the collapse of a marriage as brief as the parenthetical (picnic, lightning) with which Nabokov does away with Humbert Humbert's mother in *Lolita*. I met Daniel a few long and solitary years later when he moved to Israel on a fellowship to complete his PhD in comparative literature. Although Daniel is also American, we wanted to make our home in Jerusalem because here we were surrounded by people who shared our values, including a passion for texts both sacred and secular. Jerusalem, we knew, was where we wanted to unpack our books.

When Daniel and I got married, we merged our libraries and our lives, reading novels aloud to each other and studying Jewish texts together. We worked side by side in our spare bedroom and ate dinner when we'd finished the chapter, even if that meant the food got cold. It was art and ardor, love's labor not lost—time together did not mean less time reading but more time reading together. And then everything changed.

When our eldest, Matan, was born, I was in the middle of a chapter. I was reading Shirley Jackson's *Life Among the Savages*—the savages of the title are Jackson's children, whom she raises in a house full of books. When Jackson ought to be rushing to the hospital to give birth, she is instead reading a mystery novel; when she arrives in the maternity ward, she quotes Shakespeare to the obstetrician. Birthing my child was an awe-inspiring religious experience, in which I felt closer to God as Creator than I ever had before. Yet this awareness did not stop me from reading between contractions. I gave birth on the same page as Shirley Jackson, and I finished the chapter during my earliest hours as a mother. Now, a decade later, it often seems as if I am still working through that same chapter—about reading and mothering and the connection between the two.

❧

As a parent, I continue to read to myself at every opportunity, but I am no longer the one who decides when to put the book down. Moreover, if I am reading, there is always something or someone I am neglecting. The first time I ever gave up on a novel was after Matan was born; finally, I felt brazen enough—or perhaps just busy enough—to pronounce a book unworthy of my time.

I never appreciated time as much as when my babies were napping, especially when I had newborn twins, who rarely slept at the same time. If they were both calm and settled at once, it was like a total eclipse of the sun, an eerie, otherworldly stillness in which I tiptoed around the house, too terrified of waking them to do anything at all.

In those early days with the twins, I divided activities into three categories: tasks that required two hands (cooking, cleaning, writing), tasks that required one hand (reading, texting), and tasks that could be done with no hands at all (dreaming, despairing, plotting my own escape). I knew that when the babies were sleeping, I should attend to my two-handed tasks, but more often I read through their naps. When they awoke and I brought them to the couch, I continued to read—holding one baby in my arm and rocking the other with my foot on her swing.

As my children got older, they began to need me present in mind as well as body. They counted on me to watch, to soothe, to listen, to advise. There was no way I could do any of this while reading a book. What had happened? How had I signed on for a full-time job that prevented me from doing what I had always loved most?

🦋

One afternoon when my children were still very young, a friend came over to borrow a book. She was also a mother, but her children were in high school, and she looked at the books strewn across our living room table and nodded approvingly. "You know, the best way to raise your kids to become readers," she told me, "is for them to see how you read to yourself all the time." I looked at her in dismay. I found it extraordinarily difficult to read when my children were underfoot. I hoped my friend was wrong.

Even today, when my oldest son is ten, my twin daughters are eight, my next daughter is five, and my youngest son is turning three, I can rarely read to myself when they are around. And so I read to my children instead. In the middle of our kitchen table sits a *shtender*, a wooden stand more commonly used to support volumes of the Talmud and other heavy religious tomes. Ours features a decorative calligraphic aphorism from the ancient rabbis: "Do not say: When I have time, I will study; lest you never have time." When I bought this *shtender* nearly two decades ago, I had far more time to study than I do now, but I have repurposed it as a stand for the picture books we read at the table, including several food-related favorites: *The Watermelon Seed*, a minimalist masterwork in pink, green, and black, in which the alligator protagonist panics when he swallows a seed; and *Spoon*, in which the eponymous utensil wrestles with a sense of worthlessness and low self-esteem. Perhaps someday we will manage to eat together as a family, but at this stage of life, mealtime is when they eat and I read, turning the pages with one hand and spoon-feeding the toddler with the other.

Bedtime is arguably the most popular time for parents to read aloud—there is no frigate like a book to row a child out into the deep sea of sleep and dreams. But in our family we read all day, in every imaginable context. While I am walking the kids to school, I recite to them from the books I've committed to memory. Many of these memorized books are accompanied by tunes I've made up, a tune that fits the rhythm and matches the mood of the book. Sometimes the kids join in, belting out nonsense verse from Dr. Seuss's *One Fish, Two Fish, Red Fish, Blue Fish* as we cross the busy road, the drivers inching up to the crosswalk and eyeing us oddly: "We saw some sheep / take a walk in their sleep."

When we have time in the day for more complicated narratives—while waiting our turn at the doctor's office or sprawled on a blanket in the park—I read the kids longer picture books. Together we run away from the hat shop with *Otto: The Story of a Mirror*, share an ice cream cone with Frog and Toad, and follow the robin to *The Secret Garden*. The room in which we are reading becomes a wardrobe leading to an enchanted Narnia where we watch the snow descend by the lamppost in the wood.

Our favorite books become a private language of allusions. My children love the Miss Nelson series, about a teacher who dresses up like a mean substitute named Viola Swamp to bring her mischievous students back into line. Whenever there is a knock on the classroom door, the students bristle, worried that it might be "the Swamp" again. "Slowly the knob turned," we are told each time the suspense mounts, until it becomes an ominous refrain. One evening when we were eating dinner, we heard a knock on the front door. We were all home, and we weren't expecting anyone. "Slowly the knob turned," my toddler son piped up without missing a beat, and the rest of us burst out laughing. I'm not even sure he knew what those words meant, but he understood enough about the book to recognize that they were appropriate—and funny—in this context.

The books we read expand my children's range of associations and broaden their imaginations, but they also make it easier to parent. When we are waiting by the pool during my daughter's swim lesson and my son bursts into tears because he wants to go in the water fully clothed, I sit him down on my lap on a plastic chair and distract him with the incantatory refrain of *Hello Lighthouse*; together we watch the waves crash against the shore as the sailors are rowed to safety. When my daughter is trembling with fear before her first real haircut, I'm relieved I can soothe her with the jaunty cadences of *Ella Kazoo Will Not Brush Her Hair*. I would accomplish so much less if I did not have a ready supply of children's books to amuse, distract, and calm my children as we go about our day. Oh, the places we wouldn't go!

Reading with my children has taken us far, and it has also brought us close. I look forward all day to snuggling with my children, reading together beside a small bedside lamp. My five-year-old daughter has already figured out that she can stay up later if she engages me in conversation as we are reading stories at bedtime, and so every page becomes a springboard for her own musings. One night we are reading about a girl who is teased by her classmates for wearing the same faded blue dress every day even though she has a hundred dresses at home, she claims, all lined up in her closet. Shalvi interrupts my reading to tell me that two girls in her class made fun of her that morning because she wore the same skirt two days in a row, and she was so embarrassed. It is clear that she wanted to tell me about this incident, but if not for *The Hundred Dresses*, she might never have. The more we read together, the more I come to know my children. And the better I am at reading them.

⚜

Even after I began carrying around books for my children, I never stopped bringing a book for myself. But to my dismay, I was rarely able to read more than a paragraph at a time. It took me so much longer to get through each novel that I found myself growing tired of the characters before I had finished their stories. At some point I realized that it made more sense to bring a small paperback copy of the Five Books of Moses, and to use the little time I had to prepare the biblical verses I would be chanting in synagogue that week.

Jews read from the Torah regularly as part of the synagogue service. One person who has prepared in advance serves as the reader, standing before a table in front of the congregation and chanting aloud the verses written on the parchment scroll. The words of the scroll appear without punctuation, vocalization, or musical notation, and so the reader has to be thoroughly familiar with that particular section of the text before chanting it publicly.

I have been reading from the Torah for as long as I can remember. Each week I spend several hours going over the verses until I can chant them nearly from memory; in so doing, the words become inscribed on my heart, which is indeed an explicit biblical injunction. As God tells Moses, "These words which I command you today shall be on your hearts" (Deuteronomy 6:6). The words of the Torah I chant weave their way into my thoughts and into my speech; I speak of them when I am at home and away from home, when I rise up and lie down.

When I chant from the Torah in synagogue, it is in accordance with a fixed schedule of weekly portions that Jews all over the world follow, proceeding in synchrony by a few chapters each week. In the fall, at the start of the Jewish new year, we read about the world created in Genesis and nearly destroyed by flood. As the autumn chill sets in and the nights grow longer, we follow the patriarchs and matriarchs, who look up at the stars and journey through the desert assured by the divine promise of numerous descendants. In the coldest and darkest days of the year, we read of Joseph's descent into the pit, cast down by his jealous brothers, only to rise to prominence in Egypt as the winter days begin to grow longer and more hopeful. Wells and wombs give way to power and persuasion, and sometime around the start of the secular new year, we come to Exodus, completing the narrative of the Israelites' deliverance from Egyptian bondage in advance of Passover.

Around the beginning of springtime, with the shift from Exodus to Leviticus, redemption gives way to ritual. We immerse ourselves in the details of sacrificial worship, reading of sin and purification as the first flowers break through the softening soil. Just when it starts to get warmer after Passover, we trek with the Israelites through the desert, and then, when it's too hot to move forward anymore, we stop to hear Moses recount it all over again in Deuteronomy during the dog days of summer. No sooner do we finish reading the Torah than we start all over, scrolling back to Genesis and reading from beginning to end each year anew.

The beginning of each year's Torah reading cycle coincides with the start of the school year, and all of my children's first experiences with learning to read and write were bound up in the weekly Torah readings. In preschool, their teachers taught them to form the letters of the alphabet by instructing each child to copy the name of the weekly Torah portion off the class whiteboard onto a piece of paper, and then illustrate the page based on the stories they had heard. In elementary school, when they began learning how to read, they came home every Friday with "parashah sheets" summarizing the weekly Torah portion. In first grade there were only a few sentences on each weekly page, but from year to year, the parashah sheets grew increasingly complex, including more and more biblical commentaries in smaller and smaller print, with less white space on the page. The children's job was to read the sheets out loud to us; our job was to listen, sign the page, and encourage them to read more.

The words of the Torah were the first words my children were taught to shape and recognize, and the first words they read to themselves. Sitting in synagogue each week, they learned to listen for the names of the biblical characters and identify them on the printed page. Then they began following along as the Torah was chanted, taking note of the cycle of readings. As they came to appreciate, we return to the same passages of Torah year after year, such that we are always in the middle of reading from the sacred scroll. Everything else we read—from *Goodnight Moon* to *The Moon by Night*—takes place in the context of that ancient story.

⚜

The Torah, like all great books, can be read at any age. The text speaks to us wherever we are in our lives. When Jews read the Torah year after year, we trust that each time, we will find new meaning. One year I am focused on Rebecca's pregnancy because I, too, am pregnant with twins. Another year I am struck by the image of Pharaoh hardening his heart when my son slams his door in anger and refuses to let me in. If the text seems different with each rereading, it is because I—the reader—have changed.

The notion that every new encounter with the text has the potential to elicit new sympathies and yield new insights underlies the entire enterprise of Jewish textual commentary. Each generation's commentary informs the next generation's reading of the text, such that all reading is cumulative: The Talmud and midrash quote from the Bible; the medieval commentators reference the Talmud, the midrash, and the Bible; the modern commentators invoke all those who came before. Each new work engages, whether consciously or unconsciously, with its predecessors, and so even when we move on to later texts, we never stop reading earlier ones.

Children like to hear the same books again and again. There is comfort in the familiar ending, in already knowing that *Brave Irene* will succeed in delivering the dress to the duchess, and *Mike Mulligan and His Steam Shovel* will dig out the cellar in time. No sooner have we turned the last page than my children ask me to start over. Once they move on to longer books, I continue to reread, because I have five children, and each child reads many of the same books that his or her older siblings read with me just a couple of years earlier. And yet each time, the experience is different. Each child pays attention to different details and asks different questions, offering a window into what they are thinking and feeling at that particular moment in time.

Parenting reminds me regularly that it is not just texts but also people who are sources of meaning and insight. But we have to know how to pay careful attention, and the study of Torah provides, perhaps surprisingly, a compelling model. Jews have traditionally read the Torah very closely. The enterprise of midrash—the rabbinic commentary on the Torah—is grounded in a belief that each phrase and each word in the Torah is significant and deserving of our attention. Like the verses of Torah that give rise to new insight no matter how many times we read them over again, my children, too, are infinitely rich texts. Perhaps both reading and mothering can be, each in its own way, an act of sacred devotion.

✣

When I read to my children aloud, it is primarily in English—the language we speak at home, and the language they speak to one another. Hebrew is a sacred language—the language of the Bible, the language in which we read from the Torah in synagogue, and the language in which we recite all our prayers. It is also the language my children are taught to read in school, and the language they use to communicate with their friends in the classroom and the playground. They absorb Hebrew effortlessly. But their reading in English is dependent—for the most part—on the books we share with them.

Many of the books I read with my kids are books I first encountered long ago, when I was their age. To some extent this is circumstantial; our local public library does not have a large budget for acquiring new books in English. But even when I stumble upon newer titles, I generally gravitate toward the books that instilled a love of literature in me.

Rereading books from my own childhood with my children has taught me that even though the books are the same, I am not. *A Wrinkle in Time* is not just about children in search of their missing father but also about a mother managing her family on her own and protecting her children from her concerns about her husband's welfare. The Ramona books are not just about growing up; they are also about women's liberation. Reading from the perspective of a parent, I have different questions and different allegiances.

Life so rarely affords us the opportunity for second chances. We live just once, unable to turn back the carousel of time. Toddlerhood is over. Childhood is over. I'll never be a teenager again, and thank goodness for that. Now in my forties, I've been cycling through all those life stages anew. The story of my life has become not just the story of the books I am reading but also the story of the books I read with my children, and reencounter through their eyes.

✳

When I read Torah with my children, it is different from reading any other book, because we are the characters in the drama. It is not just the children of Israel who experienced the Exodus, but we—their descendants—who see ourselves as if we went out of Egypt, as we are commanded to remember each Passover. It is not just the Israelites who received the Torah at Sinai but we—their descendants—who are heirs to that sacred text. The Torah is the story of our people's history, but it is a way of telling our story, too.

In this memoir I tell the story of my family's reading life through the lens of the Torah. Each part of this book corresponds to one of the Five Books of Moses. In the first part, on

Genesis, I write about the beginnings of our children's lives as readers. The second part, on Exodus, is about the journey toward the liberating experience of independent reading. The third part, on Leviticus, centers on the Tabernacle—the portable sanctuary constructed by the Israelites in the wilderness—as a metaphor for the library, which is also a sacred shrine of sorts. The biblical book of Numbers tells the story of the Israelites' wandering through the wilderness; in the fourth part I chronicle how our family navigated the wilderness of the Covid pandemic by reading aloud as we wandered along our own uncharted path. The fifth part, on Deuteronomy—the book in which Moses gives the people of Israel his own account of the past forty years—explores the challenges of autobiography, and the ways we tell and retell our own stories.

Each year, as we read through the Torah, I am aware of different parallels between the experience of reading with my children and the Torah's narratives and themes. Over time, and over a decade of Torah reading cycles, the way I connect with my children through literature has changed. In this memoir, I chart those shifts as they echo the progression of the biblical narrative—from the first picture books that create my infant's world through language, to the moment my children begin reading on their own and leaving me behind, atop the mountain, as they enter new lands.

In writing about my family, I have been deliberately selective. My children appear not as fully fleshed-out characters but as readers. I seek to tell stories from their reading lives while also protecting their privacy. My husband, though he plays only a peripheral role in these pages, plays a key role in the day-to-day functioning of our family. Daniel shares my dedication to Torah and has made a career out of teaching and writing about literary texts. No doubt his account of our family's reading life would be different, and would ring equally true.

The story of our family is, in large part, the story of the books we have read. It is a story that takes us from our kitchen table to the park to the secret garden beyond, from Coney Island to Klickitat Street, from Narnia to Neverland to Eden and the Promised Land. Together we have traveled by tesseract, by phantom tollbooth, by Terabithia bridge, and by eagles' wings. These journeys have taken us to worlds beyond, but also to worlds within. In sharing books with my children, I have gained intimate access to the breadth of their imagination and the depths of their understanding. Reading together has taught me to draw out their stories, and—in the pages that follow—to share my own.

GENESIS

Sunset at the Dawn of Time

IN THE BEGINNING, GOD CREATED THE WORLD THROUGH words, speaking each aspect of creation into being. Last of all God created human beings, both male and female, and placed them in the Garden of Eden for a short while, until it was time for them to move on. After nearly destroying the world in a flood and then thwarting humanity's efforts to build a tower to the sky, God established a relationship with one family line—Abraham and his descendants—whose stories of intergenerational conflict, sibling rivalry, and reconciliation inform and shape our own family dynamics. When I began reading to my children in infancy, I was creating their world through words, summoning objects into being by speaking their names and pointing to them on the page. But like Adam and Eve's brief sojourn in the Garden, the simple joy of "board books" proved all too transient, giving way to more complex picture books about parents, children, and siblings who didn't always get along but whose stories provided us with a way of relating to one another. During the early years of my children's lives, I learned to think of reading less as a way to avoid the messiness of life and more as a way of imposing some semblance of order on the chaos—which is how the book of Genesis begins.

1

⁊ℰ

Trailing Clouds of Glory

THE MOMENT MY OLDEST CHILD WAS BORN, I BEGAN
reading to him from an anthology of Romantic poetry that
I have owned for decades. No sooner was the red, squirming
newborn placed on my chest than I reached for the worn paperback copy and opened to the first dog-eared page: "Sweet joy
befall thee," I read through tears of joy and gratitude, bestow-
ing a blessing with Blake. I had not planned to read this poem
aloud. I had brought the book to the hospital for myself, along
with Shirley Jackson's memoir and a pile of well-worn novels,
because I'd imagined that I would want to be surrounded by favorite writers during a moment of such magnitude. But as soon
as the baby was placed in my arms, I was overcome by the desire
to share my love of literature with him, and so it seemed only
natural to begin reading aloud.

I had read to myself more or less continuously since I was
a child, with a few breaks here and there for dinner, or math
class, or college graduation. I couldn't imagine why anything
should change now that I'd become a parent. Even so, it felt
rude to keep my eyes in my book when there was a baby in my
arms who, I had been told, was born with the capacity to see
only as far as his mother's face—*my* face. Surely I ought to pay

him some attention? I resolved that I would keep reading aloud instead of reading quietly to myself. Now that I was a mother, reading would be the place I'd escape to with my child, drawing him into the text alongside me.

I continued to read aloud to my son throughout the three days I spent in the maternity ward, much to the dismay of the other new mother sharing my hospital room. There were constant interruptions, and so it was hard to get through a chapter, let alone an entire novel. During the busy hours of the day, I read poetry, where each stanza—and sometimes even each line break—was an occasion to pause. Lying on my back with my head propped up by a thin hospital pillow, I read Coleridge's "To an Infant" and Wordsworth's "Ode: Intimations of Immortality," leading my soon-to-be-named Matan through meadow, grove, and stream and witnessing through his fluttering eyelids a landscape still appareled in celestial light. "Trailing clouds of glory do we come, from God who is our home: Heaven lies about us in our infancy!" While my son slumbered peacefully in my arms, I filled the interspersed vacancies with these lines, as if all the nursing and diapering and soothing were secondary to this literary ministry.

A few weeks later, when a friend visited me at home and asked me which board books I owned, it occurred to me that I ought to read Matan books with pictures he could see and pages he could touch and chew. It was my first experience of maternal guilt: Why had I assumed that Matan was also interested in a novel about a reclusive translator stumbling upon dead bodies in the frozen Polish woods? Since when do newborns care about the Nobel Prize in literature?

Thanks to gifts from friends and family members, we already owned several board books. I'd read that infants could see only black and white during their early months of life, which presumably explains why we'd received a very simple board book with no words except the title, *Black and White*. The book unfolds like an accordion: One side has a series of white objects depicted against a black background, and the other side has a series of black objects depicted against a white background. I took a deep breath, as if warning Matan that what he was about to hear would sound very different from Blake, or Coleridge, or even Olga Tokarczuk. I pointed to each object and made up a tune that I sang as I "read" the book aloud—bottle and book and boat and car; rattle and truck and cup and dog. Read that way, it was almost like poetry.

The first board books I read to Matan had very few words. In this sense, too, they resembled poetry. Unlike prose, poetry is printed with relatively few words of text per square inch of paper, so that every black word has ample white air to breathe. In a Torah scroll, which even in modern times is calligraphed on parchment using ink and a quill, each letter must be fully surrounded by white background, so that no letter touches the adjacent one. The black words of the Torah exist against a backdrop of sublime, ineffable white parchment, like the words of a poem, and like the images in *Black and White*.

As I unfolded and refolded the accordion board book, I wondered how much Matan was absorbing. He was soothed by the cadences of my voice, but I couldn't tell if he was able to focus his eyes on the various black and white objects. At that point he was sleeping through much of the day, and up crying in the wee hours of the night; like most newborns, he was still adjusting to the pattern of day and night. Had he already learned to distinguish black from white, darkness from light?

The book of Genesis teaches that one of God's first acts in

creating the world is the separation of light and darkness. Only when there is light that is distinct from darkness is it possible to discern black shapes against a white background, or white shapes against black. Each time I read *Black and White* to my son, I imagined that we were drawing back the darkness so that the light might appear distinct and his world might sharpen into focus.

Although the Bible begins with the creation of the world, the midrash—the rabbinic interpretive tradition—tells a different story. According to the rabbis, two thousand years before the world was created, the Torah existed. The rabbis teach that just as an architect cannot build a palace without a blueprint, God could not construct the world without the blueprint that is the Torah. The world was preceded by and predicated on a book; God looked into the Torah and created the world.[1]

Books are guides to the world. When I read to Matan, I am teaching him how to make sense of his world—how to discern the bottle and the boat in the black space that is not the surrounding whiteness, and then, later on, how to separate good from evil, kindness from cruelty, right from wrong. I am teaching him the distinctions of light and shade that will shape not just his visual perception but also his moral sensibilities. *Black and White*, so deceptively simple, is the first book to constitute his world.

※

While he was still an infant, the delight of reading to Matan lay not in the pages we turned together but in the wheels that seemed to turn in his mind as we read. I was reading a board book, but I was really learning how to read my child—the flicker of recognition in his eye, the trace of a smile that assured me that reading together was bringing him pleasure.

Though the board books we read were short and simple, they nonetheless contained more words than my cooing, gurgling Matan knew how to speak. One of his favorite titles was *Baby's First Words*, featuring full-color photographs of a series of labeled objects from a baby's everyday world: spoon, cup, plate on one page; tractor, train, truck on the next. I watched in wonder as my son learned to point with his tiny finger as I read aloud the name of each item on the page: Spoon! Cup! Plate! He beamed in proud delight each time he identified an object on the page, excited to hear me speak its name.

The book of Genesis teaches that God spoke the world into existence. God said, "Let there be light," and by the power of God's word alone, there was light. At the beginning of time, the formless void of creation was like an enormous echo chamber in which every word spoken by God resonated with such force that it constituted the sun and moon, the trees and shrubs, the beasts and fish. Utterance by utterance, the world of Genesis resounded into being.

When Matan learned to speak his first words, he began "reading" *Baby's First Words* to himself. "Spoon!" he cried excitedly, pointing to the image on the page, and it was as if the spoon were being summoned into existence for him then and there. The spoon on the page became a sort of platonic, primordial spoon, a template for every spoon he would subsequently encounter. Thanks to this spoon, he would dip into bowls of applesauce and rice cereal, then Cheerios and chicken soup, and then into vaster depths. Cynthia Ozick, in an essay titled "The Ladle," writes about this common kitchen utensil as a metaphor for all the ways we dip into knowledge and draw up wisdom, such that the ladle in a kitchen drawer leads her to the Big Dipper and Joseph's pit and the wells dug by the patriarchs in the book of Genesis. As my infant son delighted in identifying the spoon on the page, I gazed at the perfect roundness of his head, a ladle dipping into the eternal well of pictures and stories, drawing up wisdom.

2

By the Light of the Moon

A DECADE HAS PASSED SINCE I BEGAN READING TO MY oldest child, Matan, and now my youngest, Yitzvi, is already two. He goes through phases with books, and these days he is obsessed with *The Very Hungry Caterpillar*. This is all he wants to read, all day long, by the light of the moon and the light of the sun, his appetite for the book insatiable.

Meanwhile, his sister is learning stories from the book of Genesis in preschool—how God began with the earth unformed and void, and then filled the world with the sun, the moon, the trees and grasses, the fish and birds and cattle and human beings, before, finally, resting. Each day after school, five-year-old Shalvi wants me to read it all to her from the illustrated children's Bible. She thrusts the book into my lap, on top of *The Very Hungry Caterpillar*. But Yitzvi is unrelenting. "Hung-ee catapilla," he insists, dropping the illustrated Bible to the floor.

I look at Shalvi sympathetically. She is going to have to turn the pages by herself, or wait patiently for one more *Hungry Caterpillar* rendition. She sighs with visible annoyance as I begin to read to Yitzvi, though this time I read through the lens of the Bible stories my daughter wishes I would read instead.

At first the world is just darkness and potentiality—a tiny

egg in a dark world illuminated only by the light of the moon. This is the darkness of the start of creation, when the world is still unformed and God creates light, but life has not yet emerged. And then there is a sun, and the first creepy-crawly things appear, and "pop"—the caterpillar emerges. On each subsequent day, the caterpillar eats more than the day before, and the pages unfold as a series of flaps that grow wider and wider—one apple, two pears, three plums . . . Each day follows the same formula: The caterpillar eats, but he is still—I draw out the final "l," then pause and look at Yitzvi—"Hung-ee," he concludes. In the book of Genesis, too, each day of creation is narrated with the same repetitive formula: "God said 'Let there be' . . . And it was so. . . . God saw it was good. . . . And there was evening and there was morning." Each day, God creates more and more, but the world is still incomplete.

On the sixth day of the caterpillar's life, his appetite peaks. Over the course of a full-color two-page spread, he eats every kind of food—cake, ice cream, cheese, salami, a lollipop, a piece of pie. This explosion of bounty has its parallel on the sixth day of creation, when God makes "every kind of living creature, cattle, creeping things, and wild beasts of every kind" (Genesis 1:23), as well as humanity, created in God's image. God charges the man and woman to be fertile and multiply and to fill the earth. But the tiny caterpillar in the bottom right-hand corner of the page is full already. He has a stomachache and can't possibly eat another bite.

Then comes a period of dormancy, of sitting still and holding tight. God sees all that He has made and finds it very good. And the heaven and earth are completed, in all their array. What is left for the seventh day? The caterpillar builds his cocoon and remains inside for two weeks. It seems as if nothing is happening.

The cocoon is large and brown and it fills the whole page—for the first time, we don't see the caterpillar, with his wide smile and big green eyes. This is Shabbat, the day of rest, when we are commanded to imitate God and desist from the work of creation.

We might think on Shabbat that nothing is happening. What could possibly come of resting and staying put, holed up in the cocoons of our homes? Quite a lot, apparently. At the end of the book, when the caterpillar emerges from that cocoon, he is a beautiful butterfly, his dazzling multicolored wings spread across two facing pages.

"Again, again," Yitzvi insists when we turn the final page, and I know he will give me trouble if I try to read his sister's book. "Yitzvi," I say to him calmly, in my most authoritative voice, "it's Shalvi's turn now. You can listen to her story, and then we'll read the *Hungry Caterpillar* again." The corners of his mouth turn down and he lowers himself to the floor, preparing for a tantrum. But then Shalvi surprises me.

"It's OK," she says. "You can keep reading to Yitzvi. I'll look at the pictures in my book for now, and then you can read to me later." It is unusual for Shalvi to cede so graciously to her younger brother—usually she competes fiercely for my attention. Whence this newfound maturity? How did I miss this transformation? I notice, then, that her brightly colored sweater is getting small—she won't be able to wear it much longer. She flies off the couch, alighting on the armchair beside me as her squirmy brother crawls back into my lap to hear his story again.

✶

Reading the same book over and over again to my child has taught me a lesson in how to pray. The challenge of prayer is to try to find meaning in reciting the same psalms and blessings day after day. Our prayers are not supposed to be rote; we are supposed to pray to God from the fullness of our hearts. But how is this possible when each day we open to the same page and begin with the very same words?

In synagogue the prayer service is led by a member of the congregation, who chants the liturgy that the congregation then repeats aloud or murmurs silently. As I read to Yitzvi, it is as if I am the prayer leader and he is the congregation's most vocal member. I chant the words in a tune that has become familiar to us both, pausing each time in the same places: "By the light of the—" I pause, and Yitzvi bobs his head excitedly: "Moon!" We read it the same way each time.

One afternoon I come into Yitzvi's room, where he has been napping. I find him sitting up in his crib with *The Very Hungry Caterpillar*, reciting the book to himself. He misses a few words here and there, but he is clearly not paraphrasing; he knows the rhythm of each page, and when he doesn't know a particular word, he replaces it with a similar sound: "By a light on a moon, a li'l egg, on on on leaf!" It is as if the words of the book have a certain sanctity, and he knows he must remain faithful to their rhythm. He is so absorbed that he doesn't notice me, and I think of the rabbis' image of a person so immersed in prayer that he doesn't stop even when a snake curls around his ankle.[2] I tousle his hair, and he thrusts the book at me, tugging at my sleeve: "Read it! Read it!"

As I read the book yet again, I remember that prayer is not supposed to be an intellectual exercise but an act of devotion. I am not trying to discover something new in the words on the page; I am trying to transform myself. And perhaps that is my son's experience, too.

Does Yitzvi know what a cocoon is? A stomachache? He

never stops to ask what a word means, because for him, meaning is largely irrelevant to the ritualized experience of reading. He wants to hear the story not to find out what happens but to lose himself in the phrases that have become intimately familiar even if they elude comprehension. By the end of the book, he will be in a different place, just as we are ideally in a different place after each time we pray. Something has lifted off within us. The egg on the leaf on the book's opening page inevitably morphs and spreads wings.

ᴶᵍ

Ideally our prayer is not just an occasion for transformation but also a means of connection. The rabbis of the Talmud credit the forefathers in the book of Genesis—Abraham, Isaac, and Jacob—with the establishment of the daily prayer services.[3] Abraham instituted the morning prayer when he prayed on behalf of Sodom; Isaac instituted the afternoon prayer when he went out to the field in the late afternoon; and Jacob instituted the evening prayer when he dreamed of a ladder of angels. They were not reciting a fixed liturgy; they were talking to God. In its most fundamental sense, the point of prayer is not the words spoken or the text recited but the connection forged.

I try to view the fixed, unvarying text of a board book as an opportunity for connection. I look into my son's animated eyes as we come to his favorite page, on which the caterpillar eats the cake and the ice cream and the pie, and each time, unfailingly, "He was still hungry." How is it that Yitzvi never tires of the refrain? In a psalm recited as part of the Shabbat morning liturgy, the phrase "His graciousness endures forever" repeats twenty-five times. I marvel to think that God's patience could be as enduring as God's graciousness. Does God never tire of our prayers? Is God still hungry for more?

The Talmudic rabbis note a subtle inconsistency in the Bible's description of the creation of the world. Although grass was created on the third day, until the sixth day "no shrub of the field was yet on the earth" (Genesis 2:5). The rabbis explain that for three days, the grass stood poised beneath the surface of the earth, waiting to grow until Adam came along and prayed for it to emerge. According to the Talmud, "God desires the prayers of the righteous," and thus aspects of the creation of the world were contingent upon human prayer.[4] God created an imperfect world so that human beings would have reason to call out to God.

If only we could recite our prayers with the same eagerness and devotion with which God, in this Talmudic passage, receives them. If only I could read to my child with the same excitement the words seem to awaken within him. I summon my patience and endurance and return to the first page to start reading the book all over again, from the beginning.

3

Far from the Tree

IN THE MIDDLE OF THE SIXTH DAY OF CREATION, SOMEthing changes. God has already created light and darkness, all kinds of vegetation, the sun and moon and stars, and swarms of living creatures. God surveys all of creation, and it is good. But until the middle of the sixth day, there are no people.

Many children's books take us back to the middle of that sixth day, to a world without human beings where to be individuated meant to be Frog waking up Toad in the springtime, or Elephant sharing an ice cream cone with Piggy. The landscape of children's literature is populated by highly anthropomorphized animals—from Pearl, the pig who finds an amazing bone, to Frances, the badger who eats only bread and jam. Sometimes the anthropomorphism can lead to confusion. The first time I took Yitzvi to the dentist at age two—he was merely tagging along while his older siblings were getting their annual cleanings—he looked around, bitterly disappointed. "Where are the animals?" he asked when we walked in. It took a few minutes before I realized that he must be thinking about William Steig's *Doctor De Soto*, the bespectacled mouse dentist who bravely risks his life by climbing into the mouth of one of his patients, a wily fox suffering from a terrible toothache.

Featuring animals instead of people in children's books may be a way of eliding distinctions such as race and gender that might not be explicit in the text but are evident from the illustrations. After all, once the pictures disappear—once children move on to chapter books without illustrations—the characters, by and large, are human again. So long as there are no illustrations—or so long as the illustrations liberate rather than constrain the imagination—readers are free to see themselves in the characters.

In the book of Genesis, God creates human beings in an attempt to see God's self in creation. "Let us make man in Our image, after Our likeness," God declares (1:26). The use of the plural is understood in the midrash as including the angels, whom God consults before creating humanity.[5] But perhaps the plural is employed to reflect the notion that God contains multitudes, and thus it is possible that all human beings the world over are created in God's likeness. To be human is to have the potential to act like God, regardless of external distinctions. The midrash on the book of Genesis comments that the first human being resembled God to such an extent that the angels got confused, and nearly prayed to Adam.[6] And so God put Adam to sleep, and then the angels realized the difference. "Behold He neither sleeps nor slumbers, the Guardian of Israel," says the Psalmist (121:4). It is only God who neither sleeps nor slumbers.

When I share the early stories of Genesis with my children, I want them to identify with Adam, a model of what it means to strive, even if to fail, to live up to the divine image in which we were created. It seems like a realistic expectation, especially in light of the account in the first chapter of Genesis: "And God created man in His image, in the image of God He created them, male and female He created them" (1:27). This first human being, like the animal characters in children's books, was both male and female, dark-skinned and light-skinned. Adam, created from the earth, is a creature that any child could imagine as progenitor.

But by the second chapter of Genesis, Adam is no longer as universal. The Adam of the second chapter finds himself alone, and so God creates a second human being—a woman—to keep him company. The woman is a derivative of him, created almost as an afterthought. Unlike Adam, who was formed from the earth, Eve is fashioned from Adam's side, and he feels proprietary about her from the outset: "This one at last is bone of my bones and flesh of my flesh" (2:23). When Adam is accused of wrongdoing, he immediately points his finger at Eve, and she, too, denies responsibility. They are each punished: He will be the one to work the earth, and she will be the one to bear children. The dynamics of gender will shape who they become and how they relate to one another for millennia of human history.

As we read our way through the Garden of Eden, I worry about the extent to which my sons will identify exclusively with Adam and my daughters exclusively with Eve. If only we could go back to the original Adam, created both male and female, or perhaps back even further, to the middle of the sixth day, when the world was populated only by animals—Elephant and Piggy and Frog and Toad. It was all so much simpler back then, before humans came onto the scene.

❧

Adam and Eve are the first couple, and their relationship is presented as a model for committed partnership—it is the model invoked in the blessings recited under every Jewish wedding canopy. But theirs is not a partnership of equals, nor is it how I want my children to think about the relationship between man and woman, or husband and wife. To the extent that I hope the books I read to my children will model the values worth emulating, the relationship between Adam and Eve leaves me uneasy.

One of my favorite couples in children's literature is not married, nor are they even, well, human beings. But they are a model of intimate partnership nonetheless. James Marshall's George and Martha—two gray, toothy hippopotamuses—appear in thirty-five very short stories, each as dense and concise as a poem, with spare illustrations that convey a mind-boggling array of emotions and expressions using just black dots for eyes, concentric circles for nostrils, and an enormous hippo overbite. George and Martha argue, they blame each other, they make fun of one another, and they make up—before hurting each other all over again. It is not that their relationship endures in spite of their wrangling and reconciliations—these disagreements are, in fact, the warp and woof that binds them.

All the George and Martha stories are short—just a few hundred words, spread over four or five pages. But each story packs a punch. Many explore the tension between honesty and harmony. Martha makes split pea soup, but George can't stand it, so he hides it in his shoes. Martha notices and demands to know why he wasn't frank with her. George says he didn't want to hurt her feelings, and Martha insists that "friends should always tell each other the truth." Other stories are about protecting privacy within a relationship: George wants to read his book undisturbed, but Martha can't stop fidgeting at his side. George and Martha enjoy each other's company—most of the time. Their pranks and spats challenge us to think about how we carve out space for ourselves in a relationship without making the other person feel shut out.

The George and Martha stories treat many of the issues

that come up in long-term partnerships. How much can we expect to change the other person? How do we navigate the line between good-hearted teasing and hurtful insult? What is the place of "I told you so," and what is the place of "I'm sorry"?

George and Martha get angry at each other in nearly every story, but they rarely stay angry for long. When George can't resist spraying water from a hose at Martha, who had been reading peacefully in a hammock, she insists that they are no longer on speaking terms. But the next morning, she reads a funny story and wants to share it with George. The first autumn leaf falls and it reminds her that it is George's favorite season. Martha has had enough. She goes straight to George's house and forgives him because "good friends just can't stay cross for long."

The Bible doesn't tell us whether Adam and Eve stay cross at each other. At least initially, they seem too busy casting blame to apologize or forgive. Neither rushes to defend the other; they are interested only in covering their own sin, and then their skin. This dynamic of blunder and blame is one I know all too well from the domestic disputes in my own home, where Daniel and I are often quick to point fingers and evade responsibility. Every partnership is, to some extent, heir to the legacy of Adam and Eve. But we can aspire—like George and Martha—to set things right.

🌿

Adam and Eve's sin is to eat from a tree that sits in the center of the Garden. Its fruit looks delicious, and Adam and Eve surely pass by every day. But they have been commanded to keep away. I think of a book that sits at the center of our bookcase, where it catches my eye each time I scan the shelves: *The Giving Tree*. It is a favorite from my childhood, and so of course I want to reread it with my children. But when I revisit *The Giving Tree* as a parent, I am troubled and alienated by a story that was once so beloved and familiar. Do I really want to share the fruit of this tree with my kids?

The book tells the story of a boy and a tree. The boy is referred to as a boy throughout, though he ages from page to page—from a boy swinging on branches to a world-weary elder who has energy only to sit and rest on the tree's stump. As time passes, the tree changes, too—not because of age but because it is stripped bare of its leaves and then its branches and finally its trunk, all of which it gives willingly and selflessly to the boy. The older the boy gets, the more he needs and the more he takes, and the less the tree has left to give.

Each time I read *The Giving Tree*, I cry. I identify with the tree's desire to give everything. It can be very reassuring to know that as a parent, my questions of purpose and self-worth are answered for me: I am here on this earth because there are little creatures who need everything I have to give. But I also know enough to interrogate these emotions, and to regard them through a critical lens.

I am not the only reader who is troubled by *The Giving Tree*. Once read as a moving if sentimental tale about unbounded generosity, Shel Silverstein's classic has more recently been critiqued by parents, educators, environmentalists, and feminist scholars, who question the book's message—do we really want to teach children that it is all right for the boy to take and take, without any thought for the giver? How can the boy strip the tree of its natural beauty with such rapacious abandon? Why is the tree a "she"?

The Talmud tells the story of Elisha ben Abuya, a learned scholar who strayed from the path of Torah and became a heretic. Even so, his disciple Rabbi Meir continued to study Torah with him. Rabbi Meir's colleagues were troubled; how could he learn Torah from a man whose lips sang secular Greek songs, and whose lap was covered with heretical books? The Talmud's answer is that Rabbi Meir found a pomegranate; he ate the inside and threw away the rind. He knew how to pick out the good—the wisdom still implanted in Elisha—and discard the rest.[7]

Like Rabbi Meir, I'm not prepared to throw the pomegranate away. Instead I try my hand at replanting *The Giving Tree* in more fertile contextual soil. The Bible teaches that God places Adam in the Garden "to work it and to protect it" (Genesis 2:15). The midrash adds that first God led Adam around all the trees of the Garden and said to him, "Look at my works, how beautiful and praiseworthy they are. And all that I have created—for you I created it. Be careful that you do not corrupt and destroy my world, for if you do, there is no one to repair it."[8]

If *The Giving Tree* were replanted in the Garden of Eden, we might remember that trees, like all of God's majestic world, were created for human beings to enjoy, but we are meant to do so in a way that respects and protects that beauty. Later in the Bible we learn that it is forbidden to eat a new tree's fruit for the first three years after it is planted; that fruit is considered sanctified to God (Leviticus 19:23). By waiting, we remind ourselves that the world's fruits are not just ours for the taking.

My daughter Shalvi, at age five, is learning about giving and taking. She shares a room with her younger brother, and sometimes she is the first to hear him cry in the mornings, rattling the sides of his crib and pointing excitedly at the first rays of light streaming through the window. She gets out of bed, drags over a wooden stool, and wraps her arms around him to pull him out of his crib. In the afternoons, when we walk through the park on our way home from preschool, Shalvi and Yitzvi pick mulberries—they ripen in the spring from a pale cream to a deep crimson, and the two of them sit under the tree and eat them together, licking their stained fingers. They both prefer the darkest-colored ones, though sometimes there are only a few. "OK, this one is for you, but the next one will be for me," she tells Yitzvi with a smile, and he takes.

Someday I trust that Yitzvi will learn from his sister to give generously, and not merely to take. It is a lesson he might learn from a Talmudic parable about trees and giving. The parable begins with a hungry, thirsty, tired man who was walking through a desert. He found a tree with sweet fruit and pleasant shade and a stream of water flowing beneath, and he ate the fruit, sat in the shade, and drank the water. When he wished to depart, he said, "Tree, tree, how shall I bless you? If I say that your fruits should be sweet, they are already sweet. If I say that your shade should be pleasant, your shade is already pleasant. If I say that a stream of water should flow beneath you, a stream of water already flows beneath. Rather, I will bless you as follows: May it be God's will that all the saplings which they plant from you be like you."⁹

I imagine writing a version of *The Giving Tree* in the context of the Bible and Talmud, lending the book new meaning beyond its celebration of boundless giving. In my version, a weary old man walks through the desert when he comes upon a tree. He eats from its fruit and sits underneath its shade and blesses the tree, admiring its beauty. Then on the next page, the tree appears again, and the man's son—who looks much like the man, just a bit younger—comes to eat from that tree and bless it. Then on the next page, the tree appears again, and the man's grandson—who looks much like the man, but even younger—comes to eat from that tree and bless it, and so forth. On each page the boy is happy. On each page the tree is happy. Really.

♒

The parable about the desert traveler concludes with a blessing for the tree: "May it be God's will that all the saplings which they plant from you be like you." And yet it is so rarely the case that our offspring are like us. "The apple doesn't fall far from the tree" goes the adage, but as Andrew Solomon showed in his monumental book that plays off this idea, often quite the opposite is true.[10] No matter how much we give of ourselves to our children, there are no guarantees that our children will embrace our values or uphold our ideals. Often they will define themselves in opposition, choosing to be exactly what we are not.

The notion that the apple falls far from the tree is another way of thinking about the curses in the Garden of Eden story. God's curse to Adam is a curse upon the trees he plants and the fruit they will bear: "Cursed be the earth because of you; by toil shall you eat of it all the days of your life: thorns and thistles shall it sprout for you" (Genesis 3:17–18). Adam will sow seeds only to reap thorns and thistles. The earth will not always yield the bounty we hope and expect of it, no matter how much we tend and water and care for the saplings and sprouts. Eve's curse, too, is about the discrepancy between what we sow and what we reap. God tells Eve, "I will greatly intensify your pain and your pregnancy; in sorrow shall you bear children" (3:16). The Talmud explains that this pain is "the pain of raising children."[11] Indeed, the same Hebrew word is used to refer to Adam's toil and to Eve's pain, suggesting that the two curses parallel one another—just as the earth does not always yield what we hope for, our children do not always become the people we envision or embody the values we try so hard to instill.

It seems built into our modern ethos to want our children to surpass us, such that every generation is an improvement on the one that came before. But the traditional Jewish blessing that parents bestow upon children conveys quite the opposite message: "May the Lord bless you like Ephraim and Menashe" for boys, and "May the Lord bless you like Sarah, Rebecca, Rachel, and Leah" for girls. We bless our children that they should be like their ancestors. We, their parents, strive to emulate the values of those who came before us. We hope our children will do the same.

Matan, who is ten, has decided for the time being that he is not interested in going to synagogue on Shabbat morning. He tells us, rightfully so, that it is his only day to sleep late—like most Israeli elementary schoolchildren, he has school six days a week. He is not averse to prayer—he will pray at home once he wakes up, bending over his prayer book in the living room and mouthing every word. But, as I try to explain to him, praying alone is different from experiencing the power of communal prayer. I wake him on Shabbat mornings, and then, when he doesn't rouse, I wake him again, until I cannot wait any longer.

Our synagogue is just two blocks away; Matan can easily get there on his own. But most weeks we come home to find him still asleep. He knows that it is important to us, his parents, that he come to synagogue on Shabbat mornings. But I'm wary of a dynamic in which the more I push, the more he pulls back, so I try to contain my disappointment.

One Shabbat morning I walk into our building from synagogue and run into my neighbor Liat, a Moroccan mother of seven children in their teens and twenties who is renowned, among all the tenants in our building, for her extraordinary hospitality—every Friday afternoon she delivers a platter of homemade salads to all her upstairs and downstairs neighbors, insisting that it is the way she honors the memory of her grandmother, who used to do the same. Liat might be heading out the door, but she is never too busy for a conversation. She sets down the paper bag she is carrying and gives me a hug. "Shabbat shalom, how are you doing?" she asks, reaching behind her head to the nape of her neck, where she secures the knot of the kerchief covering her hair.

I tell her, with a sigh, that I'm upset that once again my son did not make it to synagogue. Liat looks at me with an expression that is at once sympathetic and stern. "Oh yes," she tells me. "I used to have the same problem with my oldest son. He never could wake up on Shabbat."

"What did you do?" I ask.

"I once asked him, if someone offered you a thousand dollars to do a job, would you take it? And he said of course. And then I told him that the reward for coming to synagogue and keeping mitzvot and living a life in accordance with Torah is infinite— surely he wanted that infinite reward?"

I look at her skeptically. "Did it work?"

"Of course not." She smiles gently. "But it helped me. I realized that the only way I can try to change my child is by praying for him. And so every week I would go to synagogue and instead of being angry at my son for not being there, I would pray to the Holy One Blessed Be He to help him find his own way back to prayer."

I sigh again. Liat puts her hands on my shoulders and looks me directly in the eye. "I promise," she tells me. "Don't give up on the power of prayer. A mother's prayers are so powerful. They go straight up to the throne of God's glory. Straight up," she repeats as she picks up her paper bag by the handles and pulls open the door to our building. Her long dress reaches all the way down to the floor, and she seems to glide out the door, leaving me to wonder—not for the first time—if Liat is really Elijah the prophet in disguise, sent down to earth to act as a heavenly intercessor.

On the wall behind our Shabbat candlesticks hangs a prayer that I received, calligraphed and framed, as a gift from a group of women I once taught. It is a prayer for raising children, written in eloquent poetic Hebrew:

> May it be your will, O Lord our God, to teach us to accept the sorrow bound up in raising our children. Teach us how to know when to laugh with them and when to rebuke them, so that we are not strict when they need us to be gentle, and so that we do not permit what ought to be forbidden. Grant us the wisdom to guide them so that they may grow up to praise your name. Amen.

Shabbat, like raising children, is about recognizing the limits of our agency. For six days we can try to change the world, but there comes a time when we have to step back. I light the candles, say the blessing, and step back to watch the dancing flames.

4

⟨ᴏᴄ⟩

Going, Going, Gone

AFTER ADAM EATS FROM THE FORBIDDEN TREE OF Knowledge and is banished from the Garden, he experiences another kind of loss. The Talmud teaches that when Adam noticed that the days were growing shorter with the approach of the world's first winter, he grew terribly frightened: "Perhaps because I sinned, the world is growing dark all around me, and will return to a state of chaos and disorder?"[12]

Like Adam in the antediluvian world, a baby has not seen enough sunsets to understand that "so long as the earth endures, seedtime and harvest, cold and heat, summer and winter, day and night, shall not cease," as God promises Noah after the flood (Genesis 8:22). For a baby, every nightfall marks the end of a wondrous Edenic daytime, rejoicing in one new discovery after another. Then the child is placed in a dark room, sometimes all alone. It is a scene replicated in countless children's books, like *Goodnight Moon*, in which a rabbit goes to sleep in a large bedroom with a window looking out to the starry sky, taking leave of one object after another. Even if the little old lady whispering hush is in her rocking chair, she will not be there all night; she vanishes, almost unnoticed, on the book's final darkened page. The window is illuminated by moonlight and twinkling stars, but after the rabbit bids farewell to all the items that are so delightful in daytime, the lamp ceases to cast its glow. No wonder babies wail at night—how terrifying it must be to feel the world is drawing to a close.

Goodnight Moon is a *Paradise Lost* of sorts, an affecting poetic description of a fallen and all-too-fleeting world. The child hearing the story in bed can rehearse each valediction in the safe space of parental presence. When I read the book to Yitzvi, he points to each item in turn, confusing only the moon and the red balloon—they sound and look the same, each a round object depicted as about the same size. The balloon is like a moon closer to home, still high above but accessible with the tug of a string. In spite of the disappointments of nightfall—the lost splendor of sunlight—at least the balloon in *Goodnight Moon* never wanes and never pops. The same cannot be said for the other balloon book we love.

Though I read to my children primarily in English, a notable exception is *A Tale of Five Balloons* by Miriam Roth, one of the most famous Israeli children's books of all time. The five balloons—green, yellow, purple, blue, red—are the only colorful illustrations in the otherwise black-and-white pages. When the book opens, Ruti's mother brings a present—five balloons, one for each delighted child. But delight is followed by a series of disappointments. Uri runs and jumps with his green balloon until it is punctured by a thornbush. Ron's yellow balloon is so large that it bursts. Sigalit's balloon is torn apart by a cat. Ruti hugs her blue balloon so tightly that it rips. On every page we find the same singsong refrain. "Don't be sad, don't be forlorn," each child is told. "That's the fate of all balloons."

Instead of popping like the others, the fifth balloon in Roth's book, the red one, goes on a journey. A strong wind lifts it up, up to the clouds, as all the children watch sadly and wave goodbye.

For the first time, they are able to take their leave of one of the balloons, whose departure is less sudden and dramatic than the others. The children do not weep to see this last balloon go; there are none of the tear-floods or sigh-tempests that so often accompany loss, which John Donne writes about in "A Valediction: Forbidding Mourning." Donne contends that it is only the virtuous who are fortunate to depart this world peacefully, without resistance and regret. But another poem, "Do Not Go Gentle into That Good Night," by Dylan Thomas, urges us to hold on as long as we can. According to Thomas, none of us ought to go gentle into that good night, like the child who refuses to let go of the parent's hand after that last goodnight.

Roth's book ends when all five balloons are gone, never to return. Disappointment comes inevitably to every child, and love always carries with it the risk of loss. "Shh, shh," I repeat to Yitzvi from his bedside, until his breathing begins to rise and fall with the cadence of my voice. At some point I will free my hand from his grasp and creep out. At some point, someday, I will no longer be there with him.

⚘

So many of the books we read at bedtime are about the fleetingness of time and the impossibility of holding on forever. I'd like to think I am teaching my child to accept loss, but perhaps I am really teaching myself—as a parent—about the poignance and pathos of childhood's ephemerality. At every single moment of my child's life, I am letting go.

I am reminded of this lesson each time we read *Freight Train* by Donald Crews, a book about a passing train and the passage of time. The book is deceptively simple, with the entire plot unfolding in the first sentence: "A train runs across this track." The track, in lieu of a storyline, runs through every page of the book and is visible in all the illustrations. For the child it's the narrative thread, but for the parent, it's also a lifeline. On the very first page, where the opening sentence appears in beige type, we see the track but not the train. Aside from this one sentence hovering at the top margin and the track that runs beneath, this first page is blank. It is the blankness of anticipation, like that moment when we hear the whistle growing louder but can't quite make out anything else.

Turn the page, and all at once, an explosion of color! Three train cars appear on the track. First is the red caboose, like a baby suddenly birthed red and wailing after months of silent, hopeful gestation. Next come the orange tank car and the yellow hopper car, dazzling in their bright intensity. But the eyes can't linger, because the hopper car is connected by a black line to the green cattle car on the next page, so we flip quickly and are met, too, with the blue gondola car and the purple box car. For Yitzvi it all still lies ahead—these colorful years of childhood with their vivid intensity, their full spectrum of emotions, their never-a-dull moments.

As the book goes on, and as we age, the moments unfold in more subdued hues. The purple box car is followed by the black tender and the black steam engine, and then we see the entire train, each car a clearly defined shape with the smoke billowing overhead. Is this the peak of our lives, though we won't ever know it until it's behind us? On every subsequent page of the book, as the train hurtles through tunnels and barrels over bridges, the cars appear blurry—the train is moving so fast that we can no longer make out each car's distinct color. I know this blurriness well—it is only in the early pages of the book, and in the early years of our lives, that time unfolds slowly enough for each year to have its own distinct hue. I went from forty-one to forty-two in the blink of an eye, and yet apparently it was in that same period of time that Shalvi turned four, then four and a quarter, then four and a half, then four and three-quarters, then "almost almost five," and then finally finally (up late at night, unable to sleep because tomorrow was the big day) five.

Donald Crews's freight train rushes on, moving through darkness and daylight—through the dark times of our lives and the brighter moments. Then, all at once, it is "going, going, gone." All we see on the final page is the word "gone" and the last billowy plumes of smoke. "More!" Yitzvi cries like the soul in e. e. cummings's poem "Summer Is Over," refusing to accept that all "sweet things are until."

Though the book ends, we read it anew every evening at bedtime, and often at naptime, too. All the days in which Yitzvi and I have read this book are strung together, and the freight train of my life flashes before me with each rereading.

Donald Crews wrote *Freight Train* the year I was born— I know this because the four digits appear not just on the copyright page but also on the black tender beside the black steam engine, like a memento mori. The book is dedicated to "the countless freight trains passed and passing the big house in Cottondale." I wonder if Crews, like my parents, took his children to the railroad crossing to watch the trains go by on long summer afternoons. I remember that each time it seemed like the train would go on forever, car after car after car, until suddenly—going, going, gone—the train disappeared, and I lost count.

I am still losing count. We have read *Freight Train* far too many times to enumerate, and Yitzvi has grown faster than I can document. The week he was born, a friend gave us a baby book in which to record his milestones, but I kept forgetting to jot them down. All I have are these words, which I scribble on paper as he falls asleep for his midday nap. I write against the clock, conscious that at any moment, his older siblings will lose patience and barrel into the bedroom to find me, waking him up if I don't emerge first. I am scrambling to get the words down, conscious that all my writing is an attempt to hold on to time, even as I know it can't be done; I can see the balloon drifting up into the sky and the train disappearing from view. Footsteps in the hallway. My time to write is over. The words have hurtled past and they are going, going, gone.

5

Serious Silliness

THE BOOK OF GENESIS CONTAINS SEVERAL LONG GENE-alogical lists of who begat whom. For generations we learn very little about biblical figures aside from their names, and perhaps how many years they lived. Time seems to rush forward in these verses, with one generation following another in rapid succession, until we come to a figure like Noah, or Abraham, and the story slows down to zoom in and take note.

My experience of time as a parent of young children is somewhat reminiscent of the pacing of these genealogical passages. One day leads to another with little to differentiate the daily pattern of mundane tasks—dressing, feeding, diapering, bathing—until we come to a milestone occasion, and suddenly I am cognizant of how much our kids have changed and grown while we were too busy to notice.

To the extent that my husband and I note time's passage, we have our children to thank. They won't let us get away without a birthday celebration for each member of the family, even for those of us who might prefer to let the occasion pass unmarked. Over the years, we have developed the custom of creating a sort of birthday tableau, organizing the celebrant's place setting with a cake, small individually wrapped gifts from various family members, and handwritten cards that we'll then leave on the windowsill for a few weeks. Every tableau also includes Sandra Boynton's *Birthday Monsters!*, a board book about a reclusive hippopotamus who is rudely awakened by a group of rowdy party animals.

Birthday Monsters! is narrated in the second person, so that the narrator is addressing not just the hippo lying in bed on the morning of his birthday, but also the child being read to, and also, perhaps, the reader. Whenever I read *Birthday Monsters!* I identify with the introverted hippo who can't understand what all those monsters are doing in his house and what they want of him. Always loath to be the center of attention, I never wanted my family to make me birthday parties when I was a child, and I attended even friends' parties reluctantly.

As a parent, my aversion to birthday parties persists; I'd rather be carted down the stairs by a team of furry monsters at 6 A.M. than host my kids' classmates for two hours of party games. But while my attitude to parties has not changed, I no longer agree with my younger self, who thought that birthdays were no big deal. If there's anything I've learned from being a parent, it's that turning one year older is a big deal indeed.

I first learned this lesson when Matan was three and the twins had just turned two, and our daily life was still rowdier than the wildest party. It was shortly before Passover. While we were all busy preparing for the holiday, my daughter Liav had a terrible fall and lost two teeth. Her mouth was bleeding for several days, and she had to relearn first how to drink and then how to start eating again. When we sat down to the Seder later that week, we made the blessing recited on Jewish festivals and major milestones: "Blessed are You, O Lord Our God, King of the Universe, who has kept us alive, and sustained us, and enabled us to reach this day." Those words took on new meaning with my daughter on my lap, happily sucking on her matzah.

Liav's injury sensitized me to how lucky we were that things were not worse, and that sensitivity persists even now. Every day there are countless dangers in our path, and no, I'm not referring to the unlikely possibility of a birthday monster invasion. I worry about Yitzvi on the sidewalk pointing excitedly to the tractor on the other side of the street, and I worry about the older kids who are now starting to walk home after school on their own. I worry, too, because I am raising my children in Israel, where we live through wars and rocket sirens. Each night my kids slumber soundly in bed is a small miracle.

Birthdays serve as punctuation, forcing us to pause so that the years do not unfold like a run-on sentence. I won't be sentenced to running after a toddler forever, because at some point that stage of life will be over, period. Already my children are different from the way they were just one year ago; we have cards on our windowsill to prove it.

❧

Now that our youngest is two, my husband has started threatening to give away our baby gear. He's already donated all our infant clothing; one afternoon I found him loading the bags of onesies and footsie pajamas onto the large bucket seat of his bicycle, hauling them off to a local charity. He's told me it's only a matter of time until he does the same with the board books. "All of them?" I ask. And before I can feebly mutter something about pregnant friends, he nods vigorously. "But not the hippopotamus, right?" I ask with a sly smile.

But Not the Hippopotamus is one of our favorite Sandra Boynton board books. The cover features a forlorn gray hippo staring worriedly into the distance as he huddles behind a tree, or perhaps hugs the tree in lieu of a friend. Every other animal has a rhyming playmate: the hog and the frog cavort in the bog, the moose and the goose drink juice. But nothing rhymes with hippopotamus, and so "but not the hippopotamus" is not just the title of the book but also the sad refrain of the lone gray beastie surrounded by a host of creatures sporting their colorful bow ties, beaks, and baseball bats.

It is not good for the hippo to be alone. The second chapter of the book of Genesis teaches that Adam was initially created on his own and placed in the Garden of Eden, where he named all the animals. The midrash provides a bit of backstory. God brought each species before Adam, male and female, for Adam to name. Adam said, "Everyone has a mate, but I have no mate."[13]

Like Adam, Boynton's hippo is clearly not alone by choice; he wants to join in the fun, but he doesn't know how. Each time I read the book I am transported—to junior high school dances where I stood on the sidelines like a wallflower; to kiddush receptions after synagogue, where everyone schmoozes over grape juice and crackers and I scan the room for someone to speak with; to the park after preschool pickup, when the other moms chat animatedly and I pretend my daughter needs my full attention as I push her on the swing. We've all been the hippo at some point, and some of us still are.

God, observing Adam's loneliness, creates Eve as a helpmate and partner. And Boynton's hippopotamus, too, does not wallow for long. The animals scurry back, inviting the hippo to join in their fun. For a moment the hippo hesitates, before leaping up in great delight to join them. Happiness can be a choice, and not just for hippos—at least that's the lesson that I, and I hope my kids, take away. We can spend our lives alone and forlorn, feeling like no one else desires our company. Or we can leap up and take the risks that being with others inevitably entails. They may reject us. They may run too fast. But if we don't try to catch up, we'll never know.

Boynton could have chosen to end *But Not the Hippopotamus* there, with the hitherto lone hippo finally joining in with the rest of the animal pack. But she is after a more nuanced message. Although the hippo is no longer lonely, the existential condition of loneliness persists—the hippo joins the fun, "but not the armadillo," as we learn on the book's final page. There, a dismayed armadillo with a protective gray shell stands just as isolated as the hippo once was. It is another lesson I hope my kids internalize: Even if our own loneliness is alleviated, there will always be someone else out there waiting to be drawn in.

I have read this book countless times over the past decade— to Matan, to my twin daughters, Liav and Tagel, and then to Shalvi. But now, as I read this book to an increasingly rambunctious Yitzvi, I am conscious there is no baby who will read the book with me next. On this rereading, it seems, there is no armadillo waiting in the wings.

But Not the Hippopotamus reminds me that the time will come when I will not have young children anymore. I have already begun looking at pregnant mothers and marveling at how young they seem. After five children born in relatively quick succession, can that stage of life—diapers, pacifiers, midnight wakings—already be behind us? I remember the exhaustion of those days when there was always a baby who was completely dependent on me. I had no physical or mental energy to spare, and so I was rarely plagued by existential questions. But now that my youngest is no longer a baby, I am wary of what the next stage of life will bring. I'm not ready to give away the board books; I'm not ready to let go.

What was Adam and Eve's last day in the Garden of Eden? Were they banished immediately, or did God give them time to take one last look at the leafy trees, the lush fruits, the flowing rivers? Did they know, when they woke up on that fateful morning, that it would be their last day in paradise? When I became pregnant with Yitzvi, I knew he would be my last. I still experienced the excitement of every "first," but it was tinged by the wistfulness of every "last." By the time he learned to walk, I knew it was the last time I would witness one of my children take those hesitant, proud first steps. Once he could walk, it wouldn't be long before he began cavorting with his siblings, the rest of the animal pack. Surely I ought to feel thrilled for him, and for all of them.

Why then do I feel like huddling, forlorn, behind a tree?

※

It's difficult to remain forlorn for long when reading Sandra Boynton, and perhaps that's the point. "Serious silliness for cool little kids," says the back of one of the books, but in a title published just a few years later, her publisher seems to have reconsidered: "Serious silliness for all ages," the back of that one reads. Her books make me smile, and they make my child laugh. Perhaps that's why so many of her books feature hippos—the word "hippopotamus" is such a ridiculous word that I wonder, for a moment, if perhaps it rhymes with "preposterous," which of course it does not. That would be preposterous—the hippopotamus is one of a kind.

But there are other animals, too: pigs with pink snouts, rabbits with long ears that wave behind, moose with their antlers.

All these creatures are featured in *The Going to Bed Book*, a tale about a bedtime ritual that takes place not in a bedroom, or even in a house, but aboard a large multidecked ship that bears a striking resemblance to Noah's ark. If *But Not the Hippopotamus* is a musing on Adam's condition in the Garden of Eden, then *The Going to Bed Book* might be a sequel set during the great flood.

When the book begins, the animals are watching the setting sun from the top deck of the ship. Soon it is time to descend into the hull and take a giant bath all together. The animals hang up their towels, find their pajamas, and brush their teeth while clustering around a big sink. And then comes the surprise.

Just when we expect the animals to settle into bed—perhaps with a book, perhaps with soft music—they all race back up topside to exercise. The pig stands on its head. The moose lifts a dumbbell. The elephant jumps rope. Each time I read *The Going to Bed Book*, I wonder about this page. Who exercises after bathing?

But then I think about the bedtime ritual in our home. It begins a good two hours before the kids actually fall asleep. You might say it starts with dinner, which serves as the first sign the day is winding down, even if the sun is still high in the sky in the summer months. When everyone finishes eating, Daniel and I rush the kids down the hall to bathe. They don't always need a bath—there are days when they don't leave the house—but it's part of the ritual, so we do it anyway. Everyone brushes their teeth before bathing, and then we try to lift them straight into the tub before they run down the hall naked to jump defiantly on the couch. After baths, while Daniel or I get started on cleaning up dinner, the other starts reading to the little ones. Meanwhile, the big kids are supposed to read to themselves in bed, until one of us can come in to read with them or to them. That's how it's supposed to work. That's how I'd write our going to bed book. But the kids have a different story to tell.

After bath time, inevitably the kids get hyper. I'm not sure why; isn't warm water supposed to be calming? Instead of proceeding toward bed, they suddenly start with the silly ideas. They take their pajamas out from under their pillows and wear them on their heads. Or they pull off their blankets and spread them out between their beds to make a fort for their stuffed animals, all the while singing at the top of their lungs. In fact, compared to the wild postprandial antics in our home, going up on deck to exercise sounds rather mild. Instead, my kids are increasingly intoxicated by their own exhaustion, and I can only stand by and anticipate the inevitable crash.

Perhaps that's why Sandra Boynton's *Going to Bed Book* takes that surprising turn. Kids don't want to go to sleep just because the moon is on the rise; they want one last hurrah, and then, if they can get it, one more. The post-bath exercise up on the ark deck, like a wild pajama party, is every kid's fantasy, and every parent's nightmare.

Sometimes the more I reread a book with my kids, the better I understand them. And sometimes the more I observe my kids, the more deeply I understand the book. *The Going to Bed Book* reminds me that it is not just my own children who go wild in the evenings. If my children give me so much trouble about bedtime, how did Noah ever get all those animals to settle down at night?

The Bible tells us very little about Noah's experience on the ark, but the rabbis offer a vivid reimagining. They teach in a midrash that Noah was unable to sleep on the ark because he was so busy feeding all the animals; at every hour of the day, there was some creature who required his attention. At one point, he was late in feeding the lion, and it bit him so severely that he left the ark limping. His lack of sleep affected his health in other ways, too; by the time the floodwaters receded, he had a terrible cold and was coughing and spitting blood. Noah survived the flood, but he barely survived the ark.[14]

The final page of *The Going to Bed Book* features a halcyon image of the ark floating on the waves beneath a moon high in the sky, as the animals inside—so we are told—rock to sleep. All seems quiet, but sometimes I imagine that if I look through one of the round portholes in the illustrated ark, I'd see Noah still scurrying around to prepare breakfast for the next morning. Then again, perhaps I'm just projecting. In our house, even after all the kids are asleep, the kitchen is usually still a mess. The counter needs to be sponged. The floor needs to be swept. The bread needs to be defrosted to pack in tomorrow's school lunches. Daniel usually assumes responsibility for most of these tasks, but it's too much work for one person, and we are both eager to get to bed. Before we know it—perhaps even before morning dawns—the kids will rise and shine and give us their glory.

6

Babel Builders and Beyond

YITZVI, WHO IS TWO, IS OBSESSED WITH CONSTRUCTION. Every Friday morning, when his day care is closed but his siblings are in school, we set out for a walk but rarely get far; inevitably he insists that we stop to watch the first construction site we come across. He is mesmerized by the workers in hard hats. "Oh look!" He turns to me when he spots a worker up on the roof. "So high! So high!" I want us to keep walking—we were on our way to buy challah, or deliver cookies to a friend, or run one of our other pre-Shabbat errands—but no. Yitzvi wants to watch until the building is finished—until the elevator shaft is completed and another story is added on to the apartment complex. He sits upright in his stroller, riveted by the erection of scaffolding and the pouring of concrete. Meanwhile, I stand behind him, leaning on the handles as I read the novel I brought in my shoulder bag.

Yitzvi cannot see me as I stand behind his stroller reading, but passersby often glance at the two of us and smile in amusement. It is clear that we are each absorbed in our own separate worlds. That night in bed, I will read him *The Children's Encyclopedia of Trucks*, or *Goodnight, Goodnight, Construction Site*. When it comes to picture books, I prefer a narrative arc to the taxonomy of heavy machinery, but these are the books he chooses. I smile as he pretends his arm is the boom of an excavator that he is slowly lowering into his lap.

The next day, on Shabbat, we are all home in the afternoon reading on the couch and playing games on the floor. Yitzvi, as usual, is trying to build a tower out of wooden blocks, convinced he can add yet another story without the entire structure toppling. He is happy for his sisters to help, but only if they share his single-minded focus on building the tallest tower possible. When Liav tries to add Fisher-Price people and wooden trees from our Brio train set to one of the lower stories, he pushes her away. "No people! No trees!" Shalvi adds another layer of blocks on top and Yitzvi eyes her suspiciously; if her block makes the tower tumble, he will lunge at her in anger. "It's Yitzvi's tower," he tells us, speaking in the third person to allay any doubts.

In the book of Genesis, the story of Noah's flood is followed by an account of an ambitious, if misguided, construction project. The builders of the Tower of Babel wish to reach all the way to the heavens and to make their name great: "Come let us make a city and a tower with its top to the skies, to make a name for ourselves" (11:4). The Babel builders, who all speak "the same language and the same words," are united in their goal of building the highest tower possible. The midrash teaches that if one of the workers fell from the tower and died, the other builders would not even notice him; but if a brick fell to the ground, they would weep over the loss. At Babel, the project mattered more than the people.[15]

In a way, the Babel builders were like toddlers, insistent that everyone speak their language and share in their goal. My son with his blocks lacks the sophisticated vocabulary or the open-mindedness to engage with his older sister when she tells him, "We can take the little people and put one on every story of the building, and then the tower will have color and look nicer, and the people can play with each other—they can be a whole family." He shakes his head vehemently. "No people!" With an angry flick of Yitzvi's arm, the freckled Fisher-Price boy with the red baseball cap is precipitously plunged to the floor.

The Babel builders, despite their goal of making a name for themselves, remain anonymous. It is only in the next chapter of Genesis, with the introduction of Abraham's family, that the characters become individuated again. God promises Abraham, "I will make your name great" (12:2). The story of Abraham and his descendants will continue throughout the rest of Genesis, becoming the story of the Jewish people, of which we are a part. But for now, I am still caught up in the narrative of the builders. As so often happens, it is the biblical story that frames and makes sense of my own.

On the floor of our living room, my son's tower sways precariously as he tries and fails to add another story. "No! No! No!" he cries, his already-limited toddler vocabulary contracting into this single angry word. I crouch on the floor amid the scattered blocks and try to explain, speaking his language, how this story might go on.

※

Most of the book of Genesis—after the creation of the world and Noah's flood and the Tower of Babel—recounts the lives of the patriarchs and matriarchs. We learn about parents and children, and about the complex emotional dynamics within families: favoritism, jealousy, enmity, spite. These biblical characters are not always paragons of virtue—they sin, they make mistakes, and they suffer the consequences of their behavior. The Talmud invokes the term "measure for measure" to refer to the phenomenon whereby the punishments meted out to biblical characters correspond to the nature of the wrongdoing.[16] Jacob stole the birthright from his older brother, Esau, usurping his place as the firstborn; he received his punishment when his uncle Lavan switched his daughters, wedding Jacob to his sad-eyed firstborn daughter, Leah, instead of her more desirable younger sister. Joseph's brothers did not treat him like a brother when they sold him into slavery; Joseph metes out punishment by pretending not to recognize them when they come in search of food during a famine. Justice is retributive, and it reflects the nature of the offense.

In our house, we rarely punish our children for inappropriate behavior, even though many of our favorite books seem to assume that punishment is warranted and efficacious. When the bear in Jon Klassen's *I Want My Hat Back* finally discovers who has taken his missing hat, he promptly devours the leporine culprit. When Max makes mischief in *Where the Wild Things Are*, he is sent to bed without supper. Our kids take each other's hats (and dolls, and Matchbox cars), and they are forever making mischief of one kind or another. But most punishments seem like more of a burden to me than a deterrent to my children. If I punish my daughter after a tantrum by telling her she can't have dessert, she'll likely just have another tantrum over the treat she is denied. If I tell my son that he can't go to the park with his friend because he hit his sister, he'll be home stewing in anger and driving me crazy the entire afternoon, instead of running around outside and letting off steam. It's difficult to find a punishment that will cultivate genuine remorse.

Beyond "measure for measure," there is another principle that is frequently invoked in the rabbinic commentaries on the book of Genesis: "The actions of the fathers are a sign for the sons." We aspire to the faith and fortitude of Abraham and the magnanimity and munificence of Joseph, modeling ourselves on the examples of our forefathers. With this principle in mind, I try to act in a way that I want my children to emulate. Often I do not succeed, and then I fall asleep regretting that I picked up my daughter late from a birthday party, or yelled at my son for not finishing his cereal. When I fail—and often I do—I lament my failures openly in front of my children. No one gets devoured by a vengeful predator, and no one is sent to bed without supper. But hopefully we all go to sleep at night resolving to do better next time.

⚘

At night after my children fall asleep, I sometimes take walks with my neighbor Katrina. We met when we were both living in the mixed Jewish-Arab neighborhood of Abu Tor, situated on a high hill overlooking the valley of Hinnom, which borders the Old City of Jerusalem. It is rare for Jews and Arabs to live in such close proximity in this city, but Katrina and her husband, Jethro, are neither Jewish nor Arab, and their family stands out even in this religiously diverse landscape. They are evangelical Christians, on a mission from their church in Texas to bring more Christian pilgrims to the Holy Land. They are also the only neighbors with small children in our building, and for as long as we live there—until my oldest is seven—their children and my children are close friends.

Katrina homeschools her kids, so they are almost always around and eager for company when I bring my kids home from school. Sometimes it seems like her eldest son, Xavier— the same age as my eldest, Matan—spends his afternoons looking out the window longingly until we return, but the feeling is mutual; when Matan sees Xavier, he will often head over there even before stopping at home to drop off his backpack or have a snack. We keep our doors open so the kids can move freely from one apartment to the other. I've spent more time in Katrina's home than in any other friend's house, and I know the rhythms and patterns of her domestic life almost as well as I know our own.

Often during our evening walks, each of us reviews the day that has passed, which in my case usually involves confessing my regrets and enumerating all the ways I think I failed as a parent and as a person.

"I wish I had woken up earlier today," I tell her. "Shalvi woke me at 6:30 because she wanted me to do a puzzle. I got out of bed with her, but I was annoyed, and I'm sure she could tell—even though I was sitting on the floor with her, my mind was elsewhere. I was thinking about how I'd really wanted to go for a run."

"I don't know how you could possibly go running before your kids wake up," Katrina tells me.

"I have to," I try to explain. "I need to feel like I've gotten something done before I give myself over to the kids. Otherwise I resent them for taking up all my time. Don't you know what I mean?"

"Not really," Katrina admits. "Zarah woke me at dawn this morning, but we had so much fun snuggling together in bed. I couldn't imagine anywhere else I'd rather be at that hour."

I admire the sense of fulfillment Katrina derives from caring for her children, and I marvel at how her home runs so smoothly, given that she has no time to herself. She cooks with her kids, cleans with them, and takes them on outings around town, where she manages to make each errand into a fun and educational activity—she dictates her shopping list to her seven-year-old, and challenges him to arrange the items in groups by the section of the supermarket in which they are sold. She instructs her daughter to read the bus map and plot their route. Her kids are adventurous, independent, and responsible, and while sometimes I wish my kids were more like hers, I know that it's not about them. Really I wish I were more like her.

Katrina tells me she hasn't read a single novel since her oldest child was born. When I ask her if she ever wishes she had more time alone, she seems puzzled. "I was alone for long enough. The Lord did not bring Jethro into my life until I was thirty-seven. I don't know why, though I know He has His ways. Perhaps He wanted me to be grateful, every single day, for the miracle of marriage and motherhood." It took me a while to grow accustomed to Katrina's manner of speaking; when we first became friends, I didn't realize how frequently she used pronouns to refer to God. "Who?" I made the mistake of asking her on more than one occasion. "Who are you talking about?" She couldn't comprehend how I, the most religious Jew she's ever met, didn't understand that of course she was referring to the Lord. I had to explain to her that although we Jews talk *to* God all the time—at least three times a day, in prayer—we rarely speak *about* God in casual conversation. For Christians like Katrina, God is a character in the story of their lives; for Jews like me, God is the author of our story.

Katrina does not think of herself as a reader, and yet when she and I walk together, we nearly always talk about books. Sometimes we speak about children's books—we are both always on the lookout for quality picture books in English, and we use each other's homes as lending libraries. But more commonly we talk about the Bible, the book of books, which she, like me, has never stopped reading. Katrina prepares the readings for their Sabbath prayer meetings in church, and she asks my thoughts on the passages she's chosen.

One evening she tells me she wants to walk to the promenade overlooking Mount Zion, just south of Mount Moriah. It was here that God commanded Abraham to sacrifice his beloved son Isaac, and Abraham—steadfastly committed to fulfilling God's word—was prepared to obey, until an angel intervened. As we walk, I wonder what Abraham thought in that moment when he imagined giving up his son, his only son, his beloved son, for something he thought might be even greater. Could there be anything greater than one's child, any purpose more lofty, any pursuit more deserving of our finite time? I think about Sarah, who is not mentioned in this story, though the midrash teaches that when she learned what had transpired between father and son, her soul fled her body and she died.[17] I wonder what Katrina, as a mother, makes of this story, but her thoughts are elsewhere. Whereas I am pensive, she walks quickly and excitedly. "What a dream come true, to be living in the land of the Bible."

Katrina finds it deeply moving to be making her home in the Holy Land, the land where the patriarchs and matriarchs pitched their tents and the land where Jesus preached. On weekends she and her husband take their children to visit important biblical sites—Shiloh, Bethlehem, Capernaum. They invite us to come with them—not to the Christian sites but to the Jewish ones. "Don't you want to see the tabernacle where Hannah brought Samuel?" she asks me. I don't quite know how to explain to her that it is not the tombs and tabernacles that move me religiously, but the texts and traditions. When I read the Bible, I connect not to the sites but to the stories.

As Katrina and I walk along the promenade, I think about Abraham and Isaac walking together, the father with a broken heart, and the son still bewildered by the situation. "Abraham set out for the place of which God had told him. On the third day, Abraham looked up and saw the place from afar" (Genesis 22:3–4).

I cannot imagine raising a knife to a child—I don't even deprive my kids of dessert. But I can identify with what it might have been like for Abraham to be both present and elsewhere, his eyes looking off into the distance to see the place from afar instead of gazing into the eyes of the child standing at his side.

The Torah tells us that Abraham woke early that morning, a detail that seems extraneous to the narrative—what difference does it make when Abraham awoke? Katrina would never agree, but I suspect that maybe, just maybe, before he set off with his son, Abraham needed a few moments of quiet to himself.

7

Tell Me a Yitzvi

MANY OF THE STORIES IN THE BIBLE FEATURE CHIL-
dren who struggle to define themselves in relation to their parents and siblings, from Abraham, who leaves his ancestral home
in response to God's command, to Isaac, who is nearly sacrificed
by his father, to Jacob, who must flee his parents' home to escape his brother's wrath, to Joseph, who loses touch with his
family for decades. Abraham becomes the father of a great nation, Isaac becomes a wealthy herdsman and farmer who sows
and reaps a hundredfold, Jacob frees himself from the grip of
his uncle and reconciles with his brother, Joseph rises to power
in Egypt and saves his family from famine. The multigenera-
tional arc of the book of Genesis reminds us that eventually our
children grow up.

Yet our children don't always grow up at the pace we would
want, or at the pace we'd expect. Sometimes I will plead with
my children for weeks to assume responsibility for a particular
task—to remove their lunch boxes from their schoolbags in the
afternoons, to practice their instruments without being reminded.
And then suddenly they'll surprise me by taking on more responsibility than I'd ever have thought to demand of them.

I don't expect my youngest children, at ages five and two,

to get themselves ready for school in the morning. And so I was taken aback when one day I returned from an early-morning run to find Shalvi and Yitzvi fully dressed and eating breakfast on the kitchen floor. It was 7 A.M., and the house was otherwise silent. "Is everything OK? Why are you eating on the floor?" I asked. Shalvi smiled up at me as she spooned cornflakes into Yitzvi's mouth.

"Because of Yitz-a-vi," Shalvi said matter-of-factly, adding another syllable to her brother's name as she is wont. "He was hungry and I couldn't put him in his high chair, it was too high for me. So I decided we would both sit together here. I even set the table."

I looked up at the table, which was set with three bowls. "But you're eating on the floor," I pointed out.

"No, Ima, I set the table for the big kids, for when they wake up. They don't have to sit on the floor. Only us."

"Who else is awake now? Did Abba go to shul?"

Daniel usually waits to go pray until I get home from my run. I don't run every day, and he doesn't make it to the synagogue every day, but we each try our best.

"No, Ima, don't you know?" She looked at me as if impatient with my ignorance. "Abba is sleeping," Shalvi told me, and Yitzvi lit up at the sound of his name.

"Ababababababa," he said excitedly, looking around to see if Abba had made an appearance.

"Shh," Shalvi told him. "I told you that Abba is sleeping. We have to be quiet."

I was confused. If Abba was sleeping, who got Yitzvi out of his crib and dressed?

"Shalvi," I said, sitting down beside her as I untied my sneakers. "Explain to me. What did you do this morning?"

"I woke up. I mean, Yitz-a-vi woke me up. He wanted to get out of his crib. So I took him out of his crib. I took off his pajamas and put on a shirt. I told him I would give him a passy if he let me put it on." Wow. I thought only I knew that pacifier trick!

"No more jamamas," said Yitzvi proudly, pointing to his onesie.

"You got him dressed by yourself?"

"Yes," said Shalvi. "But I didn't change his diaper." She wrinkled her nose as if to explain why not. "Ima, I also made my bed. And I brushed my teeth. And I got dressed for Gan. And then we were going to play *Milchama*." Whenever my kids use a Hebrew term, I know they are referring to something they learned in their Hebrew-speaking schools, in this case, the card game War. I nodded, glancing at the playing cards strewn across the kitchen floor. Lately Shalvi was so obsessed that she would often play a version of the game in which I was her opponent without even needing to be there—she'd draw a card for herself and then for me and update me every few minutes about how poorly I was doing. Had Shalvi played War on Yitzvi's behalf as well? "He couldn't play, Ima," Shalvi continued, as if reading my mind. "It's too hard for him, he doesn't know the numbers. He was hungry. So now we are eating breakfast."

Yitzvi had dried milky cornflakes stuck to his chin and to his white giraffe onesie, which was unbuttoned; the cotton fabric with its open snaps hung loosely over his full diaper. Shalvi's neglected bowl of cereal looked soggy, suggesting that she was dutifully committed to feeding Yitzvi first. "And no one helped you?" I repeated, duly impressed. Shalvi bent her head to meet her upraised shoulder, the way that Israeli kids answer in the negative.

"Shalvi," I told her admiringly, "that's amazing. And it reminds me that I have to tell you a Mitzi."

As is so often the case, I found myself in the midst of a moment that is best captured by a book. Originally published in 1970 and familiar from my own childhood, *Tell Me a Mitzi* is a collection of stories about a sister and brother who look like they are exactly the ages of Shalvi and Yitzvi. Mitzi likes to be the big sister and take charge, and Jacob repeatedly says, "Dadadadada," which always makes Yitzvi burst out laughing. They live in an apartment on Manhattan's Lower East Side at some point in the last century—the lintel of their building is engraved with the numbers 1938, and a street vendor with an umbrella-shaded cart sells sweet potatoes for ten cents. In the first story, which has always been my favorite, Mitzi wakes up before her parents and attempts to take Jacob in a taxi to visit their grandparents. Mitzi, on her own, makes Jacob his bottle. Each part of this process is described in painstaking detail, time slowing down as Mitzi deliberately and determinedly gets the bottle, carries it to the kitchen, opens the fridge, takes out a carton of milk, pours it in, puts the top back on . . . She climbs into Jacob's crib to change his (cloth!) diaper, then lifts him out of his crib and dresses him in overalls, a snowsuit, and mittens. They are ready to leave home, and they do.

Mitzi lifts up Jacob because neither of them can reach the elevator button. Shalvi can reach the elevator button in our building already, but she often lifts up Yitzvi, who insists on pressing it himself. "Nu, nu, nu," Yitzvi says each time, wagging his finger back and forth forbiddingly at the alarm button in the middle of the last row, which Shalvi has taught him he may not press—a lone Tree of Knowledge that never ceases to beckon.

Thankfully Shalvi has never tried to leave home alone with Yitzvi. Ultimately, though, Mitzi and Jacob don't get very far either—Mitzi does not know the address of her grandparents' apartment, so the taxi driver deposits them back on the curb, and Mitzi and Jacob return home and go back to bed, where their parents eventually discover them. "What is Grandma and Grandpa's address?" Mitzi asks her mother, without explaining why she wants to know.

My kids have never actually attempted to visit their grandparents—not surprisingly, since their grandparents live across the Atlantic—but they love to pretend they are en route. They take out our suitcases from the storage closet, use our smallest prayer books as passports, and pretend the living room couch is a giant airplane—anyone who lets their feet dangle down to the carpet is risking his or her life. This game can occupy them for hours on a Shabbat afternoon, and once or twice Daniel and I even managed to take a nap during it.

By the end of the story, Mitzi's mother still has no idea that her children left the apartment in the morning; she can't understand why Mitzi insists she is too exhausted to take off her pajamas. The book allows children to fantasize about what it would be like to have total independence, marshaling all their skills and knowledge to get as far as they can on their own, with the naïve reassurance that they can trust in the kindness of strangers to ensure they return home safely.

As a child I loved Mitzi because I admired her confidence, her initiative, her pluck. But now as a parent, I love Mitzi because of the responsibility she assumes for her brother Jacob. The story reminds me that even if I don't always notice, my children are growing up. And Shalvi knows it, too. "Ima, it's not *Tell Me a Mitzi*," she informs me when I finish the first story. "It's Tell Me a Yitzvi!"

8

⁊ℭ

Running Away

DURING THE PERIOD WHEN WE HAD FOUR CHILDREN under the age of five, I used to walk my kids to and from preschool every day. My son would ride a scooter, my twin daughters would sit in their double stroller, and the baby would nestle in the carrier attached to my stomach. The preschool was only a twenty-minute walk away, but often it took us over an hour to get home at the end of the day. My son would refuse to get on his scooter. My daughter would insist we stop at the water fountain. Her twin sister would unbuckle herself from her stroller to chase a cat. By the time we arrived home, I was exhausted and ready for the day to be over.

One afternoon we walked in the door and I realized that we had forgotten my son's scooter by the water fountain. My heart sank. I knew that I would never be able to head out again with all the kids. But I also knew that the scooter was likely to disappear if I didn't retrieve it immediately. I was the only adult in the house, and I didn't have a neighbor who could come over and watch the kids. What could I do?

I unstrapped the girls, put the baby down, and called my mother in New York, seven hours behind, where she was just starting her day. "Can you read them stories for fifteen minutes?" I pleaded. I left all the kids on the couch and gave my son my telephone; he held it while my mother began to read Anna Dewdney's Llama Llama books. The kids loved these books about a little llama who experiences all the emotions bound up in starting school, staying home sick, losing a first tooth, visiting grandparents. I told the kids I would be back very soon—their grandmother was in charge, and they were not allowed to move from the couch. I ran out of the house at breakneck speed, racing down the bike path to the water fountain, where my son's scooter lay abandoned in the bushes. I was home less than fifteen minutes later, breathless. Thankfully the kids were sitting exactly where I had left them—my mother hadn't even gotten to *Llama Llama Misses Mama*, and already I was back.

The Llama Llama books are all in rhyme, so the word "drama" appears quite frequently. But I don't think it's only because of the rhyme. With little children, there is always drama—the skinned knee, the lost doll, the hurt feelings. In our family, so much of the drama of parenting and early childhood has involved reading. At least I know that while I am reading to my children, they are not getting into trouble.

🦙

In the book of Genesis, parents don't always watch over their children closely. Abraham allows Sarah to banish his son Ishmael to the wilderness. Jacob stands idly by as his youngest son torments his older brothers. Perhaps the children grow up more quickly because their parents are not hovering. But it's a difficult balance to strike. When we are at the playground, I sometimes let Shalvi be the one to go up and down the slide with Yitzvi while I read on the park bench, glancing up at them every so often from a safe distance. Such freedom comes at a cost, and

I've had a few scares. One day I looked up from my book to find Shalvi standing with Yitzvi on the curb, peering out at the street bordering the park. Yitzvi was wagging his finger and saying, "Nu, nu, nu"—he knows he's not allowed to go into the street, but he finds it thrilling to stand perilously close.

No doubt Yitzvi would run away if he could, not because he is trying to escape from us but because he wants to squeal with delight when inevitably—he has no doubt it will happen—we find him. "Where's Yitzvi?" I'll ask the twins while we are in the kitchen making pizza, spreading tomato sauce and sprinkling shredded cheese over the dough. The girls will shrug their shoulders, and I'll run down the hall and discover him "cleaning" the bathroom, wielding a dripping toilet brush.

Usually at bedtime Yitzvi will sit on Shalvi's bed flipping through board books while I read to Shalvi, but one night, when he had no interest in sitting still, I let him run off. I assumed he would join Daniel, who was cleaning up after dinner. That night Shalvi wanted to read *Alfie Runs Away*, the story of a little boy about Shalvi's age—five, maybe six—who informs his mother that he is going to run away after she tells him that she is giving away his favorite red shoes, which he has outgrown. Instead of chasing Alfie, or telling him not to run away, his mother advises him to take the proper provisions: a water bottle in case he gets thirsty, a flashlight with extra batteries in case it gets dark, peanut butter and crackers in case he gets hungry, and a bag to carry it all. He also takes his stuffed Buddy Bear after his mother warns him that the bear might miss him, and three books, including one about a frog and a toad.

"Ima, we have that book," Shalvi interrupts me. We squint to try to make out the picture on the cover of the book that Alfie stuffs in his backpack. Is it indeed *Frog and Toad*, one beloved book hidden in the pages of another? The allusion recalls the felicitous serendipity of discovering a familiar friend in an unexpected place, like the time we ran into one of Shalvi's pre-school classmates at the zoo. Who would have thought Frog and Toad would be hanging out in Alfie's bedroom?

Alfie never gets any farther than the backyard. When he starts to get lonely, he looks for his mother's hug in the bag, and just then his mother—once again with her impeccable intuition—comes out to give Alfie a real hug and escort him home on the final page. I hope this story, like Alfie's backyard, can function as a safe space where Shalvi can imagine running away without ever having to leave her bedroom. As if reading my thoughts, she looks up from the book and tells me, "Don't worry, Ima. If I ever run away, I won't go too far." I smile.

"Thank goodness," I tell her, taking my cues from Alfie's mother, but thinking, too, of *The Runaway Bunny*. "If you ran away for longer than that, I would miss you so much."

At the end of the book, Alfie decides to put his old shoes on Buddy Bear, since they'll never grow too small for the stuffed animal. Ironically, once Alfie gets new shoes, he'll presumably be able to run even faster and farther, and it may have been his ambivalence about that prospect that in part motivated his running away in the first place. The midrash teaches that after Joseph's brothers threw Joseph into a pit, they sold him to Ishmaelite traders for the price of a pair of shoes, perhaps an allusion to their own desire to walk away from the crime.[18] It's hard to run away from home and family without some degree of ambivalence.

I tell Shalvi that now that we've finished the book, it's Yitz-vi's turn for a story—but where is he? "Daniel, I'm coming to get Yitzvi," I call down the hall.

"Isn't he with you?" Daniel calls back a bit louder than necessary, since I'm now in the kitchen, and I can see that Yitzvi is nowhere in sight. "Did we lose Yitzvi?" I ask, thinking of Alfie.

The kids rally to the task, searching for him in all the likeliest places, but alas, no Yitzvi. I know there is no point calling out his name, because that will only encourage him to play along. And sure enough, moments later, we discover a grinning Yitzvi perched on a chair on our porch wearing only a diaper and sandals. Who knew he could open the sliding door all on his own? He looks awfully proud of himself, with one pacifier in his mouth and two more in his hand. With his other hand, he's strapping and unstrapping the Velcro on his sandals—as if contemplating how far they might take him someday.

I confess I'm also guilty of running away at times, and not just in the mornings, when I sneak out of the house to jog at the first light, hoping to return before the kids rouse. I also run away in a nonliteral sense, by which I mean in a literary sense—I sneak away to read. I've learned that if I'm out of sight, the kids are more likely to solve—or at least attempt to solve—their disputes and difficulties on their own. "Ima, can you untie my shoe?" my daughter will call over to me; she hands me her shoe and I untie it. But if I'm not in the room, I don't respond. "Ima, can you untie my shoe? Ima, can you help me?" I hear her saying. "Ima, I need you to—never mind, I did it," her voice trails off. By keeping my distance, I am training my kids to untangle their own knots—or so I tell myself.

I never truly know where my own wishes end, and my kids' needs begin. After the murder of Abel, God tells Cain that "sin crouches at the door; its urge is toward you, yet you can be its master" (Genesis 4:7). At night while the kids play in the bath-tub, I crouch outside the bathroom door with a book, close enough that I can peer through the crack of the doorjamb and jump up immediately if anyone needs assistance, but hidden enough that they don't know I'm there. My kids are no lon-ger babies, and they are safe in the shallow water. But even so, maybe reading behind the bathroom door is an urge I should master.

There are times when I know that my presence is necessary. One Shabbat afternoon my daughter fell apart for no apparent reason. She claimed that her older brother was bothering her, but he had already apologized and told her that he was happy to help her with the marble slide she was constructing out of wooden blocks. She refused his help and continued to yell "go away" any time one of us approached. "Go away!" she yelled at me when I sat down beside her. I know that when a child yells at a parent to go away, she is only testing to see whether the par-ent will actually do it. But I couldn't bear to hear her screaming inconsolably. "I'm going to read in my room," I told her firmly, hoping that my tone did not betray my aggravation. "If you want my help, or you just want to sit on my lap, please come."

In the book of Genesis, Abraham's concubine Hagar is ban-ished to the wilderness with her son, Ishmael. When they run out of water, she cannot bear to stand by helplessly as her son dies of thirst. And so she leaves the child under the bushes and sits at a distance, "a bowshot away" (21:16)—not much farther than I was from my daughter, under the covers with my book.

Not long after, I came to the end of the chapter and realized the crying had ceased. I emerged from the bedroom cautiously—there was no sign of my daughter. "What happened?" I asked my son. He explained that a friend had knocked on the door with her mother to ask if my daughter wanted to play, and she had immediately rallied and gone outside. I thought of the angel sent by God who miraculously appeared and consoled Hagar in the wilderness. I wasn't sure which of my daughter's friends had stopped by, but I like to think I knew Who sent her.

❧

As a child I loved the book *Five Minutes' Peace*, about an elephant mother named Mrs. Large who needs an escape from her adorable but incorrigible three little elephants after they strew cornflakes across the breakfast table, knock over the marmalade jar, and wear their cereal bowls on their heads. With her bathrobe on and curlers still in her hair, Mrs. Large takes her teacup and newspaper and sneaks off to the bathroom, telling her children—when they inquire—that she needs "five minutes' peace." Alas, although the cover of the book features Mrs. Large luxuriating in the tub with her shower cap on and her eyes blissfully shut, her charges do not leave her alone for long.

Rereading the book as a parent, I know just how Mrs. Large feels. Sometimes on Shabbat, when Daniel and I are both home with the kids all afternoon, I tell him that I'm going out for a few minutes to take the compost to the community garden in the park outside our building. Next to the compost heap is a small garden bed with a scarecrow, a rusty barrel painted to resemble a train car, and a small hut lined with bookshelves that serves as a makeshift lending library for neighborhood residents to borrow and drop off books. No trip to the compost is complete without scanning the library to see what new books have appeared. Inevitably I pull a worn paperback off the shelf—some bestseller I never read—and read the first twenty pages or so before heading back. When I return, sometimes a full half hour later, I worry that Daniel will raise his eyebrows or make a sarcastic comment

about how long it took me to walk across the park. But he almost never does. His ability to overlook my shortcomings is one
of the many reasons we are still happily married.

Long before I met Daniel, when I was single and living
in Jerusalem alone, I was often invited to the home of one of
my teachers and mentors, a prolific scholar and mother of five
young children. Bina and her husband had designed their home
themselves—it consisted largely of open space, with a sprawling
garden out back and ample room for the children to play. At
the center of the home—between the kitchen area and the living space—was a large wooden desk where Bina sat and wrote
while her kids built block towers, climbed up and down the tall
ladder leading up to their bedroom loft, and experimented in
the kitchen. "I would never be as productive if I worked behind
a closed door," Bina told me. "I would always be wondering
what my kids were doing. This way, I can keep an eye on them
while I work—they inspire me to write more playfully." I marveled then, as I marvel now, at how Bina could concentrate with
so much noise and activity around her.

To bring children into the world is a creative act. But creative
realms are often in tension with one another. Alice Neel reput-
edly once left her baby on the fire escape of her New York City
apartment so that she could finish a painting, and Doris Lessing
abandoned her husband and children in Rhodesia to write her
novels. In Ashley Audrain's domestic thriller, *The Push*, a mother
wears headphones so that she won't hear her baby's cries while
she is writing. When I read that line, I grimaced in chilling recognition, not because I have ever willfully ignored my children's
cries but because I identify so deeply with the impulse. "It was
the nightingale, and not the lark," Juliet tells Romeo wishfully,
desperate to prolong their tryst past dawn. "Surely that is not
my baby crying, but the downstairs neighbor's baby," I've told

myself wishfully, desperate to prolong my one free hour to read or to write.

And yet I know I ought to be careful what I wish for. Not long ago, Daniel took all the kids to his sister's house for Shabbat, leaving me home alone. It was a gift to me; for the first time in as long as I could remember, I would have a day with no obligations and no interruptions whatsoever. Not five minutes' peace, but thirty hours! I took advantage of the opportunity to read a long novel—*The Luminaries* by Eleanor Catton—since I so rarely have the sustained attention for such a lengthy and involved book. I spent Shabbat in the shipping offices and opium dens of a gold rush town in nineteenth-century New Zealand, caught up in the intrigue surrounding a hermit's mysterious death in a remote cottage. I ate Friday night dinner in the smoking room of the local inn and spent the morning negotiating with a gold fields magnate. In the afternoon I took a walk with a fortune teller and a prostitute, and listened to all these individuals testify in the local magistrate's court while sitting on our porch as the sun set, the stars came out, and the kids spilled out of the elevator and bounded through the door.

"Did you miss us?" Daniel asked me later that evening, when we were unpacking the kids' clothes. I wondered how honest I should be. I didn't miss them for even a second, no. But when they returned, I was overjoyed to be reunited—to tickle Yitzvi until he agreed to get undressed for the bath, to tuck him into bed, to read to him under the covers. The knowledge that they would all be back enabled me to relish the solitude. If I harbor the fantasy of running away, it is only because, like Mrs. Large, I know it's just a fantasy. Sooner or later the kids will open the bathroom door and jump in the tub alongside me.

9

The Set Table

I ALWAYS KEEP A POETRY BOOK ON THE WINDOWSILL IN the kitchen so I can read a poem or two while waiting for the pot to heat or the next batch of cookies to bake. I know I've stumbled upon something arresting when the soup boils over or dessert starts to burn. "These cookies are brought to you by Wallace Stevens," I will tell the kids when they complain they're too crispy.

Reading in the kitchen is not just an escape from our hectic household but also a parenting strategy. My kids are not big eaters, and they don't like to sit at the table. When they were babies, I strapped them into their high chairs so they couldn't run off; now I use books to keep them put. I promise the kids that as long as they stay seated and eat nicely, I'll keep turning the pages.

I wish we were the kind of family who sat down together for dinner every night, as my family did when I was a kid. But like many families, we are rarely all home at once. Matan has robotics on Sundays; Tagel has gymnastics on Mondays and Wednesdays; and Daniel comes home late from work on Tuesdays and Thursdays. The younger kids need to eat early, while the other kids are still out at their activities, so there is no weeknight when we all can sit down together. Instead, we just strive to make sure all the kids are fed before 6 P.M., and Daniel and I try to get a bite in edgewise during the postprandial bath-time craze. We usually only eat at our table on Shabbat; the rest of the week it is strewn with notebooks and markers and scissors and glue, and we eat on barstools at the kitchen counter.

Our kids generally get along very well when they are working on a shared project—building a tower with Magna-Tiles, squeezing lemons for a lemonade stand, choreographing a dance to a popular song. But when they are sitting together in the kitchen, they inevitably start to bicker: *She took my spoon. He spilled his water on me. How come she doesn't have to finish her soup?* Instead of responding, I read, counting on the story to distract and draw them in. The kids know that if they miss a page because they're too busy getting back at a sibling, the loss is theirs; I won't go back.

One of the most important Jewish legal works of all time is the *Shulchan Aruch*, which means "set table," and is often referred to in English as the Code of Jewish Law. Composed in the Galilee in the sixteenth century by Rabbi Joseph Caro, the *Shulchan Aruch* is a comprehensive treatise covering all aspects of Jewish law, including Shabbat and holiday observance, dietary restrictions, marriage, mourning, and Torah study. The *Shulchan Aruch* primarily reflects the practices of Mediterranean and North African Jews, but it was followed by a commentary reflecting northern European practice by Rabbi Moshe Isserles—his commentary on the Set Table is known as the *Mapah*, which means "tablecloth." Neither the *Shulchan Aruch* nor the *Mapah* was intended for reading at mealtimes— the title of the *Shulchan Aruch* comes from a midrash in which God tells Moses to explain the laws of the Torah to the people of Israel as clearly as possible, "setting the laws before them like a set table."[19] The set table is a metaphor, but I think of it when I read with my kids at dinner.

At mealtimes we primarily read picture books, since they are accessible to all ages, and I can show the kids the illustrations while I read. I keep a few favorites stashed among the cookbooks in the pantry, for easy access. Some of these titles have been read so frequently over dinner that they have dried pasta stuck to the pages and breadcrumbs in the spine. These include our all-time favorite dinnertime read, *The Seven Silly Eaters* by Mary Ann Hoberman, about a family of picky eaters—"silly" is a euphemism for "picky," which describes my kids as well.

We read *The Seven Silly Eaters* about as often as we eat pasta, namely, several times a week. When the book begins, the family is small but growing, consisting of a husband with a tool belt slung around his waist, a wife who practices cello while sitting on the porch swing of their country house, and a little baby boy playing with his toes in a wicker bassinet. Mr. and Mrs. Peters have the perfect son, except that Peter is, well, picky— his milk must be exactly the right temperature if he is to drink it. But Mrs. Peters doesn't mind. She prepares his bottle again and again until it meets with his satisfaction, even when she becomes busy with her next child, who proves equally fussy—baby Lucy refuses milk, and insists on drinking only pink lemonade. Once again Mrs. Peters obliges, humoring Peter and Lucy while caring for newborn Jack, who will eat only applesauce. As one child after another is born in quick succession, Mrs. Peters caters tirelessly to their demands—Mac eats only oatmeal without lumps, Mary Lou eats only homemade bread, and the twins Flo and Fran insist on poached and fried eggs, respectively.

"It's true we're picky," Matan reminds me when I mumble

a comment about poor Mrs. Peters, who stops kneading the dough for Mary Lou's bread to pin a cloth diaper on Fran (or is it Flo?). "But at least we all eat the same thing. You would never make us five different meals for dinner."

Matan is right about that. Everyone in the family has to eat the same thing, which is why I cook only those foods that all my silly eaters agree upon. Our weeknight dinners consist of a steady rotation of pasta with tomato sauce, pasta with cheese, lasagna, homemade pizza, tofu, and omelets, supplemented by vegetable soup and salad for the brave of heart. But each week, as I fry up yet another dinner of omelets, I own up to the truth about which came first, the chicken or the egg. I make simple meals because my kids are picky, but if I invested time and thought into making more creative and elaborate dinners, I have no doubt that all of us—all seven silly eaters—would finally learn to eat well.

"You have to agree," Liav implores me. "We're so much better than the silly eaters. We don't eat bread in the living room—Abba would get so mad if we did that. And we don't let the dog lick oatmeal from our bowls."

"That's because we don't have a dog, because you won't let us get one!" Matan can't resist any opportunity to remind his parents how much he wants a dog, and how terrible we are for refusing.

"We also don't fall asleep at the table, or hang upside down over the banister, or leave our toys and shoes all over the floor," Tagel adds, pointing to the evidence in the illustrations. I beg to differ. Since when do my kids not leave their toys and shoes all over the floor?

"But we're good at being silly," says Matan with a mischievous grin. "Who am I?" he hoots. He jumps out of his seat and runs to the front door of our apartment, before making a bee-line for me, crashing into me as I stand against the stove. "Harriet the Spy!" I cry out immediately. Whenever Harriet comes home from school to her Upper East Side apartment, she runs straight into the family cook. I guess that's me.

"Who am I?" Tagel takes a turn playing along. She runs to the cupboard to grab a tin can and lifts an empty cracker box off the counter. "I'm going to eat some metal and cardboard with my pasta tonight," she tells us.

"Gregory!" We laugh, though it's been a while since we've read *Gregory, the Terrible Eater*, a picture book about a goat who insists on eating fruits, vegetables, and eggs instead of the bottle cap and piece of rug his parents serve for breakfast. His parents bring back flat tires and a broken violin from the town dump for him to sample, and Gregory gets a stomachache from all that "junk."

The kids want to keep going, invoking the very hungry caterpillar, the elf who eats only blueberry pie, and Pete who becomes a pizza. They forget about the food on their plates, and I tell them that if they don't keep eating, I won't be able to finish reading about the seven silly eaters. Reluctantly they comply.

With each page I turn, Mrs. Peters grows increasingly exasperated and exhausted. As her kids get older, they want all the same foods, except they want more of them. Her husband is always around, delivering groceries or a basket of freshly picked apples, but the burden of the food preparation falls on her shoulders. Amid increasingly unwieldly piles of unfolded laundry and a sink of unwashed dishes, her cello languishes in the corner of the room, untouched.

It was Liav who first noticed the cello. "In the beginning of the book, when she has only one baby, she can still play the cello," she commented. "But then we don't see her cello for lots and lots of pages, because she's too busy to play."

I realized after Liav's perceptive comment that in a book with such richly detailed illustrations, I had missed part of the story in focusing on the words. My kids could instead pay attention to the illustrations, which function as kind of illuminated commentary on the text, filling in gaps by answering questions that the words do not address: How many pets does the family have? Who reads to the kids at bedtime? Are there any rooms in the house without books?

The Seven Silly Eaters reaches its climax on the night before Mrs. Peters's birthday, when she retires to bed and the seven kids—who all share one room in an attic loft with cribs, bunk beds, a canopy bed, and a rope ladder—decide to make her a birthday surprise. At the crack of dawn, they creep out of bed and each kid makes his or her favorite food to give to their mother. But when nothing comes out quite right, they throw it all into a pot and stick it into the still-warm oven to hide the evidence, before heading back to bed. Later that morning, Mrs. Peters stumbles downstairs in her bathrobe and fuzzy slippers and discovers "a pink and plump and perfect cake," made from milk, applesauce, eggs, oatmeal, bread, and lemonade. The cake is delicious for all, and from then on, they make it every night for dinner. "And now Mrs. Peters has time to play music again," Liav notes cheerily, pointing out the cello's reappearance on the penultimate page.

I like to imagine that someday our kids will sit nicely at the table, and perhaps even make dinner for the family. The oven timer will go off, and the kids will take out the quiche. "Ima," they'll call to me, "it's time to eat." Most likely I won't hear them, and they'll have to call me a few times until I finally look up from my book. "What are we eating tonight?" I'll ask, excited that we can finally sit down together for a meal. The kids will respond with the title of a book, because they know that's what I'm really asking—not what are we eating but what are we reading. There are plenty of books with no meals. But a meal without books is a different story. Who would do anything as silly as that?

10

Wild About Books

THE PRIMARY REASON I READ WITH MY KIDS AT THE table is to prevent them from arguing. I know from the book of Genesis how dangerous sibling rivalry can be: Ishmael torments Isaac. Jacob tricks Esau. Joseph's brothers sell him into slavery. And I don't even want to think about Cain and Abel. But the long arc of Genesis bends toward reconciliation. Isaac and Ishmael still do not speak at the end of their lives, but after years of estrangement, they come together silently to bury their father, Abraham (25:9). Jacob and Esau, after years of rancor and rivalry, embrace and exchange gifts (33:1–11). And Joseph ultimately offers his brothers hospitality in the land of Goshen and genuinely forgives them (45:5). Taken as a whole, a key message of the book of Genesis seems to be that while it is only natural for siblings to argue, we can provide our children with models of how to reconcile graciously.

Yet it is easier said than done. All too often my kids treat each other like Judy Blume's *The Pain and the Great One*, each convinced that it is their sibling who gets the better deal. In the first half of the book, the older sister complains about her brother, the Pain, who makes a racket while she tries to talk on the telephone and is allowed to stay up just as late as she is. In the second half, the younger brother is jealous of his older sister, who thinks she's the Great One just because she gets to feed the cat and knows how to play the piano. Both halves of the book end the same way, with the disgruntled narrator lamenting that the parent loves the other sibling more. There is no reconciliation, except in the mind of the reader, who realizes that brother and sister are both right.

We own many books about sibling rivalry, but when my kids squabble, I prefer to be distracting rather than didactic. When Tagel protests that she got the smallest piece of cake, I don't read to her about Alexander, who was convinced that his brothers had all the luck in Judith Viorst's *Alexander and the Terrible, Horrible, No Good, Very Bad Day*. When Matan refuses to switch seats with his younger sister and drips strawberry juice on her lap, I don't remind him about Peter, who ultimately agreed to paint his favorite chair pink and give it to his baby sister in Ezra Jack Keats's *Peter's Chair*. Instead, I think about which Shel Silverstein poems will make them both laugh so hard that they fall over one another in spite of themselves. I pick whichever William Steig book we haven't read in a while, so that they'll all listen up until Spinky has stopped sulking, or until they've forgotten why they were angry in the first place.

Sometimes I feel like Molly McGrew, the librarian in Judy Sierra's *Wild About Books*, who accidentally drives her bookmobile into the zoo and, upon finding herself there, begins reading aloud to the animals. The first book she reads is by Dr. Seuss, to whom the book is dedicated. Sierra, like Seuss, is a master of anapestic tetrameter, a meter ever so slightly reminiscent of an animal stampede—da da DUM, da da DUM, da da DUM, da da DUM. And a stampede is indeed what happens, as every beast in the zoo comes flocking.

Before long, the animals are itching to read on their own. Molly McGrew helps each species find the appropriate genre from her bookmobile: tall books for the giraffes, dramas for the llamas, and joke books for the laughing hyenas. Even the wildest animals are tamed by a passion for books. Indeed, the Tasmanian devils find books so exciting that they start authoring their own, giving up fighting for writing. Then the other animals follow suit, writing with their tails and quills. The hippo's memoir—perhaps ghostwritten by Sandra Boynton?—is so remarkable that it's awarded the Zoolitzer Prize.

This richly illustrated and delightfully entertaining picture book concludes with the author's sheepish apology, because now that all the animals are absorbed in their reading, there's not much to see at the zoo anymore. On the final page, the bored, disappointed visitors stand behind a wall with their colorful helium balloons, as each animal is holed up on a comfortable perch or in a cozy den, wild about books.

❧

As a parent, I sometimes feel like a cross between a zookeeper and a librarian, domesticating my charges by trying to select the right books at the right times. When my daughter is having a tantrum—when she lies on the floor screaming, "You don't love me! No one loves me!" or some such disturbing refrain—I have learned that there is nothing I can say that will calm her down. She feels too hurt, too unloved, too unlovable perhaps. But I can sit down with a book and begin reading so softly that eventually she quiets down to listen.

The book I often turn to in such moments is *Before You Were Born* by Howard Schwartz, a vibrantly illustrated picture book in which a father tells his child what happened in the womb. The book is written in the second person, as spoken by the father, so it is unclear whether the child—dressed in gender-neutral one-piece red pajamas—is a boy or a girl. Any child listening to the story becomes the child in the book, snuggling in the parent's arms to listen closely.

Before You Were Born is based on an ancient rabbinic teaching about how the soul of every child that will someday be born was fashioned during the six days of creation.[20] When a child is about to be conceived, God informs the angel in charge of conception, known as Lailah, to summon a particular soul and bring it before God. God then charges that soul to enter the womb of the mother, and although the soul is reluctant to leave eternal life in Eden, God insists that its time has come. The soul is implanted in the mother's womb, where it sees from one end of the earth to the other. A candle is placed on the child's head, and Lailah teaches that child about good and evil, about where that soul will live and where it will die. According to some versions, Lailah teaches the child the entire Torah—the book that existed even before there was a world.

When it comes time to be born, the child's soul is once again reluctant to move on, so the angel strikes it above the lips with the candle and it forgets all it has learned. In the original midrash, the angel adjures the child, "You know, my son, that you were formed against your will; against your will you will be born; against your will you will die; and against your will you are destined to give an accounting before the King of Kings, the Holy One Blessed Be He."

This is not exactly the version that appears in *Before You Were Born*, which is a cross between a midrash and a fairy tale. In the womb, Lailah reads to the child from the "Book of Secrets," a gilt-edged tome illuminated with mysterious symbols and pictures—a swan, a snake, a sun—with feather quills inserted as bookmarks. The child, in this version, hears many stories from the angel—about pumpkins and golden crowns and red-capped mushrooms and runaway gingerbread men. The angel teaches the child seventy languages, the languages of all the animals, and then, in one breathtaking caesura, we turn the page and there is a magnificent two-page spread with no words at all, just the child in pajamas walking with the angel through a flurry of snowflakes—suggesting that some of what the angel teaches the child is beyond the capacity of human language.

I linger on this wordless page, taking a moment to bask in that wintry wonderland. I consider pointing out to my daughter that each snowflake is distinct and unique, and no two snowflakes—like no two children—are ever exactly the same. The beginning of the book of Genesis teaches that every human being is created in God's image, and yet no two human beings are identical. The book concludes, many generations later, with the blessings Jacob confers on each of his children and grandchildren, each of whom has distinctive traits and talents: Judah is the king of beasts; Issachar is a strong-boned ass; Dan governs his people. I want my daughter to realize that she is beloved and unique, and the world is in need of the flurry of gifts that only she can share.

But my daughter, who long ago forgot her tears, has no patience for my musings; she is eager for the child to be born. She turns the page for me so that it is autumn now, with its swirl of bright and colorful leaves, and the child in the womb is learning the language of the wind. And then it is time. In the book the angel does not hit the child with the candle—that would be too violent—but presses her finger to the child's lips, reminding the child to keep everything she has been taught a secret. The child will forget it all when leaving the womb, but a whole lifetime lies ahead. On that last page, the child—now a bit older looking, perhaps, but with the same red pajamas—lies in bed with an A to Z alphabet book, suggesting that the soul that learned seventy languages is beginning all over again.

We read *Before You Were Born* in moments of distress, but also on special occasions. Often we return to it on birthdays, not just because it is a book about being born but because the book reminds me of the inherent value of each individual— each soul chosen by God to enter a particular seed at a particular point in time.

The midrash on which this picture book is based teaches that just as every soul is reluctant to enter the world, every soul is reluctant to leave. We do not choose when we will be born or when we will die. Nor do we choose the pace at which our lives seem to unfold. We do not even always get to choose the books we read. Sometimes these books are chosen for us, and sometimes they choose us, insisting—like the child's hand tugging at my sleeve—that this is the story I must read right now. I have no choice but to take the book down from the shelf and bring it to the bed, or the kitchen counter, or the floor where my child is crying, or feeding her brother breakfast. "Listen," I say, but I need not say anymore, because the story is already unfolding. The pages turn as if of their own accord; the story we are reading is our own.

EXODUS

The Journey to Freedom

THE BOOK OF EXODUS NARRATES THE ISRAELITES' JOURNEY from slavery to freedom and the giving of the Ten Commandments at Sinai. It is a story of moving from a place of complete and total reliance on others to a place of independence. And it is a story about receiving the gift of a text inscribed on stone that will become a source of meaning and a guide to life. As a parent, I have accompanied my children on the journey to independent reading, watching them stumble over letters and words—like Moses slow of speech and tongue—until the signs on the page transform into the wonder of stories and ideas. As my children have developed their own reading preferences, they have also individuated and become their own people, blessed with texts that inspire and guide them on their journey.

1

Signs and Wonders

ONE OF THE FIRST BOOKS I EVER TRIED TO READ ON MY own is the Haggadah, a collection of prayers, blessings, biblical verses, and rabbinic interpretations recited each year at the Passover Seder. As my family sat around a long table, joined by guests who more than tripled our number, I snuck frequent glances at my father, who conveniently marked our place in the text with his finger. I wanted to know what we were up to in the Haggadah, and I wanted to be able to read aloud when it was my turn, even though I was still learning to recognize the Hebrew letters on the cover—Hey, Gimel, Dalet, Hey.

I learned to read by sounding out those letters: "Ha-Ga-D-aH." It is a form of the Hebrew word "to tell," based on the biblical injunction to "tell your children on that day: It is because of what God did for me when I went free from Egypt" (Exodus 13:8). The Passover Seder is all about teaching the next generation about the liberation of the Jewish people from bondage in Egypt, which is the subject of the second book of the Bible. I was interested in learning about the Exodus, but I was far more interested in learning how to read.

Even at a young age—I wasn't yet in kindergarten—I understood that true liberation would come when I was able to read on my own. I no longer wanted to be at the mercy of a parent who might or might not have time to read to me, or a librarian who might or might not hold story hour that particular morning. When I could read independently, I knew, I would be able to be anywhere I wanted at any time—in the jungle with the wild things, at the carnival with Harlequin, or out building pyramids with the Israelite slaves in the Egypt of my illustrated Bible.

Perhaps because I read to them so frequently, my children did not internalize this lesson to the same extent. I was happy to drop everything and read whenever any of the kids presented me with a book. Not surprisingly, none of my kids learned to read in Hebrew before first grade, when they were taught in school; and it wasn't until third grade that my older kids showed any real interest in learning to read in English. During those early years of grade school, when they were able to read to themselves only in Hebrew, I read aloud to them many of the books in English that I had enjoyed when I was their age—*Little Women, The Railway Children, Five Little Peppers and How They Grew*, and my favorite of all—*The Secret Garden*.

All these books required a fair amount of explanation for my kids, who were growing up in a very different cultural context. As we sat on our porch overlooking a dog park and playground, I told them about the windswept moors and the heather-scented air of Yorkshire. The park outside our apartment building is surrounded by building complexes like ours with a large underground parking garage; my kids marveled at the notion of a manor house so large that there were still new wings to discover and little girls in gingham who traveled by stagecoach. They interrupted to ask about wartime telegrams, organ grinders, doctors who paid house calls, and children who had broth for dinner because their parents could not afford mutton. These were the episodes and landscapes that had cultivated my imagination when I was a young reader, and it felt important that my children, too, discover the secret garden, overhear the mysterious crying in the corridors, and witness the invalid's miraculous return to health as the lilies bloomed and the roses climbed the garden walls.

It is hard to imagine that my Israeli children will ever read such books to their own children, certainly not in English. I imagine the stories will seem too foreign and removed, like a garden overgrown and locked away. But no matter. They will choose other books to share. Though the stories may change, it is the tradition of telling stories to the next generation—the tradition of the Haggadah—that I hope will endure.

ℳ

The first chapter book I read with each of my children, *Charlotte's Web*, was also the first chapter book I read to myself. The book lay on the shelf in my childhood bedroom for a long time before I felt confident enough to pick it up. I wondered about the curious girl on the cover, who I assumed was named Charlotte, and the sad-eyed baby pig she clutched under her arm, its tail curled up beside the Newbery Honor medal. For a long time I didn't even notice the spider hanging down from the letter C, or the intricate web woven around the letters of the book's title. But as soon as I began reading, I got caught up in its gossamer threads.

Charlotte's Web begins not with Charlotte, who is in fact a spider, but with a farmer who has decided to do away with one of the pigs born in his barnyard the previous night. The pig is a runt, and the farmer has no use for it—runts make trouble, he tells his daughter. But big-hearted Fern cannot bear the thought of her father killing one of the newborn piglets. In the first illustration, she is grabbing the axe from her father's arms. Eventually her father relents. The piglet—whom Fern names Wilbur—is sold to Fern's uncle Mr. Zuckerman, and Fern comes down the road almost every day to visit, sitting on an old milking stool and observing his pen from a distance. Wilbur is spared, at least for the time being.

The Exodus story, which is retold each year at the Passover Seder, begins with a newborn who is fated to die. Born to a couple from the tribe of Levi, this baby, like all other Israelite infant boys at the time, is to be drowned in the Nile as per Pharaoh's decree: "Every boy that is born, you shall throw into the Nile!" (Exodus 1:22). But there is something special about this child—the Talmud teaches that when he is born, the whole house fills with light.[21] Instead of drowning him, his mother hides him for as long as she can, and then places him in a basket in the Nile, leaving her daughter to observe from a distance. The baby's sister, Miriam, watches over him devotedly from among the tall reeds that grow by the banks, concealing her from sight.

As Fern watches over him, Wilbur enjoys the comforts of Mr. Zuckerman's barn, where he is fed warm milk, potato skins, and a pail of slops poured into his trough. But when he learns from the sheep that he is being fattened for slaughter at Christmastime, he is outraged at the injustice of his fate. He panics, screams, and then bursts into tears. "I don't want to die," Wilbur moans, throwing himself to the ground.

Moses is raised in the comfort of Pharaoh's palace, where he is brought by Pharaoh's daughter after she discovers him crying in his basket in the Nile. When he gets older, he leaves the palace and goes out among his people. He witnesses an Egyptian beat a Hebrew slave, one of his kinsmen. Outraged by this injustice, he strikes the Egyptian and buries his body in the sand. Moses learns that the entire Israelite nation is crying out under the burden of Egyptian slavery: "The Israelites were groaning under their bondage" (Exodus 2:23). Who would hear their cries?

At their first encounter, Wilbur does not notice Charlotte—he hears only a voice calling down to him in the barn. It is a while before he realizes where the voice is coming from and looks up at the spider hanging from her web in the corner of the lintel by the doorpost. When Charlotte introduces herself, she tells Wilbur that she traps flies in her web and drinks their blood, to Wilbur's horror. She also tells him that she is nearsighted and can hardly see him; and yet she proves the most farsighted of all, for she devises a way of saving Wilbur from the terrible fate awaiting him: "I am going to save you," she announces from her perch. "Stop your crying!"

At first when God calls out to Moses, Moses is taken by surprise. He is out shepherding in Midian, where he fled after he killed the Egyptian taskmaster and became a fugitive from the law. Suddenly his gaze is arrested by the sight of a bush that is aflame. A voice calls out to him from the bush: "Moses, Moses!" It is the voice of God, promising to save the Israelites: "I have marked well the plight of My people in Egypt and have heeded their cries. . . . I have come down to rescue them" (Exodus 3:7–8). God charges Moses to free the Israelites, and when Moses protests that he is unsuited to the task, God tells him, essentially, to stop crying and listen up. God will save the people, and on the eve of their liberation, the Israelites will place blood on the lintels of their doors so that God might pass over them and strike the Egyptians.

It takes Charlotte a while to figure out how to save Wilbur.

The idea that comes to her is nothing short of a miracle, and indeed, the chapter describing the plan that the noiseless, patient spider hatches is called just that—"The Miracle." Charlotte launches forth filaments, unreeling them until she has woven a message in the center of the web: SOME PIG. When Mr. Zuckerman's farmhand catches sight of the web in the morning, he drops to his knees in prayer. "There's no mistake about it," Mr. Zuckerman reports to his wife. "We have received a sign.... A miracle has happened and a sign has occurred here on earth, right on our farm."

God takes the Israelites out of bondage by means of a series of signs and wonders. First God teaches Moses to turn his staff into a snake, and to place his hand into his bosom and draw it out covered in leprous scales. These signs are followed by a series of others, known as the ten plagues. Initially Pharaoh's magicians try to replicate the miracles on their own, but when it comes to the third plague, lice, they have to admit defeat. "This is the finger of God!" they cry, conceding that they are at the mercy of a far greater power (Exodus 8:15). The plagues culminate in the death of the Egyptian firstborn sons, at which point Pharaoh is all too eager to let the Israelites go. By means of these miracles, God redeems the Israelites—not because they are inherently special but because God loves them and has chosen them, of all the nations in the world, to be God's people.

On the Zuckerman farm, the first miracle of SOME PIG is followed by a series of others. The Zuckermans are duly awed, convinced that they, too, have seen the finger of God. They resolve that rather than slaughtering Wilbur for Christmas, they will exhibit him at the county fair in the spring. Wilbur's life is miraculously spared—not because he is inherently special but because Charlotte loves him and chooses him, out of all the animals in the barn, to be her friend.

Or so I thought, until I read *Charlotte's Web* again with my oldest son, Matan. "Why do you think Wilbur is saved?" I ask him when we are midway through the story, wondering if he has any insight into the inscrutability of divine favor. Matan's answer surprises me. "Wilbur is saved because Charlotte is a good writer. She knows that if you use the right words, you can basically do anything." It isn't what I'm expecting him to say, and I can't help wondering if Matan is telling me the answer he thinks I'd want to hear. I am forever extolling to my children the value of literacy. "If you learn how to read, you'll never be bored," I tell them when they complain that neither of their parents has time to play Candy Land or to take them out to the playground before dinner. There was one day when I expected to get home a little later than usual, so I left a note on the door for the kids to find after school: "Welcome home," I wrote, even though I knew it would be hard for them to sound out all the words. "There are fresh cookies in the pantry." I want my children to know that good things come to those who are literate.

It seems miraculous that a spider can weave words into her web, but the act of making meaning out of phonetic symbols is no less wondrous. One afternoon I discovered Tagel picking out a library book and trying to sound out the words on her own. "A New Co-At for Anna. What's a Co-At? What's a Co-At, Ima?" she called, and I told her to look at the picture, which featured the red woolen coat that Anna's mother makes for her in the early days after World War II, when they are too poor to purchase new clothing. In Harriet Ziefert's text and Anita Lobel's illustrations we witness the shearing of sheep, the spinning of wool, and the boiling of lingonberries to make a deep red dye—but the true miracle is watching the flying shuttles weave the pattern of the story in the enchanted loom of my daughter's mind.

✵

The miracles wrought by reading and writing are a theme in many books for young readers. Annie Sullivan is *The Miracle Worker* because she manages to teach Helen Keller to associate things with words and then to palm-spell, thus conveying meaning through language. In Roald Dahl's *Matilda*, in a chapter titled "The Third Miracle," the heroine saves her beloved teacher, Miss Honey, from the brutal headmistress, Agatha Trunchbull, by using her intense powers of concentration to manipulate a piece of chalk to write a threatening message on the blackboard. And in *Mrs. Frisby and the Rats of NIMH*, several rats who have been captured and taken to a lab at the National Institute of Mental Health (NIMH) manage to escape after they are taught to recognize the letters of the alphabet. This last novel made the greatest impact on my children, perhaps because—as they pointed out to me—it was only the literate rats who made their way to freedom.

In the book's opening chapter, we meet Mrs. Frisby, a widowed mouse with four young children and a problem on her hands: Her house is about to be destroyed by Farmer Fitzgibbon's plow, but she cannot relocate, because her youngest son is sick and frail. Mrs. Frisby takes counsel from a wise owl, who at first is dismissive. But then, as she is about to leave, he asks her name and learns that she is "Mrs. Jonathan Frisby."

Suddenly the owl is eager to help the poor mouse mother. He instructs Mrs. Frisby to go to the rats that live in the rosebush on Farmer Fitzgibbon's farm, and to be sure to tell them who she is. Mrs. Frisby does not know why, but she is learning

that her husband's name opens doors that would otherwise remain firmly shut.

"What does this remind you of?" I ask the kids. I am
greeted with blank stares. I tell them that when God redeemed
the Israelites from Egypt, it was by the merit of their ancestors:
"God heard their moaning, and God remembered His covenant
with Abraham and Isaac and Jacob. God looked upon the Israelites and God took notice of them" (Exodus 2:24–25). God
saved the Israelites because of a promise to their forefathers—
Abraham, Isaac, and Jacob. In Jewish tradition this is known as
zechut avot, ancestral merit. Jews begin praying by reminding
God of the covenant with our forefathers. The idea is that once
we remind God that we are their descendants, God is more
likely to heed us.

At the burning bush, God tells Moses, "I am the God of your
father, the God of Abraham, the God of Isaac, the God of Jacob"
(Exodus 3:6). And at the rosebush Mrs. Frisby tells the rats that
she is the wife of the late Jonathan Frisby. This term confuses my
children until I explain that Mrs. Frisby's husband is not delayed,
but dead. Mrs. Frisby learns that all the rats knew her husband,
as they were all captured together by lab technicians working at
NIMH. The rats were placed in cages and injected with steroids
to boost their intelligence. Then technicians began showing the
rats a series of pictures and symbols. For several weeks they saw
a picture of a rat, followed by an R, an A, and a T; they stared at
the symbols in much the same way, I imagine, that I stared at the
Hebrew letters on the cover of our family Haggadah.

Eventually one of the rats was able to read the sticker on
his cage that said, "To release door, pull knob forward and slide
right." By learning to read, the rats broke free from their cages
and ultimately masterminded their exodus from NIMH.

Although Mrs. Frisby's husband, Jonathan, escaped successfully, he later died heroically on behalf of all the other rats. By his merit, the rats living under the rosebush are ready and willing to help Mrs. Frisby escape Farmer Fitzgibbon's plow. When the book draws to a close, Mrs. Frisby's son is recovering and the family has settled comfortably into their new summer house in the garden. One evening after supper, Mrs. Frisby calls her children to gather around. She wants to tell them a story—a very long story.

By the time I come to the novel's final pages, it is two weeks before Passover. The kids have already begun practicing a skit about the Exodus to perform at our Seder—they will dress up as Israelites in long robes, place baby Yitzvi in our laundry basket, and pretend to set him in the Nile, a blue towel spread out on the floor. They will push one living room chair against another so they can then pull them apart and run through, as if it is the parted sea. They will sing wildly and triumphantly to celebrate their liberation. "In every generation, a person is obligated to view himself as if he has come out of Egypt," the Haggadah reads. My children take this injunction seriously.

But for now, they are sitting at the table calmly eating lunch after school as I read them the final paragraphs in which Mrs. Frisby shares with her children the story of their father's capture and escape from NIMH. She is the first to tell the story of the rat exodus to the next generation, and her children listen raptly. Someday they will sit around the table and tell this story to their children, and their children to their children, and on and on.

2

‚◎

The Top Ten Commandments

THE PURPOSE OF THE EXODUS FROM EGYPT IS FOR THE
Israelites to serve God, as Moses is told explicitly at the burning
bush: "When you have freed the people from Egypt, you shall
worship God at this mountain" (Exodus 3:12). The mountain
God is referring to is Horeb, also known as Sinai, which is both
the site of the burning bush and the place Moses will ascend to
receive the Ten Commandments and then, upon his descent,
give them to the Israelites, who must live in accordance with
God's word. The Israelites are liberated not so that they will be
free to do whatever they wish but so that they will be free to
follow God's commandments.

According to many Jewish commentators, it was not just
the Ten Commandments that the Israelites received at Mount
Sinai, but the entire Torah. The purpose of the Exodus, then, is
to receive a book—the Five Books of Moses. Now that my kids
are comfortable sounding out words on their own, I am excited
to share with them all the early-reader books I remember from
my own childhood—*Clifford the Big Red Dog, Danny and the
Dinosaur, Little Bear*. One afternoon I climb up to a high shelf
to retrieve the box where I stored these paperbacks after salvag-
ing them from my childhood home over a decade earlier.

When I climb down the step stool with *Morris Goes to School*, pointing to the picture of the big-antlered moose trying to do sums on the blackboard, I can tell that the twins are not interested. They don't want to hear about anthropomorphized animals; already at age six they are prancing around the house in hot pink plastic high-heeled shoes and asking for "flippy shirts" with sequins that change color when you run your hand over them.

I call my friend Ariana, the mother of my twins' best friend. Ariana is what my kids call a "cool mom." She is ten years my junior, which accounts for some of it, no doubt. But she is also far more creative and artistic. She is the kind of mother who dresses fashionably even when she is just dropping off her kids at school, orders wallpaper online to decorate her daughters' bedroom, and asks her kids weeks before the holiday how they want to dress up on Purim, so that she can sew their costumes herself. I often think how lucky her kids are to have a mother who is so talented and devoted.

Ariana, who is also American-born, reads voraciously, and she is always on the lookout for new books in English for her children. She subscribes to children's book blogs, reads book reviews, keeps lists of recommendations, and orders all her books online. Most of the books she shares with her children are contemporary—the kinds of books that weren't around when I was first learning to read. It was Ariana who introduced us to Chirri & Chirra, a series of picture books about two Japanese girls who bike through fields and forests together and eat mouthwatering treats described and depicted in delectable detail—acorn coffee, clover blossom tea, and strawberry jam sandwiches on walnut bread. I know Ariana will have an idea for me when I lament to her, "Forget Morris the Moose or Sammy the Seal. My kids have even started rolling their eyes at Amelia Bedelia!"

Ariana laughs. "So does Mia," she says, referring to her oldest daughter. "Amelia Bedelia wears a sunbonnet and an apron. Mia says she's too old-fashioned, and in a way she's right. I don't want my daughters reading about a nanny who spends her days dusting drapes and baking pies, and occasionally filling in for the doctor's assistant. Let them read about girls—I mean, young women—who become doctors themselves."

I ask Ariana if she knows any easy reader books about women doctors. "I don't," she admits. "But you have to start with characters they can relate to—characters who look the way our daughters want to look, whose bedrooms resemble the kind of bedroom they'd want for themselves. I bet your twins would love Fancy Nancy," she suggests.

I have to confess to Ariana that I've never even heard of Fancy Nancy—as I discover, the first book was published in 2005, after I'd already graduated college and nearly a decade before my daughters were born. But Ariana's recommendation proves spot-on. My twins take one look at the cover and immediately lunge for the book—they want to know more about this girl in a purple bathing suit, red high-heeled shoes, and a floral crown. Like Liav and Tagel—and unlike their very uncool mother—Fancy Nancy loves jewelry and clothes. She wears tutus and tiaras and strings Christmas lights around her bedroom mirror. The only problem is that Fancy Nancy wants her whole family to be as fancy as she is, and soon my girls follow suit.

"Ima, why do you always wear your hair in a braid?" Liav asks me, looking up from *Fancy Nancy and the Mermaid Ballet*. I tell her it keeps my hair out of my face. Then Tagel wants to know why I wear the same skirt several days in a row; I tell her

I hate doing laundry, and so I wear my clothes until they need to be washed. "But why don't you ever wear shirts with designs? Your clothes are so boring." I sigh. "I guess those are just not my *middot*," I tell my kids, speaking in a mixture of Hebrew and English. The word *middot* means both sizes and attributes—it is used to refer to clothing sizes, but also to a person's moral characteristics. I'm more concerned with conduct than with clothing, but when I tell this to the girls, they roll their eyes.

"When you were our age, did you also wear such plain and boring clothes?" they ask me, and I shrug. I don't really remember very much about what I wore, though I could tell them what I read. One day I was sitting in the elementary school cafeteria reading Louisa May Alcott's *An Old-Fashioned Girl* when a boy in my class pointed to my outfit—a shapeless floral jumper that looked as if it were sewn from window curtains—and said, "Look, she's reading a book about herself. She probably even wrote that book." Fancy Nancy, who likes fancy words as much as she likes elaborate accessories, would have had the proper multisyllabic comeback: "Excuse me, are you referring to my autobiography?"

One afternoon I pick the twins up at school wearing a pair of earrings that I once purchased on a whim in an accessories store in the Jerusalem central bus station when my bus was running late. The twins notice immediately. "Ima, wow, you're wearing jewelry today," Liav comments approvingly, reaching out to put her small finger through the metal hoops. "Why are you so fancy today?" Tagel wants to know. I think for a moment about how to respond. "I was teaching Torah this morning, so I wanted to look nice," I say.

In the book of Exodus, the Israelites build a golden calf while Moses goes up to the top of Mount Sinai to receive the

Torah. The people are supposed to wait patiently at the foot of the mountain, but they despair of Moses returning. Unable to handle the notion of an invisible abstract God unmediated by Moses, they decide to make their own god instead. They give their gold jewelry to Aaron, who melts it down and molds it into a calf. While Moses is communing with God at the top of the mountain, the people at the foothills are dancing and bowing to the calf in frenzied excitement.

I think about the contrast between Moses on the mountaintop and the people down below when I head into the twins' room one evening with a new book. They tell me they want to skip a story that night; they are too busy setting up a "makeup corner" in the space between their closet and their bed, filled with the only "makeup" they own—face paint, flavored chapstick, and the sparkly nail polish I once bought for them in the pharmacy in a moment of weakness. I sigh. I've come down the mountain bearing a book, but they're preoccupied with other matters down below.

"Can I put jewelry and makeup on you instead of reading a story tonight?" Tagel asks. "And I'll do your hair," Liav offers, bringing the sparkly silver box of hair bands that my sister bought her a few years ago, along with hot pink plastic high heels. "Even if you wear a braid every day, you don't have to wear the same plastic headband," Liav counsels me. "You could match it to your clothes, if only your clothes were more colorful." She opens her closet to show me what she means, and I think of Fancy Nancy, who hangs up a sign on her fridge for her family to read: "Learn to be fancy with lessons from Nancy." It seems my lessons have begun.

When Tagel finishes my makeup and Liav finishes my hair, they lead me to the bathroom mirror to examine their handiwork. In the midrash on the book of Exodus, the Israelite women are praised for their vanity. The midrash explains that when the Israelites were enslaved in Egypt, Pharaoh decreed that the men were not allowed to sleep at home, as a means of population control. The Israelite women, who refused to give in to Pharaoh, would take their mirrors out to the fields where their husbands were working and gaze at their own reflections flirtatiously, seducing their husbands in order to be fruitful and multiply. Later, after the Exodus, they donated these same mirrors for the construction of the Tabernacle, so that they might continue to perform a sacred function.[22]

We have plenty of mirrors in our home, but the girls are convinced that if we're all going to be fancy like Nancy, we need more supplies. They beg me to take them to Top Ten, an accessories store at our neighborhood mall. "Ima, we know you would never go to Top Ten, but please, just once." They're actually wrong about that. I've been to Top Ten several times, in the guise of the tooth fairy, stocking up on headbands and ankle bracelets to sneak under the girls' pillows each time they lose a baby tooth. Most of the accessories my girls own came from the tooth fairy, but as far as they are concerned, that has nothing to do with me.

I tell the twins that once they finish their English workbooks, I'll take them to Top Ten, and for better or for worse it works; the spelling exercises are completed in no time. "You promised, Ima," the girls insist, and of course they are right. Shalvi, as usual, wants to tag along. "Ima, do you think they will have things in my age?" She is confused about "size" and "age," and gives us trouble about wearing any items of clothing that don't have a 5 on the tag. "But Ima, it says 6, it's going to be too big. It's not for my age yet," she'll protest when I hand her a skirt to put on in the morning. It seems she, too, could use a lesson in *middot*.

Trying to redeem our trip to Top Ten, I tell the girls they can each pick one item in the store, subject to my approval, and then we'll save it to wear on Shabbat. "Why can't I wear my new headband to school tomorrow?" Liav wants to know, and I remind her that the ancient rabbinical sage Shammai would save everything special he found during the week to enjoy on Shabbat, the day we are supposed to make special and sanctify, as per the fourth commandment.[23] When the three girls have finally settled on their choices and I'm ready to pay, the saleswoman notifies me that it's "buy three, get one free," and I must choose something else.

"I know," exclaims Liav, "let's buy something for Ima!" Is this how they understand the fifth commandment? They rummage around excitedly, settling on a bottle of sparkly purple nail polish. "We'll save it for Friday, so we can polish your nails in honor of Shabbat," Liav assures me. Tagel, who notices my still-furrowed brow, knows just what to say. "Don't worry, it's not really purple," she tells me, trying to win me over with a literary allusion, now correctly pronouncing a word she had struggled to sound out the night before. "It's Fancy Nancy's favorite color—fuchsia."

3

❦

Left to Their Own Devices

AS MOSES LINGERED ON MOUNT SINAI, THE ISRAELITES grew impatient. Why was Moses late? Had he simply abandoned them? If the people no longer had Moses, they no longer had their link to the God Moses kept telling them about. Why then not fashion an idol?

Now that my kids are more independent, I am not always home when the older ones return from school. On days when I won't be there to greet them, I leave a note on the whiteboard affixed to our kitchen windowsill, indicating when I'll be back and what the kids can eat and any activities they have scheduled: IMA HOME 3:30. FRESH BREAD ON COUNTER. T GYMNASTICS 3 P.M., L VIOLIN LESSON 3:15 P.M.

Usually I am home soon after, but I don't rush. I want the kids to learn how to be responsible for themselves. They know the rules, both the positive and the negative commandments: Do homework. Practice instruments. No junk food. And above all—the rule that is most frequently violated—no screens. No games or YouTube videos on the tablet. No devices whatsoever when there is no parent home. But it turns out that knowing the rules is one thing. Following them is another.

While Moses is still on the mountain, God tells him to

hurry down because the people have built a golden calf. Moses descends in fury and is outraged to see that the people are dancing excitedly around an idol. He hurls the tablets, which shatter at the foot of the mountain, before proceeding to rebuke Aaron and the Israelites. The people had been told explicitly that they may not worship other gods or create sculpted images or likenesses—they just heard these words spoken from Sinai in thunder and lightning. How could they disobey?

It is a scenario that happens so frequently in our home that it seems disingenuous to narrate it in the past tense, as if it were an isolated occurrence. I come home from work, carrying in my backpack the books I've used to teach and study Torah that day, as well as a few groceries I picked up for dinner. I am tired, but I'm also eager to hear about what happened to each child in school, and how they fared in my absence. I open the door and the house is silent. I see only Matan in the living room, playing with his Rubik's Cube or building with Legos or poring over the *Guinness Book of World Records*. He runs over to me. "Ima, the girls have been on the tablet since they got home. I told them to stop but they didn't listen. They should be in big trouble."

I know this is one of those parenting moments when I ought to stop for a moment and take a deep breath. After all, there are many valuable ways to use screens. One could practice the multiplication tables, or research an interesting question that came up in history class, or study Torah. But I know how my twins use devices, and I have no doubt about what they are doing. Like Moses, I am filled with rage. How could they disobey? For a moment I imagine myself smashing the tablet, but I restrain myself and use my words.

"What were you thinking?" I question the girls angrily

when I burst into their bedroom and discover that they are watching a video about cupcake decoration. "You know you are not supposed to watch videos when I'm not home." Liav looks at her watch. Am I earlier than she expected? Had she despaired of my return? Or had she lost track of time, one YouTube clip leading to another in an endless loop, like the Israelites dancing around the calf?

"When I tell you that you're not allowed to watch videos, I mean it. It's like what I always say about junk food," I admonish them. Generally I try not to lecture my children, but this time I can't hold back.

"When you come home from school hungry, the easiest thing to do is just to open the junk drawer and take out a handful of pretzels. You don't have to think about it, you don't have to warm anything up, you don't even have to dirty a plate. So easy, right? But then a half hour later, you're hungry again, because pretzels don't fill you up. That's why you can never eat enough pretzels or watch enough videos." I hope the message is clear. I'm trying to teach them to take the time to think about and plan for what they want to eat and how they want to spend their time. When my children do not have the option of turning on screens, they are endlessly creative in their play: They build forts. They make lanyard bracelets. They dress up and put on plays. But once they have access to a device, every other option suddenly seems boring and unexciting. Nothing can compete with the immediate gratification of pushing a button and watching the screen light up.

Idolatry provides immediate gratification: We can see and touch the object of our worship. As Aaron explains to Moses after the building of the calf, "I hurled the gold into the fire, and out came this calf!" (Exodus 32:24), as if the idol were fashioned of its own accord, instantaneously. Belief in God, on the other hand, requires time and patience and discipline. At the core of my faith lies the conviction that if we take the time to train ourselves to be sensitive to God's presence, ultimately our lives will be fuller and more fulfilling.

Part of the reason I read with my children is that I want them to learn the value of slow pleasures. Reading did not come easily for most of my kids. I sat with them as they puzzled over silent letters, confused homonyms, and stumbled over sentences they did not know how to parse. But each of my kids is learning that if they are patient, the letters on the page will reveal themselves to be conduits of meaning. Sentences combine into paragraphs that tell a near-infinite number of stories, rich with images not manufactured for them but born of their own imaginations.

"Why can't we watch stories on screens?" my kids protest. "We learn so much from videos," they try to persuade me. They're not wrong about that, but it's not the same. In most of the video clips my children watch, the work of making meaning is done for them, the images flashing fully formed before their eyes in bright, dynamic color. But when we read, our minds have to supply the visual imagery. Often we have to wait until the words mean something to us, until we have read enough to conjure an image of the character or scene in our mind's eye, filling in the colors and contours gradually. We may have to sit with the discomfort of not fully understanding, working through those uncertain hours of waiting at the foot of the mountain. It's so much harder when we can't simply turn to our idols.

The rabbis of the Talmud teach that "a person does not understand words of Torah unless he stumbles over them."[24] Not only do my kids still stumble when they read aloud; they also struggle to understand some of the stories I read to them. They need me to explain—why was Moses late in coming down the mountain? What does it mean to be late—not dead, but delayed—and how are we to occupy ourselves in the interim? I reassure them that even if it takes a while to figure it out, they are not alone. When the Israelites heard the Ten Commandments spoken on Mount Sinai, they told Moses, "We will do and we will listen" (Exodus 24:7). The term "we will listen" is often translated as "we will understand," suggesting that the Israelites knew that first they would have to live by the Torah, and only then would they understand it. In speaking these words, they were giving voice to their patience and commitment to stumble over the words of the Torah again and again, however long it would take.

❧

I don't know if Moses was literate, but he definitely struggled to get his words out. "I am slow of speech and slow of tongue" (Exodus 4:10), he objects at the burning bush. "Who am I to go to Pharaoh and free the Israelites from Egypt?" (3:11). We don't hear about his speech impediment in the later books of the Bible. Perhaps the more he spoke, the more comfortable he became.

With time my children—who at first stumbled over every word—became more fluent and competent readers, until they were ready to begin studying the Bible in school. In Israel the Bible is an integral part of the school curriculum in religious as well as secular schools, both of which are part of the public school system. The kids begin studying verse by verse as soon as they can read competently, generally in second grade. To mark this milestone, the school holds a ceremony in which every child is presented with his or her own *Chumash*—the Five Books of Moses.

We first attended this ceremony when Matan was in second grade. The event was held in a local synagogue because the school lobby, which also functions as an auditorium, was not large enough to contain all the parents, grandparents, and siblings who came to celebrate the occasion. The spacious high-ceilinged sanctuary was decorated with branches and flowers to resemble Mount Sinai in bloom during the revelation, when the Torah was given. The children sang and danced and paraded before us in their "festive dress," as it is known—white shirts and dark skirts or pants, their foreheads adorned with a paper crown featuring a cardboard pop-up of the two tablets with the Ten Commandments. One by one they were called up by the principal and the school rabbi, who shook their hand and handed them a certificate; then their teacher hugged each child and presented them with a *Chumash*, embossed with their name and the name of the school. Afterward the students and parents lingered by a long table decorated with homemade cookies and cakes brought by each family, savoring the sweetness of the moment.

Two years later, on the morning of the twins' *Chumash* ceremony, Liav awoke with a stomach virus. To her dismay, it was clear by the afternoon that she would not be able to attend the ceremony. For weeks she and her classmates had been preparing for the event—learning the words to the songs they'd sing, practicing the choreography for the various dances they'd perform, memorizing their lines in a short skit about the giving of the Torah. The Torah teaches that prior to the revelation at Sinai, God gave the Israelites three days' notice, instructing Moses to "go to the people and warn them to stay pure today and tomorrow. Let them wash their clothes. Let them be ready for the third day; for on the third day the Lord will come down, in the sight of all the people, on Mount Sinai" (Exodus 19:10–11).

Liav and her classmates had been preparing for much longer than three days; in her eyes, her *Chumash* ceremony was an event as momentous as the giving of the Torah on Sinai. How could she possibly miss it?

In the end, Daniel took Tagel to the *Chumash* ceremony; I stayed home with Liav. That evening Tagel returned with Liav's *Chumash*. When I entered the twins' room the next day, Liav—now starting to feel better—was sitting on her bed with her new *Chumash*, her eyes brimming with tears. "I'm so sad I missed my *Chumash* ceremony, Ima. There was music and dancing and all the teachers were there, and everyone got called up one by one to shake the principal's hand. There were flowers and cookies.... And I wasn't there."

I gave her a hug. I felt so sad that she had missed the ceremony, the excitement, and the recognition. As I watched Liav page through the *Chumash* that had become hers just one day earlier, I thought about the private revelation that takes place for Moses alone, after the smoke and fire and the mountain ablaze.

Following the giving of the Ten Commandments, and following the golden calf episode, the Torah tells of an intimate encounter between Moses and God. Moses, having pleaded with God to forgive the people for the sin of the calf, requests to see God's glory. God responds, "You cannot see My face, because man cannot see Me and live" (Exodus 33:20). However, God allows Moses to see His back. God instructs Moses, "Station yourself on the rock and as My presence passes by, I will put you in the cleft of the rock and shield you with My hand until I have passed by. Then I will take My hand away and you will see My back, but My face must not be seen" (33:21–23). Unlike the grand theophany at Sinai, this episode in the cranny of the rock is a sort of private revelation, for Moses alone.

The *Chumash* ceremony—with the crowds and the singing and the dancing and the synagogue all decked out in greenery—was like the public revelation at Sinai, where God came down in a cloud of fire with thunder and lightning, accompanied by shofar blasts. Liav wanted to be part of that sublime drama, and I understood why. But I wanted her to realize that there was also the more subdued revelation that took place without all the special effects, when Moses stood alone in the cranny of the rock and saw God from behind. That, too, was a numinous experience.

The rabbis teach that God is present wherever people sit and study Torah.[25] Even if only one person is engaged in the study of Torah, the divine presence rests upon that individual. Studying God's Torah is how we draw close to God, which is why in Jewish tradition, literacy is not just an end in itself but a means of engaging with the sacred. I told Liav that whenever she opened her *Chumash* to read from it, the divine presence would be right there with her. Each time she studied Torah—every time she encountered the text that Moses had received from God on Mount Sinai—she was experiencing a private revelation. She was coming as close to Sinai as most of us will ever get.

4

☙

The Unicorn and the Scroll

JUST BEFORE SHALVI TURNED FIVE, I ASKED HER WHAT she would like for a birthday present. She told me that she wanted "either a dancing unicorn or a Sefer Torah," and I could only laugh. The dancing unicorn was actually a gift her twin sisters received two years earlier from my mother-in-law— the furry stuffed animal, equipped with a set of AA batteries, danced and sang a repetitive song about prancing on rainbows when the button on its horn was pushed. The song drove me crazy, especially because I was forever knocking the button inadvertently when cleaning up the kids' stuffed animals or climbing over their toys. At some point I conveniently "lost" the stuffed unicorn, slipping it into a bag of giveaway clothing, but apparently it had not been forgotten.

A Sefer Torah, though, is a different story. We own many printed editions of the Five Books of Moses, but Shalvi was asking for a Torah scroll, like the one we read from in synagogue. A Torah scroll is made of parchment and is handwritten with ink from a quill, wrapped around two wooden rollers and encased in a velvet mantle with an ornate crown. A proper Torah scroll— one fit for ritual use—costs tens of thousands of dollars, but as I learned from a bit of googling, it is possible to buy a "toy" scroll that contains the entire Five Books of Moses computer-printed on a long sheet of white paper wrapped around lightweight wooden rollers with a faux velvet mantle and metallic ornaments. Confronted with the choice between a dancing unicorn and a Torah scroll—between a golden calf and the Ten Commandments—I knew what Shalvi was getting for her birthday.

I ordered a toy Torah scroll from a Judaica shop in Geula, an ultra-Orthodox neighborhood in northern Jerusalem. It arrived a couple of weeks later, just in time for Shalvi's birthday. The Shabbat after it arrived, I came back from a walk with a friend and entered our apartment building. I could hear the sound of children singing floating down through the stairwell, and I wondered whom it might be. As I began climbing the stairs, I realized that the children were singing the prayers of the Shabbat morning service. Was it the neighbors' children? But no, I had already passed the lower floors where the other young children in our building live. Could it be my children who were so devout?

The Mishnah, an ancient rabbinic legal compilation, discusses the case of a man who comes back from a trip, hears a cry of woe in the distance, and prays, "Please God, I hope that cry is not coming from my home."[26] The prayer I uttered in that moment was just the opposite: "Please God, may those be my children who are singing." Sure enough, when I walked in the door, I found them parading around the room with the Torah scroll, just like we do in synagogue, singing the prayer recited at that point in the service: "Exalt the Lord and worship Him, for He is holy." They set the Torah scroll down on our coffee table, carefully and gently.

"Come, Ima, we want to call you up to the Torah," Shalvi said. When the Torah is chanted in synagogue, a series of individuals from the congregation are called up to the podium to recite a blessing. Shalvi wanted me to have this honor. She removed the metal crown and the velvet mantle, and Matan turned the rollers until he had scrolled to the portion for that week.

Liav lifted the Torah scroll into the air, just like we do in synagogue, and the kids sang, "This is the Torah that Moses set before the Israelites" (Deuteronomy 4:44), pointing to the scroll that Jews traditionally believe, in fact, contains the very same text dictated by God to Moses on Mount Sinai.

According to the rabbis, though, there is more than one Torah. The Talmud teaches that when Moses climbed Mount Sinai to receive the Torah, the angels in heaven bristled: What business had a flesh-and-blood human being in ascending to the heavens? Why not leave the Torah with the angels instead? Moses explained to the angels that the Torah simply wasn't relevant for them. "The Torah teaches not to murder—is there murder among you angels?" Moses asked. "Do you have a father and mother to honor?"[27] Instead, according to various medieval commentators, the angels received their own version of the Torah, consisting of all the letters in order without any spaces between them. As Nahmanides explains in the introduction to his Bible commentary, the angels' Torah does not include spaces, because the angels read the entirety of the Torah as spelling out the names of God. The Torah given to human beings, however, is divided into words because that is how we make sense of it. We parse the Torah such that it teaches about permitted and forbidden behavior, purity and impurity, and the rest of the laws that are relevant to human beings on earth. The angels' Torah and the human Torah contain the same letters, but they signify very different truths.

Perhaps the human Torah is printed with spaces not just

so that we can learn its lessons but also to allow room for our readings and interpretations. Now that my older children have begun reading to me, they are the ones who insert the spaces. They can stop to ask questions when they are confused, or read onward when they are too engaged in the story to stop and ask.

Shalvi, though, is still sounding out her letters. A few months after she received her birthday Torah, our downstairs neighbor Yossi knocked on our door with a question. He works as a *sofer stam*—a scribe who calligraphs the text of Torah scrolls and other ritual objects. He explained to us that every letter has to be clearly formed—if there is any confusion about the identity of a particular letter, the scroll is not fit for ritual use. "The reason I need your help is because I know you have a daughter who is five, right?"

Yossi explained that according to the Talmud, one way to determine if a letter is written clearly enough is to ask a young child who is just learning how to read to identify the letter in question. "You can't ask anyone older, because they will be biased by their understanding of the context in which the letter appears. It has to be someone old enough to be familiar with all the letters in the alphabet, but young enough not to be capable of understanding the words based on context. Your daughter would be perfect."

Shalvi was thrilled and proud to discover that she had such an important role to play. She was going to be the one to judge the letters in a Torah scroll! She sat down with Yossi as he pointed with a toothpick to each of the questionable letters he had inked on parchment. She identified each letter, and Yossi took note of her responses, nodding and stroking his short, scruffy beard. "I get to help Yossi because I know all my letters," she told her older sisters excitedly; it was rare that she was the only one capable of performing a certain role.

Although all our kids take turns reading—or pretending to read—from Shalvi's Torah scroll, Shalvi knows that it is hers. It was her birthday present, and so she gets to decide who may read from it, and when. Thanks to her Torah scroll, Shalvi, who is sandwiched between her older and younger siblings, has carved out space for herself. And thanks to our neighbor Yossi, she has discovered that she has her own unique and important role to play, at least at this stage of her reading life. I hope that she, and all my children, will continue to find space for themselves among the letters and words of the Torah that was set before the Israelites at Sinai.

5

A Series of Their Own

THE REVELATION AT SINAI TAKES PLACE ON THE SAME mountain where, years earlier, Moses encountered God at the burning bush. Back then Moses felt woefully unsuited to free the Israelites from bondage, let alone give them the Torah. God assured Moses that he would not need to approach Pharaoh on his own—his brother Aaron would be at his side to help him get the words out.

Until the Israelites departed from Egypt, Moses and Aaron worked in tandem to communicate with Pharaoh and the people. But after the Israelites cross the Red Sea and are making their way through the wilderness, God furnishes Aaron with his own separate role: While Moses will continue to lead the people, Aaron is charged with serving as the high priest in the Tabernacle, which is constructed throughout the second half of the book of Exodus. The two brothers will work toward the same end, but they will do so by different means: Moses will continue to transmit God's word to the people, whereas Aaron will administer to their ritual needs. As prophet and priest, each brother has a unique role.

Perhaps not surprisingly, it was my twins who had the most difficulty developing independent identities. When they were younger, Liav and Tagel shared all their friends. Throughout preschool, they were together in the same class, where they played with the same group of girls. When I picked them up at school, they had the same stories to share, and at night we read the same picture books together, with one twin sitting on each side of me on their trundle bed. We were all inhabiting the same fictional world, whether it was the grassy yard where William Steig's *Yellow & Pink* tried to figure out who created them, or the city street corner where Vera B. Williams's Bidemmi purchased her bag of *Cherries and Cherry Pits*.

The girls fell asleep together, woke up together, and began learning to read in Hebrew from the same books, a series originally written in Swedish, entitled *My Happy Life* by Rose Lagercrantz. The series tells the story of Duni and Ella-Frieda, who meet on the second day of first grade and become fast friends—until, not long after, Duni learns that Ella-Frieda's family is moving "thousands of streets away" and the two will no longer attend the same school. Duni and Ella-Frieda, although initially devastated, manage to keep up an epistolary friendship. Whenever Duni misses her friend, or whenever anything makes her sad, she consoles herself by counting all the times in her life when she was most happy. These enumerations of her happiest moments become a refrain throughout the series.

Liav and Tagel did not just learn to read from Duni and Ella-Frieda; they also received a primer in friendship. When they began elementary school, we enrolled them in separate classes for the first time, hopeful that they would develop more independent identities both socially and academically. One day Liav invited a friend to come home after school and refused to let Tagel join in. Tagel looked miserable, closed out of the bedroom she shared with her sister, where Liav and her friend were playing with dolls. But Tagel has never been one to complain. Instead she took the first book in the *My Happy Life* series— a book she had finished months earlier—and curled up on the couch, finding solace in her fictional friends. She was revisiting her happiest reading moments; this was the first book she'd read to herself, and it remained bound up in her mind with the thrill of independent discovery and the pleasure of immersion. Over time, she would continue to return to *My Happy Life* even after she became a more competent reader, and even after she made her own friends.

The midrash on the book of Exodus, in reflecting on the experience of the Israelites' enslavement, recounts that the slaves suffered from the backbreaking labor imposed upon them all week long. But on Shabbat—the day of rest—they found comfort in furling and unfurling scrolls inscribed with God's promise to redeem them.[28] Perhaps Tagel, in reading and rereading the stories of Duni and Ella-Frieda, was renewing her faith in friendship, and in the prospect of one day having a best friend of her own.

During the middle of second grade, an American girl named Leah joined the twins' school, gravitating immediately to Tagel. Tagel was elated, at least at first—her new friend brought her a rainbow-colored heart she had drawn herself and invited her over to make friendship bracelets on the porch of her apartment. For a while, Tagel didn't pick up the Duni novels at all.

But then something changed. One day Tagel returned from the park where she had been playing with Leah, her face streaked with tears. "Leah's cousin came to the park and then suddenly Leah told me she was leaving. She said that even though she likes me, she likes her cousin more. How could she say that? How could she do that?" she asked me imploringly.

I gave Tagel a hug. I was sorry she was hurting. But I also pointed out to her that Leah was doing something very difficult—she had come to a new country with her family and was trying to learn a new language, adjust to a new school, make all new friends. "Being a good friend is like reading a chapter book," I tried to explain. "You learn how to feel what someone else is feeling, and to see things the way they do." I reminded her that even Duni and Ella-Frieda argued, though I wasn't sure this was the case. "That's true," she told me. "They had a fight when Ella-Frieda told Duni that she wouldn't give her the bookmark with the angel, but then they made up."

Since then, Tagel and Leah have had several arguments, and the pattern of wronging and reconciliation has come to define the fabric of their friendship. When Tagel feels hurt by Leah, she will sometimes respond by hurting Liav, and then it is Liav who will find refuge in reading. The twins still keep the Duni and Ella-Frieda books on hand—for a while they were stashed behind the toilet so they could reread them in the bathroom, cycling through the entire series. "Some of my happiest moments are reading those books, even again and again for the hundredth time," Tagel told me one day. "But my real happiest moments, in my whole life right now, are with Leah." She says this hesitantly, as if it might be a betrayal, because she knows how much I love to read. But I assure her that's exactly the way it should be.

ye

Around the time that the girls started making separate friends, they stopped wanting to read the same books. Any book that Tagel had read and loved was suddenly anathema to Liav, and vice versa. I tried to get a sense of their tastes, but they weren't really all that different. It wasn't that they each gravitated to specific kinds of books but rather that neither wished to read what the other was reading. They were learning how to make different friends both on the page and off it, with the fictional world serving as practice for the schoolyard. In the middle of second grade, when we moved to a new neighborhood, the trundle bed went to Shalvi and the twins began sleeping on opposite sides of the room. It was as if their beds were lined not just with their stuffed animals but with a new assortment of fictional friends who came to visit every evening.

Tagel was the first to express any interest in reading in English, and so initially, she was the one I read aloud with at night in bed. Meanwhile Liav voraciously devoured one Hebrew mystery novel after another on her own. Her favorite series, *The Time Tunnel* by Galila Ron-Feder-Amit, includes over a hundred tales of historical adventure set at various points throughout Jewish history. She was determined to bore her way through them all, strewing them on the floor like debris when she was finished so that I'd know to return them to the library and check out more.

The first books Tagel read by herself in English were the *Ivy & Bean* novels, a series about two best friends living a few houses over from each other on a quiet cul-de-sac in a leafy American town. Tagel fell in love with both friends, perhaps because she saw elements of herself in each: She is athletic and spunky like Bean, but also bookish and self-reliant like Ivy. If I were to draw a caricature of Tagel, she'd be reading while standing on her head, legs shooting high up against the wall and face obscured by an upside-down paperback. It sounds, come to think of it, like an illustration right out of *Ivy & Bean*.

The illustrations are part of the genius of the series. Each black-and-white line drawing is documentarily precise, capturing all the details in the text such that the young reader who does not understand a part of the story can look to the accompanying image for clues. Here too, as with many of the picture books we read, the illustrations illuminate the text while also adding detail—reminiscent of the work of Rashi, an eleventh-century French rabbi who was the preeminent commentator on the Bible and Talmud. Rashi's commentaries are regarded as such an indispensable study aid that they are generally printed on every page. Sometimes he merely explains what is meant by a given word or phrase, but often he will round out a story by filling in details from the midrash and other exegetical traditions, painting a fuller picture.

Tagel lingered over the illustrations in *Ivy & Bean* with the intensity of a scholar poring over the marginal notes in a sacred tome. She could describe each and every one of the fifty-six erasers in Ivy and Bean's eraser collection, as if she herself had sat alongside Ivy and Bean playing Eraser Valley—a game in which the various eraser figurines battle hurricanes, tsunamis, and other natural disasters. Tagel passed her finger from one eraser to another as if deciphering an ancient hieroglyph, and she wouldn't let me turn the page until we each picked our favorites. She wanted Liav to weigh in as well, but Liav refused to set foot in Eraser Valley. *Ivy & Bean* was Tagel's domain, and Liav wanted no part of it.

The more proficient Tagel became, the more I worried that Liav would never agree to start reading in English. Every time I sat down to read with her, she'd end up in tears. Eventually she became so self-conscious that she didn't want to read at all. "I am slow of speech and slow of tongue," she essentially protested, sending me away. At the burning bush, Moses tells God to choose someone else for the job of liberating the Israelites. In the midrash on this verse, Moses tells God, "It is not my destiny to lead the people into the Holy Land and to be their future redeemer.... You have many other redeemers!"[29]

I decided it was time for me to step back. Someone else would have to take over. Fortunately, Liav's grandparents were up for the task. Recently retired, my mother suggested that she and my father take turns reading with Liav by transatlantic video call. Liav was excited about the prospect of time alone with her grandparents, who started each conversation by asking her about her day and letting her speak for as long as she wanted. Each evening I would take a photo of the next chapter and send it to my parents; then during their mornings and our afternoons—after my parents in New York had drunk their morning coffee, and Liav in Israel had returned from school— she would read to them over the phone and my parents would follow along.

The first time we arranged for this reading date, I suggested that Liav start with *Ivy & Bean*, now that Tagel was already well into the series. But Liav refused. Perhaps she sensed that in the world of *Ivy & Bean*, she would always be known as Tagel's kid sister. Perhaps she worried that Tagel would spoil the ending or make fun of her for what she hadn't yet found out, twisting dramatic irony into cruelty. Liav needed her own book.

Instead of the quiet cul-de-sac of Pancake Court, Liav took up literary residence in an apartment building in Boston, where eight-year-old Clementine—the well-intentioned but troublesome heroine of the eponymous series by Sara Pennypacker— lives with her father, mother, and younger brother. Before long, Liav developed the confidence to read not only with my parents but also with me. Together we befriended Clementine's best friend, Margaret, though we agreed she was a bit stuck-up and obnoxious. We laughed together at Clementine's antics and cheered for her when she managed to shine against all odds. We both thought that the best book in the series was the one about the class talent show, in which a dismayed Clementine—convinced that she has no talent whatsoever and therefore can't participate in the show—ends up helping the principal run the entire production, proving that she has a talent after all.

"What is my talent, Ima?" Liav asked me. "Tagel is so good at gymnastics, everyone knows that. And Matan understands technology and how things work. But I don't really have a talent, do I?"

I hesitated for a moment. Should I remind her that she plays the violin? That she is a gifted and creative visual artist? Liav was certainly talented, but it was not her music or her art that made her unique, and I wanted her to know that.

"Every person is created in the image of God," I said to her solemnly. "That means that every person has a unique spark of God in them. You have talents that no one else in the world has."

Liav looked at me skeptically. "Really? Like what?"

"I don't know anyone else who understands Shalvi the way you do. Somehow you are always able to figure out what is upsetting her and how to calm her down. You are so sensitive like that. You understand how people are feeling, and you know how to make them feel better. It is an extraordinary talent, and it's part of what makes you so special."

Liav and I agreed, lying there on her bed together, that sometimes the best talent is just being who you are. As we both learned from Clementine, sometimes the art you create is not anything you sketch or sculpt or sing, but the arc of the life you live by just trying to be your kindest and most empathic self, day in and day out.

In the evenings I alternated between reading *Ivy & Bean* with Tagel and *Clementine* with Liav. Sometimes I imagined their bedroom was divided down the center, midway between their beds—Tagel's side of the room was lined with the potions Ivy had concocted in training to become a witch; Liav's side was decorated with Clementine's drawings. I tried to keep their fictional friends straight, but sometimes I'd get confused. Tagel would look at me with a puzzled expression when I referred to Yitzvi as Mushroom, and then I would remember that it is Clementine— Liav's friend!—who teasingly refers to her younger brother by the names of various vegetables.

Eventually both girls became comfortable reading on their own when I couldn't join them. I didn't usually make up the pages I'd missed, but I tried always to check in so I was up to date. "Did Clementine get sent to the principal again?" I'd ask Liav on our walk home from school, and it wouldn't seem at all strange to her that I was asking about a fictional character. "This reminds me of the secret spot in Ivy's backyard," I'd comment to Tagel when we found a quiet corner of the park in which to change Yitzvi's diaper. These comments became a way for me to connect with each twin individually—a sort of secret language that only we shared.

Clementine and *Ivy & Bean* have a lot in common. Both series feature annoying siblings, misunderstanding teachers, friends who show off too much, and parents who seem at times unfairly strict. But then again, Liav's school friends are not all that different from Tagel's; the twins gravitate to the same kinds of girls, and occasionally they end up playing all together in the yard after school. Inevitably there are arguments about who is allowed to play with whom, and who is considered a closer friend. These arguments are normal and perhaps even salutary. But Clementine will never play in the backyard at Pancake

Court, and Ivy and Bean will never ride Clementine's school bus. When it comes to Liav and Tagel's fictional friends, there is no overlap. Though they still share a room, each girl has found a series of her own.

6

꩜

Bare Ruined Choirs

ONE AFTERNOON I WAS READING *IVY & BEAN* WITH
Tagel on the couch, in that brief window when the older kids
had returned from school but it was not yet time to pick up
the little ones. Usually I spend that time working. I have certain
projects that require less concentration, and I bring my laptop
to the kitchen table and supervise the kids as I translate a children's book or proof an article. If I can't concentrate on work,
I'll get started on making dinner. But when Tagel asked to read
together, I let everything else wait. An older friend once told
me that when my child asks for a hug, I should leap at the opportunity, because the day will come when that child will refuse
all forms of affection. It's probably also true of reading together,
and so I try to say yes whenever I can.

By this point we were already up to the fifth book, *Bound to
Be Bad*, in which Ivy and Bean resolve, after Bean endures a series of reprimands, to be as good as they possibly can. Ivy, having
read about St. Francis, decides that she would like to become so
pure of heart that the animals follow her around. Tagel fills me
in on all this, because I haven't read the first few chapters with
her. In the scene she is up to, Bean walks down the path beside
Ivy's house and is surprised to see her friend standing with her

arms in the air. She asks Ivy if she's trying to fly. Ivy explains that she is attempting to be perfectly calm in the hope that birds will land on her arms. "Ivy's arms were trembling," reads the next sentence, except that Tagel was unable to sound out "trembling," nor did she know what it meant. When I saw her stumbling over the word, I tried to explain. "Shaking," I said. "Her arms were shaking from holding them up for so long."

Tagel's eyes lit up in recognition. "Oh," she said. "Like in the war with Amalek." I was astounded. I had been thinking the exact same thing. The Torah relates that immediately after the Exodus, when the Israelites were exhausted and exhilarated from the thrill of the liberation at the Red Sea, the nation of Amalek attacked them from behind. Moses stationed himself atop a mountain and held up his arms to aid the Israelites in battle. Whenever his arms were raised, the Israelites gained on Amalek, and whenever he lowered them, Amalek prevailed. But Moses's arms grew heavy from holding them up for so long, and so two others, Aaron and Hur, supported his arms until the Israelites won the war, just as the sun set.

The Torah tells us that Moses's arms were stable until sunset. The biblical word translated as "stable" is *emuna*, which means faith, and the Mishnah teaches that Moses's arms ensured the Israelites' victory: The people would see his arms, turn their eyes upward, and submit their hearts to God.[30] Moses's arms conjured an image of God's outstretched arm for the Israelites, much as Ivy's arms conjured the image of Moses's arms for Tagel and for me.

I was surprised to discover that Tagel had also thought of Moses's arms. It reminded me of the time Matan was four years old and I brought him to the pediatrician for an annual checkup. After shining a light into his ears and rapping on his knees to check his reflexes, the doctor showed Matan a series of cards, each of which depicted a scene. Matan had to answer questions about what he saw in the pictures. On one of the cards, a boy appeared to have just tripped and fallen; his cup of water was still spilling next to him. Behind him was a small rock. The doctor pointed to the boy, the rock, and the puddle, and asked my son to explain what he saw. Matan nodded eagerly—this one was easy. He pointed to the boy and explained, matter-of-factly, that it was Moses. "He was supposed to talk to that rock to make the water spill out, but instead he hit it." The doctor raised his eyebrows in astonishment. "I've been showing this card to kids for longer than I can remember," he told me. "I never heard that one before."

Like Tagel, Matan saw an image unrelated to the Bible but immediately associated it with a biblical story—in his case, the scene in which Moses raises his arms to strike the rock and give water to the querulous Israelites at a place in the wilderness called Kadesh. God punishes Moses harshly for hitting the rock instead of speaking to it: Moses will not be allowed to enter the Promised Land (Numbers 20:1–12). And yet it's not hard to understand Moses's mistake—earlier in the Israelites' wilderness journey, in the book of Exodus, Moses had a similar experience just before the battle with Amalek, at a place that became known as Merivah. The people complained about the lack of water in the desert, and God instructed Moses to strike a rock with his rod so water would issue forth (Exodus 17:1–7).

Presumably Moses assumed that just as he was supposed to strike the rock last time, he was supposed to do so this time. It is a mistake my children have often made as well. Whenever there is a special occasion in synagogue, there is a custom of handing out candy to all the members of the congregation, who then throw the candy in the direction of the person who is celebrating. My children have learned that they have to hold on to their candies until it's time to throw them, and then they can join all the other kids in gathering the candy to eat. One time when I took then four-year-old Matan to visit an elderly friend in a nursing home, she handed him a sucking candy. Matan looked at me sternly. "Don't worry, I'm waiting to throw it," he assured me, as if all candy had to be tossed before it could be consumed.

The two parallel instances of Moses striking the rock recall a formative moment in Moses's youth, when he left Pharaoh's palace and "went out" among his brothers in Egypt (Exodus 2:11). He sees an Egyptian man striking a Hebrew and strikes down the Egyptian and buries him in the sand. This incident, like the striking of the rock, plays a critical role in shaping Moses's destiny: After striking the Egyptian, Moses flees to Midian and receives his mission from God at the burning bush. Moses is thus sent on his mission because of one "striking" incident, and his mission is terminated on account of another.

Is every moment really haunted by prior ones? As Tagel understood, this is how associations work, and literary associations are no different. The image of Ivy lifting her arms in the hope that the birds will mistake her for a tree reminds me not just of Moses but also of Shakespeare's sonnet about the autumn of his life, when most of the yellow leaves have fallen off the trees and the branches resemble "bare ruin'd choirs, where late the sweet birds sang." Shakespeare's sonnet in turn recalls Edna St. Vincent Millay's sonnet in which she, too, compares herself to a tree after her lovers have all flown off and left her arms as empty as boughs in winter. Was Millay referencing Shakespeare? I suspect so. It doesn't really matter, though—each sonnet functions like a palimpsest revealing traces of the other.

Tagel's association between Ivy and Moses triggered a series of associations for me, including Matan's appointment at the pediatrician, Moses striking the rock and striking the Egyptian, and Shakespeare and Millay. And it was all because she stumbled on one word, allowing us to fill the white space on the page with our own associations.

I know that Tagel—and all of my children—will stumble again, not just over difficult words but also over difficult moments and decisions. I will not always be there to hold their hand, or to hold up their arms. Our children's journey to freedom and independence, like their journey to independent reading, is a journey away from us. But we can try to furnish our children with the associations that matter to us. We can fill their minds with allusions, in the hope that their experiences will evoke the texts they have read, and those texts will in turn evoke other texts, such that the sweet birds of recognition will alight in the choirs of their arms. Or at least, like Ivy, we can try.

LEVITICUS

The Shrine of the Book

THE BOOK OF LEVITICUS DESCRIBES THE WORKINGS OF the Tabernacle that the Israelites constructed in the wilderness in accordance with God's instructions. As a site of intimacy between God and Israel, the Tabernacle—and later the Temple modeled after it—is a model for the intimacy I seek to forge with my children through the books we discover and read together. We spend many hours in our local public library, which bears a striking resemblance to the Tabernacle described in Leviticus. Our visits to the library—a place with its own code of conduct that requires reverence and decorum—have in turn taught my children how to behave in synagogue, where we read and engage with the sacred books of our tradition.

1

༄

Pilgrimage to the Library

ON WEDNESDAYS I PICK UP YITZVI FROM PRESCHOOL and we have an hour to spend together. On this day of the week alone, all the other kids are accounted for—I don't need to drag my son to his sister's ballet lesson or race home with him to make dinner before the older kids have to rush out. "Park or library?" I ask Yitzvi as he climbs into his stroller and I fasten the buckle. "Umm . . . park!" he tells me excitedly, though I already regret having given him the choice.

I am useless at the park. "Look! Look! Watch me!" he'll cry out when he climbs the ladder to the slide, except that I never look at the right moment—I'm usually sitting on the bench with my head buried in a book, reading a novel or studying Torah. All around me other parents are perched opposite their kids on the seesaw, or pushing them on the swings, or holding their backs reassuringly as they climb the ladder to the highest slide. I am rarely that kind of parent.

Fortunately, we pass the library on our way to the park, and more often than not, Yitzvi changes his mind.

"Library open?" he'll ask me as we pass by.

"Yes, it's open."

"Go in it. Go in it," he'll tell me, kicking his feet excitedly in the stroller to urge me to turn around. I park his stroller by the elevator, unstrap him, and we walk up the two flights of stairs together. It feels like a pilgrimage of sorts. The Talmud teaches that any child who is old enough to hold his father's hand and ascend to Jerusalem is obligated to make a pilgrimage to the Temple on certain festivals.[31] Now that my son is old enough to hold my hand, grasp the banister, and climb the stairs himself, he is ready for the library.

Housed in our neighborhood community center, our local Jerusalem public library is very small—just two rooms connected by a steep staircase, with picture books upstairs and adult and children's chapter books downstairs. Yitzvi knows where his favorite books are shelved, and as soon as we walk in the door, he bounds up the stairs to find *Yellow Car* and *Green Tractor*. "Read it, read it," he tells me excitedly, bringing the books to the low table where we sit side by side. I know the drill. There is no chance he'll let us look for any other books until we have first read his two favorites, which are fortunately almost always on the shelves. We finish the books quickly, as neither has many words or much plot: A yellow car gets a flat tire and then keeps driving. A tractor gets filled with apples picked from a tree.

Only when the tire is repaired and the apples are loaded do I dare suggest that we look for another book. Yet even then, Yitzvi is most excited to discover the books we already own. "I have this book in my house!" he tells me gleefully, eager for me to read him the library copy and unable to comprehend when I try to explain why I'm unwilling to check it out. When I find new books that I think may interest him, he eyes them with suspicion, rarely willing to brave anything we haven't read before.

Visits to the library with Yitzvi are highly ritualized; I can generally predict exactly which books he will choose for me to read to him, and in which order. But the ritual is important to both of us. I think of the sacrifices the Israelites are commanded to offer in the book of Leviticus—each sacrifice must be prepared and offered exactly as God specifies, with little room for variation or improvisation. Unlike in the park, where I have a hard time paying full attention to my child, there is a devotional aspect to my library visits with Yitzvi that requires my heightened presence. If only I can understand what is taking place between us in the library, perhaps I'll understand the meaning behind the sacrificial rites that govern the book of Leviticus—the confession of sin, the ascent to the sacrificial altar, the intimate encounter in the sacred shrine.

🜨

I began taking my children to the library when they were very young. I wanted them to experience the thrill of being surrounded by more books than we could possibly read, and the excitement of pulling them off the shelf on their own. I wanted them to understand that there are spaces devoted to housing books and making them freely available to people who love them. And I wanted them to learn that such spaces have their own codes of conduct: My kids can't run wild in the library, or nibble on crackers whenever they are hungry. They have to learn to speak in a whisper, out of respect for others who are reading and concentrating. A library demands that we adhere to its rules and comport ourselves with respect and reverence—not unlike the ancient Temple in Jerusalem, or the Tabernacle in the wilderness where the Israelites worshiped God.

The Israelites construct the Tabernacle at the end of the

book of Exodus, but the sacred structure is inaugurated only at the start of Leviticus, when Aaron and his sons—who will serve as priests—undergo a week of intensive training to prepare for a life of ritual service. God, speaking through Moses, teaches exactly how they are to perform the sacrificial rites—a burnt offering differs from a sin offering, which in turn differs from a guilt offering, each with its own rules. The priests are taught how to lay their hands upon the sacrificial animal, remove all the fat, and pour the blood at the base of the altar. They learn how to lay the wood on the altar, light the fire, and place upon it the entrails of the sacrificial animals so they burn in a manner that is pleasing unto God. There are very clear rules for how to behave in the sacred precinct—the priests must drink no wine, wear sacred vestments, and remain ritually pure. Even the most minor lapses can be fatal, as we learn from the story of Nadav and Avihu, two of Aaron's sons, who bring a "strange fire" before God and are summarily devoured by flames (Leviticus 10:1).

At the library we try to follow the rules, but it's not always easy for a toddler. One of Yitzvi's favorite activities is pulling the books off a high shelf, which he can reach only when standing on tiptoe, and watching as each book falls to the floor with a thud. I furrow my brow and look at him sternly. Immediately his shoulders stiffen; he knows I disapprove. We do not dare reshelve the books he has dropped—only the librarians are allowed to shelve, and they will reprimand us if they catch us presuming to know which book goes where. Instead, we carry the books to the cart by the circulation desk, where they will await reshelving by the next librarian on duty.

When we are ready to check out our books, I approach the circulation desk near the entryway with trepidation, conscious that Yitzvi and I are likely to be admonished. Often I hold him on my hip when it's our turn, because I don't want him to run off and pull more books off the shelves. On the wall adjacent to the door is another temptation—a row of seven light switches, like the Menorah, the seven-branched candelabra in the Tabernacle. Yitzvi reaches out his arm and flicks the lights on and off, on and off, turning his head back and forth from the switches on the wall to the fluorescent strips on the ceiling to take the measure of the power he wields. "The switches—don't touch them," the librarian says, holding the due date stamp hovering over the circulation card until I either put down my child or reprimand him, or both. Only the librarians may kindle the lamps.

Like the Levitical priests in the Temple, librarians are public servants, working to maintain order. They help their patrons find the right books to engage, inspire, and inform, similar to the priests, whose duties include assisting visitors to the Temple to purify, confess, and achieve atonement. If librarians sometimes seem stern and fastidious, perhaps it is because they, like the Levites in times past, are aware of the gravity and sanctity of their work.

Librarians often play a key role in teaching children how to care for books, as I know from the first chapters of two of my favorite series for children—Sydney Taylor's *All-of-a-Kind Family* and Beverly Cleary's *Beezus and Ramona*. Sarah, the conscientious middle sister in *All-of-a-Kind Family*, has committed the cardinal sin of losing a library book; Ramona, Beezus's mischievous younger sister, has furtively and defiantly scribbled her name on every page of her favorite library book in the hope that she can then say it was hers, and thus not have to return it. Both girls have to confess to a beloved librarian in the hope that they will not be barred from checking out books again.

Fortunately, both girls are forgiven. Sarah heartbrokenly

tells a kindly Miss Allen that she loved her book, but now no one else will be able to read it again. Ramona puts on her winning smile and declares to an understanding Miss Evans, "I'm a bad girl. . . . I wrote in a book. I wrote in purple crayon and it will never-ever erase. Never, never, never." Sarah's sisters chime in, explaining that it was actually Sarah's friend who misplaced the book. Older sister Beezus, who finds Ramona's long stream of "nevers" more exasperating than endearing, interrupts to vow that she will try to keep library books out of Ramona's reach from now on. Both girls are responsible for paying what seems like an exorbitant fine to replace the lost book—a dollar in the prewar Lower East Side, and two dollars and fifty cents in Portland, Oregon, forty years later. In each novel, the library drama of the opening chapter serves as a reminder that books are valuable, and caring for them is a weighty responsibility.

In our home, the responsibility for caring for and returning library books generally falls on my shoulders. All too often one of us will accidentally shelve a borrowed book on our hallway bookcase, and I'll find myself scanning the spines in search of, say, *The Library* by Sarah Stewart—a library book we've checked out often, about "skinny, nearsighted, and shy" Elizabeth Brown, who reads all day long and amasses so many books that she eventually donates her collection to the town and it becomes the public library.

After twenty minutes of placing life on hold to track down the book—the soup is boiling on the stove, the kids are hungry for supper—I start to wonder whether we, like Elizabeth Brown, should just donate our entire collection to the public library. Daniel reproves me for being overly dramatic. "Enough! Just pay the fine, or buy the library a new copy."

Perhaps Daniel is right that I could always replace a lost library book, except that many of the books are out of print. Our Jerusalem neighborhood has a sizable English-speaking population, so the library has a relatively extensive collection in English, especially when it comes to picture books. The majority of these books date to the 1980s, when there was a large influx of American immigrants to the neighborhood. At the time, several American mothers in search of English-language books for their children joined forces to collect books from libraries and individuals in their communities of origin. As a result, many of the English children's books bear the stamps of libraries in Forest Hills, Kew Gardens, and other New York neighborhoods with large Jewish populations, where the books resided before they made aliyah to Israel—thanks to the post office's special discounted book rate. The library has a small budget and limited space, so few new picture books have been added in recent decades. When I take my kids to look for books in the library, it is like traveling back in time.

Even if I could replace a library book, it wouldn't be the same. I once confessed to the librarian that I had lost an easy reader book about dinosaurs, and she shrugged her shoulders. "Just bring us any other book on that level," she suggested, and when I brought in a story about a dog named Biscuit, she accepted it without question. I was bothered by the notion that one book could be so easily substituted for another. The sacrificial laws in the book of Leviticus (27:33) teach that if an animal designated for sacrifice is replaced by another, the original animal never loses its sanctity, and must be sacrificed as well. At some point that dinosaur book will emerge from its Mesozoic hiding spot, and I'll be sure to return it.

It seems inadequate to replace a library book with another title, because every library book belongs, in part, to those who have read it. Most of the books in our local library have been in circulation for decades; each is still handstamped with the due date on a card affixed to the back page, a testament to its borrowing history. There are dog-eared pages and underlined passages and translations of words or phrases hastily jotted down in pencil—bearing testament to past readers. In the closing stanzas of his poem "Marginalia," Billy Collins imagines the previous reader of his copy of *The Catcher in the Rye*, who scribbled in the margins, "Pardon the egg salad stains, but I'm in love." I like to know, when I'm checking out a book, that someone else enjoyed it too much to bother putting down her sandwich before turning the page.

✡

In my own copies of sacred books—in my copy of the Bible, and in my volumes of the Talmud—I have a long-standing practice of jotting down notes in the margins. I scribble lightly in pencil, with all the requisite humility. Even so, my children are horrified. How dare I write in a book?

"I'm taking notes," I tell my daughter. "I want to remember what I'm learning, and what I am thinking as I learn." She wrinkles her nose dubiously. "Then use a notebook," she retorts. "That's what we do in school." My kids' textbooks are all on loan from the school. Each book contains various labels with the names of the students who used that same copy before them, a lineage that reminds me of the opening Mishnah in the Ethics of the Fathers: "Moses received the Torah on Sinai and passed it down to Joshua, who passed it down to the prophets, who passed it down to the elders..."[32]

I pull a book off our shelves, turn to the inside cover, and show my daughter the spot in the upper right corner where I've written my name in every book I own. Above my name I always scribble a Hebrew acronym, Lamed Hey Vav, which stands for the words "The earth is the Lord's, and everything in it," a quotation from Psalms (24:1). "Everything belongs to God," my inscription signifies, "but this book is temporarily mine, so please return it to me if you find it." As I tell my daughter, I know the book is not really mine, because nothing I own is truly mine. But I write in the margins because the book is part of a conversation that has been unfolding for generations. I want to add my voice to that conversation, and someday, when she is older, I hope my daughter will, too.

⚘

In the Temple, the priests perform the exact same rituals they learned from their fathers, who learned from their grandfathers, a lineage tracing all the way back to Moses's brother Aaron, the first high priest. In the library, my children discover the same books I read as a child. When I read aloud to them, sometimes I feel as if I am ventriloquizing my own parents, whose voices echo in my ears. "Caps for sale, caps for sale," I repeat, speaking in the voice of the peddler wearing his caps for sale stacked high on his head as he walks through the village. The peddler falls asleep under a tree full of monkeys who take his caps and refuse to return them. My voice rises and falls with the cadences I remember from my father, who must have read me that book more than a hundred times, using a squeaky voice for the monkeys in the tree as they mimic the peddler, who demands, "You monkeys you, you give me back my caps!" I imitate my father, who imitated the monkeys, who imitated the peddler—successive levels of mimicry piled atop one another like a stack of caps.

Whenever we travel with our monkeys to visit their grand-parents in the United States, Daniel and I take advantage of the opportunity to visit bookstores and scout out new books for ourselves and our kids. In Israel the bookstores are generally just one room, with space for only new titles. A few years ago, I walked into our local Jerusalem bookstore and was surprised to discover that atop the stack of books for sale were several jars of instant coffee, also marked for retail. Who had designated precious real estate in our poky bookstore for caffeine? I imagined a scenario in which the head of the store had called up the owner of a major bookstore chain in the United States to ask for business advice. "The only way to run a successful bookstore these days is to sell coffee," the owner presumably responded, and the Israeli store owner must have shrugged his shoulders in puzzlement and decided to give it a try.

Visiting bookstores is one of our favorite activities when we travel, especially on those rare occasions when we can go without our kids. One evening we put the kids to bed early and borrowed my parents' car for a bookstore date. We headed straight to the children's book section, conscious that we were spending our one night without kids searching for new books to read to them. We knelt on the floor, pulling books off the low shelves and sharing amusing covers and illustrations with each other.

The bookstore featured many new hardcover titles about unicorns, mermaids, and animated race cars. But to our surprise, the real joy of our bookstore outing lay not in discovering new books but in finding the paperback reissues of titles we each remembered from our own childhoods. I felt like Yitzvi in the library, gravitating instinctually to books I had already read. Did Daniel remember *Harry the Dirty Dog*, I asked after I found the fiftieth-anniversary edition tucked away on a low shelf like the scrubbing brush Harry hides when he doesn't want to take a bath. I showed Daniel my favorite picture, where Harry's family discovers that the black dog with white spots is really their beloved Harry, a white dog with black spots who becomes unrecognizable after he slides down a coal chute and runs past the dark steam clouds of a locomotive. "I used to think I could clean the dirt off Harry if I rubbed the pages with my fingers," I told him, and we added it to our pile.

We left the bookstore with several old favorites and only two books that neither of us had previously read: an illustrated rendering of Robert Frost's *Stopping by Woods on a Snowy Evening* and a historical account of Eleanor Roosevelt's childhood. Both books unfold slowly, the narratives driven by horse-drawn carriages. Our children have not read much poetry, nor are they familiar with American presidential history. We knew that each story contained a world we wanted them to inhabit.

Our outing to the bookstore taught me how grateful I am that most of the books in our Jerusalem library are not new titles but rather books that have stood the test of time. My daughter can reach to the top shelf and pull down a small yellow-and-red hardcover featuring a woman stretching a black dress over her head, her contrabass leaning against her bureau in the background. It is *The Philharmonic Gets Dressed* by Karla Kuskin, published in 1982 and imprinted with the Bensonhurst Public Library stamp, about the members of an orchestra preparing to perform at a concert one evening. We witness as the various players take showers, trim their moustaches, fasten their earrings, button suspenders onto the waistlines of their pants, pick up their instruments, and walk out onto the big stage. *The Philharmonic Gets Dressed* is a book about people whose work is to add beauty to the world. There is no drama and no tension, and the pictures are in only a few colors. But if you listen closely, you can almost hear the black notes on the white pages transformed into a majestic symphony.

※

In our local public library the books are divided into sections based on reading level. My oldest three children have already graduated from the easy readers to the middle-grade chapter books, and they are convinced there is no going back. They are proud of their competence as readers; they don't need pictures anymore. But I bristle at the notion that a person might "graduate" from one type of books to another. A good book is not geared toward only one particular age; we can appreciate it in new ways at different times in our lives.

In Jewish tradition, too, books are divided by level—there are books we read when we are young, and there are books we can read only when we are older. The rabbis teach that children begin studying Torah at age five, Mishnah at ten, and Talmud at fifteen.[33] But the Bible is not a baby book, the Mishnah is not middle grade, and the Talmud is not for teens. A child who begins studying Mishnah does not stop studying Torah; rather, the Torah is the basis for the Mishnah's laws. Likewise, it would be impossible to study Talmud without also engaging with the Mishnah and the Torah. Indeed, much of the work of the Talmud consists of identifying the verses in the Torah that serve as the basis for the Mishnah's laws, thereby linking these texts together. All Jewish literature is cumulative; every text incorporates and is based on the texts that came before.

Part of the excitement of studying Jewish texts is that the enterprise is endless, and therefore endlessly engaging. There are a finite number of verses in the Torah, but a person never finishes studying them. Each verse becomes the basis for generations of interpretations, stories, and legal principles, which in turn inspire further teachings. Torah may be the text most accessible to us when we are young—hence children begin studying it at age five, even before they can read. But it is a text that proves just as challenging at age twenty-five, and forty-five, and seventy-five. The rabbis caution, "If you have studied much Torah, do not think highly of yourself, for it is for this reason that you were created."[34] They insist that if a person does not find meaning in Torah, it is because that person is empty, and not because Torah is empty of meaning.[35] Every new commentary or interpretation returns us to the beginning—to the Five Books of Moses—and so every time we read we are also, necessarily, rereading, no matter how old we are.

The world of Jewish learning is often compared to a sea because of its vastness and depth. As with a sea, Jewish texts can be accessed on many different levels—by skimming the surface, swimming underwater, or diving to explore the flora and fauna on the ocean floor. One can leaf through an illustrated book of Bible stories, or learn to read by sounding out the first verses in Leviticus, or study the various rabbinic interpretations of the text and their legal ramifications. No one ever outgrows the study of Torah, which is perhaps why the rabbis teach that "it is not incumbent upon you to finish the task, but nor may you desist from it."[36] The text demands a lifetime of engagement at all levels and ages; it is the book we always return to, and the book we never return.

2

ॐ

The Bad Mother

IT WAS SHABBAT AFTERNOON AND WE WERE ALL IN THE
living room except Yitzvi, who was napping in his bedroom.
Matan was fiddling with a magnetic puzzle, Liav was leafing
through a graphic novel, Tagel was curled up on an armchair
reading a historical mystery in Hebrew, and Daniel was on the
floor helping Shalvi connect wooden railway tracks. I was trying
to start reading the first chapter of a novel, but I kept getting interrupted. Matan had his legs stretched out on the couch where
Liav was sitting, and apparently, he kept kicking her, until she
snapped at him in anger. "Matan, please stop kicking Liav," I attempted, but that didn't help. Liav was increasingly annoyed at
her brother, and she wanted me to intervene. "Liav, please, work
it out with Matan," I pleaded from my perch on the other armchair. "I just want a few minutes to read while Yitzvi is asleep."

"No one in this family cares about me," Liav pronounced,
leaping off the couch in self-righteous indignation.

"Good, she finally moved," said Matan, stretching his legs
out even farther.

"You're so mean," Liav attacked Matan. "You're the worst
brother ever. And no one cares. Even Ima isn't helping me." She
glared in my direction.

Liav stormed off to her bedroom and slammed the door behind her, waking Yitzvi, whose bedroom is across the hall. Yitzvi shuffled into the living room with his blue furry blanket, rubbed his eyes, and announced to all of us, "I didn't sleep so much."

Daniel shrugged his shoulders, looked at me, and then looked back at Shalvi's train tracks. I knew what he was telling me as if he had spoken the words aloud: "I'm already busy playing with Shalvi. Yitzvi is your responsibility." But in that moment, I couldn't see Yitzvi for who he was. He was not my sweet red-eyed two-year-old but a problem I had to solve. His nap had been cut short, he would be cranky all afternoon, and he'd need constant attention. So much for the novel I wanted to read.

Then I had an idea. "Yitzvi, let's go out for a walk. We might even see a street cleaner." The sanitation department doesn't work on Shabbat, but I was desperate. If I took Yitzvi out, maybe he'd fall back to sleep in his stroller, and make up the rest of his nap. Even if he didn't fall asleep, I could push him in the stroller while reading my book.

"I want to come for a walk," said Tagel, leaping up from the armchair and setting her book face down, open to her place. She was already buckling her silver Shabbat shoes before I had strapped Yitzvi in. "No, Tagel," I told her firmly and perhaps a bit rudely. "It's not that kind of walk. I'm going to read," I confessed, hoping that Daniel couldn't hear. I didn't want this time to count against me. He and I try to give each other a little bit of alone time on Shabbat, and I didn't want to use up my precious minutes on this walk. But Tagel loves to get outside, and she'll take advantage of any opportunity. "Ima, it's OK, you can read," Tagel assured me. "I won't bother you. But I want to come."

I was skeptical. This was not going to be the walk I had envisioned, and already I was feeling resentful.

"Tagel, how will I read if you're walking with me?" I asked, trying to discourage her. It wasn't really fair, and I knew it. Surely I ought to have seized the opportunity for alone time with my daughter. Surely I should have welcomed her along, inviting her to share whatever was on her mind. The Talmud teaches that a person cannot learn Torah unless they act harshly to the members of their household, citing the example of one particular sage, Rabbi Ada bar Matana, who went off to study and left his wife with no food to feed their children; when she protested, he told her to feed them rushes from the marsh.[37] Sometimes it seems like the only way to read is to be harsh to those we love most.

But Tagel surprised me. True to her word, she walked by my side quietly. Her one request, which was only fair, was that I read aloud to her. I had yet to make headway in the novel I'd brought along, and I wasn't sure if it was appropriate for an eight-year-old. But at that point, I told myself, there was only one way to find out.

The novel, by an Israeli author I'd never read before, begins with a temper tantrum in the middle of a street. The narrator—a young single mother—tries to console her five-year-old son, who is sprawled on the crosswalk wailing. He wants a lollipop; she doesn't have one. The cars in front and behind them start honking impatiently. Desperate, she leans over and promises her son, "If you behave nicely, we'll go to Luna Park tomorrow." His older sister knows it will never happen, and tells her brother, "She's just saying that." And indeed, the next day, the mother tells her kids that the amusement park is closed for renovations, even though they see right through her lie. Theirs is not a happy family. The mother cannot make ends meet, and they are facing a very real threat of eviction. She is too depressed to work; it takes all her energy to get herself out of bed to send the kids off to school and receive them when they return. All she can give them, she feels, are her promises, even if they are vain.

I wondered what Tagel made of this depressed mother who can't afford her rent and lies to her children. Tagel didn't say a word, and I was too nervous to ask. The mother in the book believes she is not a good parent. She admits that she was too young to have children, and never really wanted to become a mother at all. She knows that it is not acceptable to voice such sentiments—to rail against the holy grail of motherhood—and yet she shares it with us, her reading audience. Except that now her audience included Tagel, who might be trying, at that very moment, to wrap her mind around what it means to be a bad mother.

I imagined what was going through Tagel's mind. Has the phrase "bad mother" ever occurred to her before? Perhaps she thinks a bad mother is one who reads on a bench in the park instead of playing with her child? Maybe, I imagined Tagel thinking, a bad mother is one who comes to pick up her kids at school at the very last minute every single day—not for any good reason but simply because she finds it agonizing to tear herself away from her work? Or perhaps a bad mother is one who keeps stealing away to her computer after dinner to type these very words, as if she can't hear the voice crying out, "Ima, please check my hair for soap, Ima, come look, did I get all the soap out?"

These are merely my projections, of course. For all I know Tagel wasn't thinking anything of the sort. Even in moments when I feel dreadful about something I've done as a parent, I try never to speak negatively about myself in front of my kids. I don't want them to grow up to be as self-critical as I am. Besides, as the mother in the Luna Park novel tells us, "Children love even a bad mother. What matters is that they have a mother."

Novelist and essayist Natalia Ginzburg writes similarly in *Serena Cruz, or the Meaning of True Justice*, her attack on the Italian magistrates who tried to separate a girl from her adopted family. She explains that it is more important for a child to have a bad family—a family that is oppressive, uncaring, or toxic—than no family at all. "Maybe he grows up unhappy in his family, he's ashamed of it, hates it, but it's an unhappiness memory can feed on. In the future he will go back in his mind to that thick and woody forest."[38] Children grow up to define themselves, for better or worse, in relation to their parents and their families. There is no way of knowing how these influences will shape a child, but children with no strong influences—no thick and woody forest—will find it harder to clear a path to who they are, and who they want to be.

We had been walking and reading for fifteen minutes when Yitzvi, who had not fallen asleep, began fidgeting uncomfortably—always the signal to turn around and head home.

"Next Shabbat we can take a walk and I won't bring a book," I promised Tagel. I felt like I was telling her I'd take her to Luna Park, but she just shrugged it off. "It's fine," she told me. "I like when you read to me while we walk. It's interesting for me to hear grown-up books. I'm learning a lot." I wondered what she was learning, but I knew better than to ask.

The next day, after the younger kids left for preschool, Tagel was proud to tell me that when Shalvi broke down in tears because her favorite shirt was in the wash, she knew just what to say. "Ima, I told her that if she got dressed and ate breakfast, you would take her to Luna Park," Tagel boasted, as if I had been reading her a parenting manual rather than a work of fiction. A shadow crossed my face; maybe that book wasn't appropriate for her after all. "Don't worry, Ima," she assured me, noticing my uneasiness. "I'll just tell her it's being renovated."

✡

Sometimes when I am reading to my children, there are passages I'm not sure I want to read aloud. This happens particularly when I am chanting to them from the Torah at bedtime, a ritual that developed in response to a perennial parenting problem: What is a parent to do when the child insists "stay with me, stay with me" and refuses to go to sleep alone?

For a long time, my kids did not just insist that I stay with them. They also wanted me to read to them or tell them a story until they fell asleep. Of course, this never worked. Invariably my stories kept them awake. But then one night I had an idea. Torah reading has been putting Jews to sleep in synagogue for ages; why shouldn't it work for my children, too? And so I began chanting verses from the weekly Torah portion, repeating the verses until the kids grew so bored of hearing the same words over and over that they fell asleep.

Chanting Torah to my kids was not just a way of getting them to fall asleep but also an educational opportunity. After years of reading and listening to Torah in synagogue on a weekly basis, I am always hearing words of Torah echo in my mind. These words permeate my thoughts and become the soundtrack for my life. I would like Torah to become the soundtrack for my children's lives, too, but they are usually not interested in sitting in synagogue on Shabbat and following along; the little kids are too young to sit still, and even the older kids would rather play with their friends in the synagogue courtyard. At bedtime, though, when they insist that I stay, I have a captive audience. I hope they'll fall asleep dreaming of a ladder of angels, but sometimes they ask questions instead.

"Why is there so much blood?" Shalvi wanted to know one night when I was reading about the Yom Kippur sacrificial rites in the Torah portion called *Acharei Mot*, midway through Leviticus. "And who would want to eat blood anyway?" I tried to explain to her that people used to worship God very differently than they do now, though even today, in our prayers, we find echoes of Temple ritual. "But we don't kill goats," she countered. "There are so many dead goats in the Torah!" I nodded. And then I told her that I would keep chanting, but she should save all her questions for the morning, because it was time to go to sleep.

In truth, though, the real reason I didn't want her to ask any questions that night was that the part of the Torah I was chanting wasn't appropriate for her. The continuation of *Acharei Mot* is about forbidden sexual liaisons—a man may not lie with a married woman, or with his father's wife, or with his daughter-in-law. . . . I didn't mind if Shalvi heard me read these verses; there is no part of the Torah I wouldn't want my children to hear. But to hear and to comprehend are two very different things.

The rabbis of the Talmud understood that not every verse in the Torah is appropriate to explain in every context. The Talmud recounts that it was customary when chanting from the Torah for a professional "translator" to explain the text in Aramaic, the lingua franca, so that the congregation would understand. This explanation, known as the Targum, was recited alternately with the Torah portion, verse by verse. But the rabbis cautioned that not every verse should be interpreted; sometimes the translator ought to stay silent. For instance, the account in Genesis of how Reuven slept with his father's concubine is chanted without Targum.[39] Some affairs, as it were, are better left unexplained.

I suspect the same holds true for my daughter. When I was a child, there were many verses from the Torah that I heard chanted before I had any inkling of what they meant; they became part of the fabric of my being even before my conscious mind had processed them. This is still true for me—not just with Torah but also with poetry. Often I will read a poem several times without any real idea of what it is about; all I know is that it is beautiful, and that this beauty is related to a commingling of sound and sense that enchants yet eludes me. I know that I will keep reading the poem again and again until I have begun to tease out its meaning. In the case of Torah, it will be a lifelong engagement. The Torah is described as "*morasha kehilat Yaakov*," the inheritance of the people of Israel (Deuteronomy 33:4), but the rabbis say to read the word *morasha* as *me'orasa*, meaning an engaged bride. I want my children to remain engaged with Torah their whole lives as I am, courting her, uncovering her layers of meaning, getting to know her ever more intimately.

But not all at once, and not all right now. Like Tagel, who doesn't need to hear about bad mothers, Shalvi does not need to hear about the forbidden relationships at the end of *Acharei Mot*. Let her think, for the time being, that "lie with" is what I am doing at that very moment—lying down next to her in bed with the verses of Torah aglow on my cell phone, chanting ever more softly as she drifts off to sleep.

3

⁊⁊

The Menorah Tattoo

WHEN CHOOSING WHAT I WILL READ WITH MY CHIL-
dren, I favor the books they are less likely to appreciate on their
own. My children will inevitably find their way to novels about
magicians and spy schools and babysitter clubs. Once they start
reading these series, they are not able to stop, which has value in
its own right: These books instill a love of reading and cultivate
the ability to sit with a book for long stretches. But I want my
children to learn to enjoy books that are not as readily accessible to them—books with long descriptive passages that slow
the plot development, books set in times and places that seem
foreign and faraway, books that make them question their as-
sumptions and imagine how different the world could be.

One of the advantages of reading aloud is that it allows for
questions. The kids can stop me when they don't understand
something, and I can do my best to answer. "Why does English
have so many words that mean the same thing?" Matan asked
while I was reading him *The Phantom Tollbooth*. We had recently met Milo, a boy of about Matan's age, whose adventures
began when he drove through a tollbooth that mysteriously appeared in his room. In the chapter we were up to, Milo had just
arrived in Dictionopolis, where all the words in the world orig-

inate. He is welcomed by the king's royal advisers, who speak in a chorus of synonyms, each using different words to echo the sentiments of the others. Milo asks a question very similar to Matan—why not just use one word? Why must each adviser say the same thing in a slightly different way?

"That's just it," I try to explain. "Each word is slightly different, because no two words mean exactly the same thing. And even if at one point they meant the same thing, the meaning of each word is affected by all the ways that word has been used in the past. That's why it's so important to choose your words carefully when you speak, and to think about why a particular word is being used in the book you are reading." Matan shrugs, opting for no words at all. He wants me to keep reading, but my thoughts have drifted elsewhere.

Why choose one word and not others? This is a question that underlies much of the enterprise of rabbinic midrash. The word "midrash" comes from the Hebrew word for searching or seeking; midrash is a way of seeking out meaning in the biblical text. The creators of midrash—beginning with the rabbis of the early centuries of the Common Era—regarded the Bible as God's sacred word. The Bible was central to their lives. Its stories were not just historical chronicles but conveyors of timeless truths, and its laws governed how they lived and organized their society. But the rabbis understood that in order for the Bible to remain vital and relevant, it needed to be interpreted in ways that would speak to readers in every generation. Midrash is a way of reading the Bible closely and creatively, paying attention to each word and its multiple interpretive possibilities.

If every word in the Torah reflects the divine word, then no single word is extraneous. The rabbis believed that every word conveys multiple levels of meaning, beyond the literal. This is evident, for instance, in rabbinic commentaries on the Torah's description of the menorah, the seven-branched candelabra in the Tabernacle. The menorah had cups, calyxes, petals, and whorls, and each cup was shaped like an almond flower. The Torah specifies that the menorah had to be made of hard, beaten gold. In Hebrew, as in English, the term "hard" also signifies difficulty, a connotation that was not lost on the rabbinic close readers.

What was so hard about the menorah? What is the Torah trying to convey by describing the menorah in this way? The rabbis explain that when Moses received the instructions for building the menorah, he was overwhelmed by how "hard" it was to craft, with all its ornamental detail. This single word in the biblical text, "hard," became the source of various midrashim about the menorah's construction. According to one midrash, God recognized Moses's difficulty and carved an image of the menorah on Moses's hand, so that he could then fashion it from this illustration. Another midrash teaches that a candelabra of fire descended from the mountain for Moses to copy. Yet another midrash proposes that in fact the entire Tabernacle was shown to Moses in four colors of fire, and then God instructed Moses to use earthly materials to construct a version of the heavenly prototype: "I remain in my glory, but you have your materials."[40] According to these sources, God shows Moses a manual—perhaps even in its literal sense, from the Latin word for "hand"—that he can replicate himself.

I think of this midrash when I sit down to write, hoping the right words will flow from my mind through my hands. Sometimes I can see a fiery model in my mind's eye of just what I am trying to say—I momentarily glimpse its blazing splendor. But then the vision fades, and I am left with the same charge God gave Moses: I must replicate that glory using my own materials, the words that are my gold. Samuel Taylor Coleridge wrote in the preface to "Kubla Khan" that the idea for this poem came to him after he fell asleep reading about the vast and stately palace constructed by the Mongol ruler. He then proceeded to have a vivid dream in which he was convinced that he had composed two or three hundred lines, "if that indeed can be called composition in which all the images rise up before him as things." When he woke, he was determined to translate that vision into poetry, but alas, he was interrupted by a knock on the door and the vision fled. The poem he wrote is less than a hundred lines and he referred to it as "a fragment." It is all he was able to salvage from his vivid but ephemeral dream.

When I write, I try to hold on to that dream, to grasp that vision. No single word has the exact same meaning as any other, as Milo learns in Dictionopolis, and so choosing the right words sometimes seems like playing with fire. Often it is difficult—as difficult as fashioning hard, beaten gold into cups and calyxes, petals and whorls. But out of this difficulty—out of the hard, beaten gold—creativity is kindled.

🜨

When I begin reading *Little Women* to my eight-year-old twins, I am wary of the difficulty. They have never heard of New England or the Civil War. They don't know about measles, telegrams, or young ladies who come out into society. But I have always loved this story about family devotion and the complexities of sisterhood and the dreams we harbor when we are young. As a child I read about the "castles in the air" that Meg, Jo, Beth, and Amy share with one another—their dreams for a future they can only imagine: Meg will be rich. Jo will be a famous writer. Beth will stay home with her parents. And Amy, the youngest sister, will travel to Rome and become the greatest artist in the world. Jo, ever the practical one, suggests that they meet in ten years and see which of their dreams have come true. I remember reading this chapter as a child and thinking, like the sisters, that ten years seemed so far away; now, thirty years later, I am thinking of my own little women. How can I not share this story with my daughters, no matter how far removed its cultural and historical contexts?

I'm astonished when, midway through the first chapter, Liav interrupts me to tell me the story is in fact quite familiar to her. "I know this book," she tells me. "It's about four sisters who live with their mom, because their father is off at war. One of the sisters gets very sick and, Ima, it's really sad. This book is going to get very sad." I turn to look at her in surprise. How does she know this story?

"I read it in school," she tells me. "One of my friends had it, and she let me read it during recess. I like the part about how the family came to be. The mom had one daughter named Meg, but then her husband left their family. And she married a man who had one daughter, Jo, and they both had dark skin. And then the mom and the new dad had two girls together, Beth and Amy, and their skin was kind of light brown."

Wait a second. Are we talking about the same book? I look at Liav quizzically. "The sisters were named Meg, Jo, Beth, and Amy? What was the book called?"

"I don't remember the name. But it was a comic book. Maybe it was the comics version of the book you're reading us?"

With a bit of sleuthing on Amazon, I discover that Liav is right. The book her friend lent her was a graphic novel version of *Little Women* set in contemporary times. It is a story about four sisters whose father is off at war, though he's not serving as chaplain in the Union army during the Civil War but fighting overseas with the American military in the early decades of the twenty-first century. Instead of telegrams, he communicates with his family by email. And yes, in the modern version, the Marches are an interracial blended family. "See, Ima, I told you I'd read this before."

As I read aloud from *Little Women*, Liav keeps interrupting me to announce what is going to happen, because she's already familiar with it all from the graphic novel. "They're going to volunteer in a soup kitchen on Christmas, and then their neighbor Mr. Laurence is going to invite them over for fancy restaurant food in his apartment," she tells me, just before I read about how the sisters donate their own breakfasts to feed a poor family on Christmas morning, and then their neighbor sends his servant over with flowers and ice cream when he learns of their good deed. Liav tells me what each sister wants for Christmas. In the version she has read, Jo longs for a copy of a Pulitzer Prize–winning coming-of-age novel about an intersex character; in the version I read her, Jo wants a German romance about a water sprite and a knight. Ultimately, the sisters pool their money to buy their mother a massage and manicure—the equivalent of the handkerchiefs and gloves they buy her in Alcott's original.

As Liav apprises me of the parallel story that unfolds in the graphic novel, I realize that the version she has read might be described as a midrash on *Little Women*—an interpretation of the original text that makes that text seem relevant and vital in light of our contemporary reality. Liav doesn't use handkerchiefs, but she knows about manicures, because she and her sisters polish their nails on Friday afternoons on the bathroom floor. As with the handkerchief-turned-manicure, midrash connects contemporary readers to a canonical text by drawing a version as if on our hands, for us to grasp. Suddenly the text is less foreign, less alienating, less difficult. We have a tattoo on our hands—a graphic version. The text still leaves its indelible imprint.

4

⁊ℰℂ

The Tent of Meeting

THE BOOK OF LEVITICUS IS DIFFICULT TO READ. IT contains long descriptive passages about sacrificial offerings, skin afflictions, and forbidden foods, as well as the rituals undertaken by the priests to cleanse, purify, and atone. After the human drama in Genesis and the first half of Exodus, it can be difficult to enter the world of arcane religious rites. But not everything we read need be immediately accessible and relevant. Sometimes we have to wait before the text makes sense to us.

In the book of Leviticus, even the priests had to learn how to wait. In the opening chapters we learn how Moses trains the priests to serve in the newly constructed Tabernacle, also known as the Tent of Meeting. But first the priests are told that they must wait seven days before the Tabernacle is inaugurated: "You shall remain at the entrance of the Tent of Meeting day and night for seven days, keeping God's charge, so that you do not die" (Leviticus 8:35). Some commentators contend that the purpose of this period is for the priests to do nothing and go nowhere, suggesting that perhaps they are simply learning how to wait.[41] In their role as priests they will not just have to wait on the people who come to the Tabernacle bearing sacrifices; they will also have to wait during the quiet times when there are no sacrifices to bring, no blood to sprinkle, no ashes to clear away. They have to learn that part of keeping God's charge is simply being present, receptive, and ready.

One of my greatest struggles as a parent is that there is so much time spent waiting, and so much time in which it seems nothing happens. I used to pride myself on never wasting a moment, because I always had a book in hand to read. As a parent, though, much of what my children need is my attentive presence. They want to know that I am there, ready to listen, able to help when they need assistance. If I am forever furthering the plot development—rushing to get things done, scrambling to check one more item off my list—I end up missing the real drama that is unfolding. Often what my kids need most from me is for me to be doing nothing at all.

⁂

It is a scene that has happened again and again, with minor variations: We are all ready to leave for school in the morning, and I know that as long as we head out in the next five minutes, everyone will arrive on time. I have been watching the clock, trying to keep us all on schedule. I put the toothpaste on all the kids' toothbrushes so that I can check if they actually brushed; I've kept a mental record of which kids used the bathroom; and Daniel has already packed all the lunches. Everyone's jackets are on, and the kids are in various stages of putting on their own or each other's shoes. But wait. Someone is missing. Where is she?

Today it's my turn to take the kids; Daniel has to leave shortly for the university. I call my daughter's name down the hall, but there is no response. I tell the other kids to wait a minute as I run down the hall to her bedroom. I find her curled up on her bed, her head buried in her hands. Her hair, which I'd brushed and braided neatly just twenty minutes earlier, is now unruly, strands standing up in the air from the static of her blanket. "Sweetie, what's the matter?" I ask her.

No response.

I come over to her bed and rest my hand gently on the back of her head. She will not let me see her face. "Can you tell me what's bothering you? We're all ready to leave, we're just waiting for you. What's wrong?"

"So go!" she barks. "Go without me. Leave me here. Just go! Go away!"

"But we don't want to leave without you. I can't leave you here alone. Please come with us."

She shakes her head, which is still pressed into her blanket.

I know that unless I figure out what is bothering her, I will never be able to get her to move. But how am I going to get inside her head?

"Ima?" I hear a voice coming from behind. I turn around to find my oldest son standing in the doorway. "Ima, we have to go to school. We're going to be late."

I nod, then turn back to my daughter. "Sweetie, I have to go for a minute, but I'm coming back." I arrange for Daniel to cross the busy street with the other kids and drop off Yitzvi at preschool on his way to the university. It's not an ideal solution, and I'm annoyed at my daughter for derailing our morning. If only I could lift her up and deposit her in school, where she will undoubtedly be fine the moment she lets go of my hand. But I know that my annoyance is not going to get me anywhere. I need to be patient.

In Jewish tradition there is a concept known as *bitul Torah*—the term literally refers to the nullification of Torah, but it is used to refer to wasting time. The idea is that anyone who wastes time that could otherwise be spent studying Torah is in fact nullifying the Torah. I live with tremendous anxiety about *bitul Torah*. Whenever I am not accomplishing something, I begin to think about all the ways I might be better spending my time. But as the rabbis also teach, "sometimes the nullification of Torah—*bitul Torah*—is its fulfillment."[42] Sometimes the only way to fulfill the Torah's dictates is by forsaking the study of Torah.

In perhaps his most famous sonnet, John Milton—who was fully blind by the time he wrote *Paradise Lost*—reflects on his anxiety about failing to use his God-given talents. "When I consider how my light is spent," he begins, alluding both to the way he spends his daylight hours and to the fact that his sight, now spent, has failed him. His anxiety yields to the wise counsel of Patience, who reminds him that there are plenty of other people who do God's bidding on earth; busy advancing the plot, they "post o'er land and ocean without rest." God does not need everyone to be racing: "They also serve who only stand and wait." Eventually my daughter will tell me what is bothering her, and we will be able to move on with our day. Eventually the plot will resume. But for now she just needs me to stay calmly at her side. I reach for her blanket and tent it over our heads, creating a space for just the two of us where she can feel safe. Here I can fulfill Torah by means of its abrogation; here, by doing nothing, I can do what she needs most. Here, in this tent, I also serve.

5

Happily Ever After

ACCORDING TO SOME JEWISH COMMENTATORS, THE Tabernacle was constructed in response to the sin of the golden calf. After the people sinned against God by building an idol at the foot of Mount Sinai, God gave them instructions to build a Tabernacle where they could bring sacrifices to atone for sin and restore their connection with God. Rather than melting their gold to erect an idol, they donated their gold to erect a dwelling place for the divine presence. The Tabernacle enabled the Israelites to atone not just for the collective sin of the golden calf but also for the sins of individuals. Any time a person committed a sin unwittingly—without intending to sin—that individual would bring a sacrificial goat or sheep to the Tabernacle. There the priest slaughtered the animal and sprinkled its blood on the altar to achieve expiation.

As a parent, I sin unwittingly all the time. I do not mean to hurt my daughter's feelings. I do not mean to yell at my son. I have apologized to my children countless times for my failings, but the regret and guilt remain. A friend once told me that every morning, she prays that she will not inadvertently say or do anything that will hurt her children. Inevitably I do, nearly every single day.

"Go away! You're the worst mother! You don't love me," my daughter shouts at me after dinner one night. She has just discovered her art project in the garbage, a leaf collage now covered in tomato sauce and pasta scraped off the dinner plates. She is deeply hurt. Surely if I loved her, I could not possibly have thrown away the work of her hands. I feel terrible, but I am also tired, and it has been a long day. And so instead of apologizing, I snap. "Do you really think I can save every art project you've ever made? Where would we keep them all? Are you going to organize them all yourself? Because I certainly don't have time for that."

I am angry. I have lost my temper. But I am determined to prove to my daughter that my mistake can be rectified. I lift her collage out of the garbage and begin scrubbing with a dry sponge, as if I can make it look new again. "I'm going to fix your collage," I insist with a resolve that borders on aggression. "I'm going to take off the stains and then we're going to put it under a pile of books so it's not wrinkled anymore. It's going to be fine," I tell her, but I've already raised my voice to a fever pitch and it's clear to my daughter that all is not fine.

My daughter looks at me in fury. "You don't love me!" she cries out, by which she means that she needs me to regain my composure, like the responsible adult I ought to be. I misread her, responding to her words rather than to her emotions.

"How can you say I don't love you?" I lash out. "I just stuck my hands into the garbage for you." She looks at me. I have lost control. She starts crying and runs to her room.

I set my elbow on the counter and lean my forehead into my palm. And in the midst of our argument, I think about *Little Women*, which we are still reading together. If only I could learn to read my daughter as well as I read to her. If only

I could learn, from the mother in the novel, how to modulate my responses. As a child, when I read *Little Women*, I didn't pay much attention to Mrs. March. I thought of her simply as Marmee, as her daughters call her—the calm, wise, and devoted mother who always knew what was best. Now I can appreciate how well she reads her daughters, and how skilled she is at communicating with them. It seems that Mrs. March knows how to do everything I am still trying to figure out.

It is somewhat comforting to know that it wasn't always so easy for Mrs. March, either. For all that Louisa May Alcott idealizes Marmee, she also makes it clear that becoming such a good mother took many long years of hard work. One evening, when Jo laments her inability to control her temper, her mother responds by telling her that she, too, has a terrible temper. Jo is astonished; she has never seen her mother angry. Mrs. March shares with Jo that she has been angry every day of her life, but she has learned not to show it. She explains that her own mother helped her keep her temper in check, and then when she met her husband—whom she describes as a paragon of patience and virtue—she asked him to help her by giving her a certain look whenever she was about to lose control. Mrs. March confesses to Jo that she still sometimes has to leave the room when she feels that she is about to utter words that she will regret.

After Mrs. March explains to Jo about her own struggle to control her temper, Jo holds her close, grateful for all that she has shared. I wonder how I can reclaim that closeness with my own daughter, now sprawled on her bed clutching a leaf from her collage, kicking and screaming, "You don't love me! You don't!"

The book of Leviticus describes that in the Tabernacle, there were two cherubs carved of gold, each atop a corner of the holy ark. The rabbis of the Talmud explain that the cherubs would face each other whenever the people were doing God's will. But when the people and God were at odds, the cherubs would face in opposite directions.[43] I look into my daughter's bedroom, and she turns the other way. How will I catch her eye again?

⚘

In the Torah, the Tabernacle the Israelites construct in the wilderness is the site of divine encounter. Once the Temple replaces the Tabernacle, the Israelites are commanded to make a pilgrimage to that holy site three times a year so as to be seen by God. But the Hebrew word for "to be seen" may also be read as "to see," suggesting that the Temple was not just the place to be seen by God but also the place to see God—a mystical, intimate encounter in which the holy gaze is reciprocated. According to the Talmud, when the Jewish people would ascend to Jerusalem on the pilgrimage festivals, the priests would roll up the ark curtain to reveal the cherubs, who were embracing each other, and say to the people: "See how you are beloved before God, like the love of a male and a female."[44]

We aspire to intimacy and closeness. Yet so often the people we most love are the people we hurt most, even when the weapon we wield is Cupid's bow. I know my husband so well that when I cast my arrows, I know just where to aim. Usually, in retrospect, I wish I had missed. But with those we love, we rarely miss.

During a period when Daniel and I squabble more than usual, our five-year-old takes refuge in fairy tales. Every single book she pulls off the library shelves is pink or purple, featuring princesses and unicorns and fairy godmothers. These books are not shelved together; Shalvi makes her way around the room like the prince with his glass slipper, searching them out one by one. Reluctantly I read about Snow White, Sleeping Beauty, and Cinderella, alongside drawings of petite maidens with cinched waists, dainty wrists, and flowy hair. In every story, the prince and the princess live happily ever after.

I am a hopeless romantic. I believe that my potential for greatest happiness lies in exclusive partnership with one other human being. But I can't suspend my disbelief long enough to get through the traditional fairy tale anymore, nor do I want to leave my daughter with the impression that all it takes for loving partnership is for her to be beautiful and trusting, and for him to be handsome and rich.

I try to present Shalvi with the feminist answer to the fairy tale, hoping she will realize that there are other kinds of princesses, other models of romantic love, other ways of cultivating intimacy. We start with *The Paper Bag Princess* by Robert Munsch, the story of a brave, smart princess who rescues her intended after he is carried off by a fearsome fire-breathing dragon; when he responds impudently to her heroism—he tells her she looks like a mess—she promptly ditches him, and they don't get married after all. We move on to Babette Cole's *Princess Smartypants*, about a motorcycle-riding princess who is too cool to get married, so she sets impossible challenges for her suitors that send them all running, leaving her to live happily ever after on her own. Neither of us is satisfied with these stories. What use is having one's pride intact if one is left all alone in the end? Is anyone really too cool for companionship?

And so instead I read her a story in which the acceptance or rejection of marriage is not the final scene but merely a thickening of the plot. In *The Queen Who Couldn't Bake Gingerbread*, a German folktale published as an illustrated children's book in English in 1975, the hapless King Pilaf is in search of a wife. He has very strict criteria for his spouse. As he tells his Lord Chamberlain, she must be beautiful enough to please him and wise enough to help him rule, and she must know how to bake his favorite gingerbread. King Pilaf searches far and wide, but it seems there is no perfect woman. Finally, the king meets Princess Calliope. She tells him that she is in fact seeking a husband, but he must know how to play the slide trombone, which he does not; nor can she bake gingerbread. However, she is drawn to his kindness, and he to her wisdom, and they decide to get married.

The two do not live happily ever after, at least not yet. One day the king and queen get into a terrible argument. "See?" I tell my daughter. "Husbands and wives argue. Not just in our house." The king tells his wife that he wishes she knew how to bake his favorite gingerbread; and she tells him that she regrets not marrying someone who could soothe her nerves with the music of a slide trombone. But thanks to the intervention of the goodly Lord Chamberlain, all is not lost. After several scorched pots, the king learns to bake his own gingerbread; and after sounding at first like an elephant blowing its nose, the queen learns to play the slide trombone.

I can abide the "happily ever after" of King Pilaf and Queen Calliope because it celebrates the partnership of mutually respecting equals, and the maturity that can develop within a relationship. King Pilaf and Queen Calliope learn the important lesson that we can't expect to change the other person, but we can change ourselves and, in so doing, transform our relationships. The king and queen don't always get along, but they live together ever after, presumably with many happy moments.

In the bond between God and Israel, too, there are moments of closeness and moments of distance, but the relationship endures. Back in Genesis, God promised Abraham, "I will maintain My covenant between Me and you, and your offspring to come, as an everlasting covenant throughout the ages" (17:7). God tells Abraham that his descendants will be slaves in a land not theirs, and God will redeem them from bondage. In the book of Exodus, God makes good on that promise, not only liberating the Israelites but giving them the gift of the Torah in a ceremony often analogized to a wedding. Now, in Leviticus, the couple—God and the Jewish people—inaugurate their new home, where God's presence might dwell amid the people.

The Tabernacle will become the model for the Temple, which the Jews will build once they have arrived in the Promised Land. That Temple will subsequently be destroyed on account of the sins of the Jewish people, and the Jews will be exiled. But as God tells Moses in the book of Leviticus, "Even then, when they are in the land of their enemies, I will not reject them or spurn them so as to destroy them, or annul My covenant with them, for I am the Lord their God" (26:44). Neither God nor Israel ends up alone forever after. They remain part of that everlasting covenant.

6

Sacrificing the Little Prince's Sheep

THE BOOK OF LEVITICUS DETAILS THE VARIOUS SACRI-
fices offered in the Tabernacle: the sin offering, the guilt offering, the peace offering, and the offering that is entirely burnt on
the altar. The Torah's word for "sacrifice," *korban*, comes from
the Hebrew word meaning "to draw close," suggesting that sacrifices are a way of forging—or perhaps restoring—intimacy.
Sometimes at night, when I come into Matan's room to read to
him, it feels as if I am bearing in my arms not just the book we
are reading—tonight it's *The Little Prince*—but also an offering
of penance for all the ways I have inadvertently wronged and
hurt him over the course of the afternoon.

Today it seems like he and I have been bickering ever since
he came home from school. "Matan, hi, how was your day?" I
ask him when he walks in the door and dumps his heavy backpack in the closet, eager to make his way to his room. It's an
innocuous question, but I know the pattern of our interactions,
and I'm already wary.

"Fine, Ima."

"Do you want anything to eat?"

"No," he tells me. "I'm not hungry."

"Do you have any homework?" I know the answer, and so
does he.

"Yes, I know, I'll do it."

Matan goes to his room and closes the door. When I knock twenty minutes later, he is sitting on his bed with his Rubik's Cube collection, his hands turning fast and furiously as the matching colors slide into place. "Matan, please get started on your homework. You also have to practice viola, and prepare your presentation for science, and—"

"Ima, I know. Leave me alone. Not now."

I remind Matan that he has only an hour until his robotics club, and when he comes home from that, he's generally too tired for schoolwork. But Matan doesn't want to be reminded.

In the opening chapter of *The Little Prince*, the narrator relates that once, when he was a boy, he drew a picture of a boa constrictor swallowing an elephant. It was his first drawing, and it was rather primitive. When he showed it to the grown-ups, they assumed it was a hat. The boy was frustrated that the grown-ups were unable to understand his artwork. So the boy drew another picture—a transparent cross section of the boa enveloping the elephant. This time, the grown-ups told him to abandon his drawings and devote himself to his studies. Alas, the narrator bemoans, the grown-ups care only about figures, and they always need everything spelled out.

I open Matan's math book and set it before him with a pencil, even as I know I am overstepping my bounds. But I can't help myself. I always try to get my work done immediately, and I can't understand why my son isn't more like me. When I return from picking up the younger kids, Matan's door is locked and he is playing music—not on his viola but on a device he is not allowed to take into his bedroom. I knock on the door, and he pretends he can't hear me.

The narrator in *The Little Prince* grows up to become a pilot, and one day, when his plane crashes in the Sahara, he meets a little prince from another planet, who demands that he draw him a sheep. Over the course of the novel, the narrator gets to know the prince, who has left his planet and the flower he loves—a small flower with just four thorns to defend herself. Matan, with his door closed and the music playing, is putting up thorns. For a moment my heart softens. If only I were able to respond out of tenderness. But I am increasingly upset that he is ignoring me, and so I knock even louder.

When Matan finally opens his door, the tension between us mounts, and both of us erupt like the two active volcanoes on the little prince's planet. By the time Matan leaves for robotics, he has completed none of his assignments, and I am so consumed by frustration that I've neglected everything else I ought to be doing. Daniel is out teaching until late, so I am on my own with the kids for dinner tonight. I head into the kitchen, and as I am banging around in search of the right-sized pot, my daughter sits down at the counter to share the latest kindergarten drama. "Ima, Yael hurt my feelings today. It made me so sad," she confides. I try to listen as she tells me about the girl who asked to borrow her colored pencils and then returned them blunt and broken, but I'm not completely following. I am rushing to get dinner ready before two-year-old Yitzvi—whose bedtime is fast approaching—collapses in a tantrum born of hunger. I'm reminded of a line from *The Little Prince*: "I am busy with matters of consequence."

The narrator speaks these words when he is trying, one day, to fix the engine on his plane. As he is unscrewing a bolt, the little prince asks him a question about flowers and thorns. The narrator does not realize that the prince is asking this question because he loves his flower dearly and is terrified that she will be eaten by the sheep the narrator has drawn for him. For the little prince, the fate of the entire universe hangs in the balance. My daughter has been trying to sketch her universe for me, but I am too busy with matters of consequence.

Once dinner is served, the younger kids are asleep, and I am loading the dishwasher in a moment of quiet, my remorse sets in. The little prince tells the narrator, when he is too busy fixing his plane to listen attentively, that he once met a red-faced businessman who spent all his time counting stars so that he might acquire more stars; the man never smelled a flower, never looked at a star, and never loved anyone. The little prince tells the narrator that this businessman is not a man but a mushroom, implying that the narrator—in ignoring the pathos-filled tale of the little prince—is acting in much the same way. Not a man but a mushroom. Not a mother but a mushroom, in my case.

My daughter is already asleep, but perhaps it's not too late to make amends with my son. I walk into his room to read to him, but the air between us is still charged; I know that if I try to apologize or broach the subject of our disagreement, he will not be receptive. Instead of sitting on his bed, I sit at his desk, a bit farther away.

We are reading about the fox whom the little prince met on his travels from planet to planet. The fox asks the prince to tame him. To tame, as the fox explains it, is to cultivate a relationship of mutual responsibility. It is to get to know another individual and to become deeply invested in their welfare. The fox explains that a person can only understand someone after taming them. He tells the prince that in order to tame him, the prince should sit at a distance; over time, says the fox, they will draw closer to each other.

When I come to that sentence, I shift over so that I am

sitting at the foot of Matan's bed. This is the moment to offer a sacrifice in the Hebrew sense of the term. And so I draw closer, stroking his hair and saying the words that I need to say, and the words that he needs to hear. In the pages we just read, the fox told the little prince that if he tames him, the fox will no longer be a fox like all other foxes. Instead, he will be unique in the world to the prince, and the prince will be unique in the world to the fox.

Shortly before instructing the Israelites to build the Tabernacle, God tells them, "You have seen . . . how I bore you on eagles' wings and brought you to me. Now if you will obey Me faithfully and keep My covenant, you shall be My treasured possession among all the peoples, for all the earth is Mine" (Exodus 19:4–5). Although the entire earth belongs to God, there is the promise of a special relationship with the Israelites, who then become—on account of that relationship—unique among the nations. Bound by an everlasting covenant, God and the Israelites tame one another.

7

The Miniature Shrine

THE TABERNACLE, LIKE THE TEMPLE MODELED AFTER it, is a reminder that true intimacy is possible. When the people build a home for God, then God will be present among them. It is not that God needs a home. After all, as God declares, "The whole earth is filled with My glory" (Isaiah 6:3). But as the prophetic books underscore, the act of working to build a home for God—the act of making the world hospitable for the divine—is what ensures that God will dwell among us.

Often when we return home from synagogue on Shabbat, my children play together with Magna-Tiles and with Fisher-Price peg-like plastic people. Nearly every time my children's imaginations are given free rein, they build a synagogue, with the people lined up in rows and the rabbi facing them in the front, praying together as the sun streams through the stained glass Magna-Tile windows. God's question echoes in my ears: "The heaven is My throne and the earth is My footstool; what house could you possibly build for Me?" (Isaiah 66:1). It seems my children have quite a few answers.

In the Bible, everyone is encouraged to contribute to the effort of building God's dwelling place, bringing gold for the altar, dolphin skins for the tent covering, and oil for kindling the eternal lamp, the westernmost light of the menorah that was always kept lit. The Tabernacle is constructed from the finest materials the Israelites have to offer, adorned in regal shades of purple and scarlet, as befits the King of Kings whose presence they will encounter within. My daughter runs to get the plastic chairs from her dollhouse, and my son retrieves small Lego squares to use as prayer books. They warn us not to come too close, lest we stumble over any part of their creation.

But neither the Tabernacle nor the Temple lasts forever. By the time of the prophet Ezra—who lived in the fifth century BCE, after the First Temple's destruction—God was no longer being sought out in the Temple but rather in sacred books: "For Ezra had dedicated his heart to seeking out the Torah of the Lord so as to observe it, and to teach laws and rules to Israel" (Ezra 7:10). The Hebrew word for "to seek out," *lidrosh*, comes from the same root as the term *midrash* and the term *beit midrash*, a place where holy books are stored and studied. The act of seeking out God in Judaism is not just a mystical pursuit but a literary one; the *beit midrash* is essentially a religious library.

Unlike a library, though, a *beit midrash* is not a place of quiet and hushed whispers. In the *beit midrash*, the learners generally sit in pairs with a book before them, discussing the text they are studying. The classic text studied in the *beit midrash* is the Talmud, which invokes the Bible to determine how Jewish law should be interpreted and practiced. The Talmud unfolds dialogically, as a series of debates and arguments among rabbis of the early centuries of the Common Era. Those arguments continue through the medieval and modern periods, as scholars in all generations reference and try to make sense of the Talmud's complex and often conflicting teachings. To this day, the conversations that take place in the *beit midrash*—and in any space where Jewish texts are studied—are a continuation of the conversations that have been unfolding for thousands of years, ever since the Torah was given to Moses. The words spoken by God at Sinai continue to reverberate within the walls of the *beit midrash*, rendering it a sacred space.

As Jews, we are not alone in enshrining our houses of study. Many of the greatest libraries in the world resemble sacred shrines: the Wren Library at Trinity College, Cambridge, with its high ceilings and marble busts; the Tianjin Binhai Library in Tianjin, China, with its miles of terraced bookshelves and luminous spherical auditorium at the center; the Library of Congress, with its copper dome and arched colonnades. Such august edifices leave no doubt that seeking out wisdom in texts is a spiritual pursuit.

There are libraries so magnificent and awe-inspiring that I have trembled at their gates. When I was an undergraduate, I received a travel grant for three days to research my senior thesis on phrenology and mesmerism in the rare books reading room of the British Library. At the circulation desk I was instructed to check all my belongings, except for a pencil and notebook. The book I requested—a medical journal from the 1830s—was handed to me on a triangular wooden "cradle," along with a velvet "book snake," which reminded me of the fabric belt wrapped around a Torah scroll to hold the wooden rollers in place. The purpose of the cradle and book snake was to prevent unnecessary contact with the fragile books; once I had turned to the page I wanted, I was supposed to set the book on the cradle and rest the book snake atop so that I might read without using my hands.

The rabbis of the Mishnah used the term "defile the hands" in speaking about sacred texts, on account of an ancient practice of storing sacred scrolls next to tithed grain consecrated for the priests. The rabbis were concerned that the mice that ate the grain would also nibble at the scrolls and desecrate them. In an effort to ensure that scrolls would be kept separately, they somewhat counterintuitively decreed that sacred texts "defile the hands" and would therefore impurify grain if stored alongside it. The rabbis invoked this phrase when discussing which books to include in the biblical canon—a book sacred enough to be part of the canon is, by definition, a book that defiles the hands.[45] In the British Library, though, the fear was that hands would defile the books.

Throughout most of my time in college I studied in Widener Library, the main research library, located in the heart of Harvard Yard. The majority of my friends preferred to work on their assignments at the undergraduate libraries, where the space was organized to allow for more socializing and study breaks. But I preferred the grandeur and austerity of Widener, ascending the wide stone staircase and passing by the marble columns as soon as the library opened in the mornings. Widener offers its patrons the privilege of open stacks; instead of requesting a book from the library staff, one can simply find it on one's own. There are ten floors of vast, cavernous stacks, six aboveground and four below, lit by dangling naked light bulbs. The perimeter of each floor is lined with unassigned study carrels where anyone might sit and study. I rarely saw another human being when I worked in the stacks, except for the occasional member of the library staff who came by with a squeaking cart to reshelve books, like a priestly functionary in the Temple silently and purposefully going about the daily rites.

Since college, I have also studied in libraries that are far less grand. But even if a library is not architecturally striking, I am still filled with awe when I enter. Libraries remind me of how much larger the world is than my own small corner. At times when I have felt dispirited or uncertain about how to face the future, the best way to emerge from the Slough of Despond—a phrase I first encountered in *Little Women*—is to walk into a library. As soon as my eyes register the vastness of book after book, shelf after shelf, and row after row, I am overcome with a desire for more: more hours and days, more years to read. No longer do I want to flee from life but to embrace it. Jorge Luis Borges once said that he imagined paradise as a kind of library. But no one takes books to the grave. When I look out at all the titles I have yet to read, life feels like a gift again, carrying with it the promise of all the books I can fit into my numbered days. Entering a library, my soul yearns for infinity.

In Jerusalem, the Israel Museum combines the library and shrine in a magnificent, iconic structure known as the Shrine of the Book, home to ancient Hebrew manuscripts dating back to the turn of the first millennium. On the outside, the Shrine of the Book appears as a white dome, built to resemble the lids of the jars in which the scrolls were discovered. On the inside, a long underground hallway with successive alcoved entryways leads into a main atrium, which features at its center a large pillar. The pillar is inset with a glass case protecting the Isaiah scroll, the oldest complete copy of the book of Isaiah, which is the most intact of the ancient scrolls discovered nearly a century ago in caves by the Dead Sea. It is not an altar that stands at the center of this shrine, but a sacred text.

The Shrine of the Book is located down the block from the National Library of Israel and not far from the Parliament building and the Supreme Court, all situated on a large hill. The mutual proximity of these buildings is not incidental; the library is located in the "National Precinct," a testament to the import and esteem in which it is held by the Israeli government and the Jewish people. I visited the National Library frequently in the years before I had children, arriving by a bus that left me just outside the main gates. When I reached the building housing the library, I checked my backpack at the desk and ascended a wide staircase to the reading room sanctuary, where scholars sat poring over their books with the rapt concentration of religious devotees. Most of the books I wanted to consult were shelved in the reading room, but every so often I placed a request for a volume from the stacks—the holy of holies—where only the library staff were permitted to enter.

When my oldest son, Matan, was born, I had just submitted a proposal for a doctoral thesis on the destruction of the Temple in the rabbinic imagination—a thesis I ultimately never wrote. During the first few months of Matan's life—when he was not yet weaned, and I could not be apart from him—I used to take him with me in a stroller to the National Library. I didn't dare enter the silent reading room with him, but I discovered a cramped, run-down side room devoted to the history, philosophy, and sociology of science, where I was generally the only patron. I wheeled Matan's stroller between the narrow stacks, took out my computer, and worked while he slept.

Sometimes, when I was struggling to find the right word or phrase, I would swivel around in my chair and gaze at my infant, sleeping tranquilly with his arms up, the rest of his body swaddled, his breathing slow and steady. I thought of Byron and the joy of "they who watch o'er what they love while sleeping." Then I thought of Dante and the lovers who read together until they are too distracted by each other: "That day we read no more." I shut my computer to gaze at my infant a while longer, until eventually I stopped coming to the library altogether. The Temple's destruction would have to wait. I was too busy building a new home.

§

Once I had babies, my academic pursuits gave way to writing and translating work that seemed more compatible with my family commitments. For the most part I worked at home, visiting the library infrequently. But any place where I am privileged to immerse myself in a book—especially with one of my children—becomes a miniature shrine.

The term "miniature shrine" appears in the Bible in the prophecy of Ezekiel, who foretold the destruction of Jerusalem in the sixth century BCE and the eventual restoration of the Jewish people to their land. Ezekiel assured the people that although the Temple would be destroyed, God would still maintain a "miniature shrine" (11:16) in Babylonia, where the people would be exiled. Over half a millennium later, the rabbis of the Talmud invoked this term to refer to a *beit midrash* or synagogue, both places where Jews gather together to read sacred books.[46] The rabbis teach that in the absence of the magnificent Temple in Jerusalem, any place where Jews gather to pore over sacred books or pray and chant from them becomes a shrine.

Just as I wanted my children to feel comfortable and at home in the library, I hoped that the synagogue, too, would become a familiar and welcome environment. When Matan was four days old and had not yet been initiated into the covenant of circumcision or received his name, I carried him strapped on my chest to synagogue. I had not counted on how often I would need to leave to feed him, and always at the most inopportune moments—when I wanted to hear the Torah reading, or recite the prayer for the sick, or stand with my feet together for the recitation of the prayer known in Hebrew as *Kedusha*, "sanctity," in which we are supposed to imitate the posture of the angels in heaven. Yet I persisted, determined that my son should grow accustomed to the rhythms and melodies of the prayer service, hopeful that one day he would learn how to follow the service himself.

The synagogue I brought Matan to was egalitarian—both men and women lead the prayers, chant from the Torah, and participate fully in all aspects of the service. I prefer to pray in a synagogue where there are no gender-based distinctions; such distinctions seem like a distraction from the truly important distinction between God and human beings, which is the reason we pray in the first place. Besides, how can we demand equality in all other spheres of our lives, and yet deny women leadership roles in synagogue? And so I brought Matan to the synagogue I had been praying at for years, where I continued to chant from the Torah—often with Matan in a baby carrier on my chest when I stood before the congregation.

Less than two years later, when the twins were born, I showed up in synagogue with my double stroller only to discover that I could no longer climb the three flights of stairs to the room where we prayed, nor did my wide stroller fit through the narrow door. Daniel, who prayed elsewhere—at the Kotel, the Western Wall, a vestige of the sacred precincts of the ancient Temple— generally joined me only at the end of the service. How was I to bring my children to synagogue if I couldn't even make it up the stairs, or in the door?

Shortly thereafter I found my way to a different synagogue, which I chose primarily because of accessibility. In this synagogue women did not participate as fully; they were permitted to lead only some of the prayers. My younger idealistic self would not have approved, but my thirty-five-year-old self saw it differently. This new synagogue had a wide ramp leading up to the sanctuary, a place for me to park my double stroller, and a children's service where my kids learned to sing many of the Shabbat morning prayers.

My children began to feel at home in the synagogue with the ramp. At first they were too young to follow along, but they would sit at my feet and play with one another. I alternated between keeping up with the prayers and attending to the kids' needs. Sometimes I had to do both at once—I'd affirm God's sovereignty and then, in the very same breath, respond to the two-year-old relentlessly tugging at my skirt that *yes, Elmo also has a tushie.* Perhaps it was for such very moments that the Talmudic sage Rabbi Shimon bar Yohai declared that he wished God had given him two mouths, one to speak sacred words and one for all other needs.[47] Eventually my children learned that there are parts of the service where I could not be interrupted unless it was an emergency. In such moments, I would press my finger to my lips and shake my head discreetly so they knew to wait.

It felt important for me to model a commitment to prayer for my children because of the centrality of prayer in Jewish tradition. Drawing on a verse from Hosea—"Instead of bulls, we will pay the offering of our lips" (14:3)—the midrash teaches that the prayers we utter take the place of the sacrifices once offered on the altar.[48] Like sacrifice, prayer is a way of drawing close to God by means of giving up something deeply valued. In our busy, fast-paced modern world, time is one of our most precious resources. When we pray, we give up some of the time in our day to God. Even so, for many years I found it difficult to resist the temptation to take time away from prayer to read in synagogue. I brought books about the Bible and other Jewish texts with me, and I would try to pray as fast as I could, to maximize my time to read.

All this has changed now that I have children. I rarely bring my own books to synagogue, conscious that I'm lucky if I have enough time simply to get through the prayers. Instead, though, I bring books for my children. The Shabbat morning prayer service is long, and if I want my children to stay inside, I need to find ways to keep them occupied. I choose books with involved, elaborate illustrations, so they can linger over every page and narrate the story to themselves. My daughter loves Dr. Seuss classics in which the logic is primarily governed by rhyme: a man named Ish who makes a wish for fish on his dish, or the Yink who winks as he drinks pink ink. She shows the pictures to her younger brother, who waits eagerly for her to come to his favorite page, about Mr. Bump.

My school-age children are old enough to pray independently. They know how to read the words in the prayer book, and they are familiar with the general choreography of the service—when to stand and when to sit, when to bend their knees and when to bow. But they rarely agree to open the prayer books I hand them when we arrive in synagogue. Instead, they bring their own books to read—Percy Jackson, Harry Potter, Magic Tree House. I follow with my finger in my own prayer book, hoping they'll take note of the place. Generally, though, they are too absorbed in their reading, as I was before they were born. I am reminded of the oft-told story about a fabled synagogue with a sign on the wall discouraging the worshippers from talking during prayer: "If this is where you go to talk, where will you go to pray?"

And yet even when they are not paying attention to the service, my children are learning other lessons—about books, and holiness, and sacred texts. They know that if a Torah scroll were to fall to the floor, God forbid, we would be obligated to fast; if a prayer book or Bible falls, we pick it up immediately and kiss it, placing our lips to the spine. They know that we never place secular books on top of sacred ones. It has been ingrained in them from a very early age that there is a hierarchy of sanctity when it comes to books.

In this hierarchy of sanctity, the Torah is the most sacred book of all. Even my toddler looks up when the Torah makes its appearance in the service. As soon as the prayer leader pulls back the curtain to open the ark where the Torah scroll is kept, Yitzvi leaps up excitedly, pointing and shouting, "To-RAH! To-RAH!"—he has been eagerly anticipating this dramatic reveal. After the reader completes the chanting of the weekly Torah portion, the Torah scroll is lifted high up into the air for everyone to see. "This is the Torah that Moses set before the Israelites" (Deuteronomy 4:44), the congregation sings, and this time everyone—not just my toddler—points a finger at the scroll. I imagine a library card affixed to the velvet cover, stamped with due dates all the way back to the revelation at Sinai, attesting to hundreds of generations of readers.

The Temple, the library, and the synagogue are sites of intimate encounter—with God, with texts, and with one another. But ultimately, as Ezekiel told the Jews on the eve of the Babylonian exile, sacred space can be found anywhere we work to create it. At night I sometimes find one of my older daughters reading under the covers with a flashlight long past bedtime, unaware that the bright beam shines through the blankets, illuminating her room like an eternal lamp. I lift the blanket like a tent flap and my daughter, startled, turns to face me; she knows she has been caught. If I am cross, it is only momentarily, because a love of reading is so much of what bonds us; I too stay up reading much later than I ought. I close her book without saying a word and set it atop the pile on her nightstand. This time it is not the book I kiss, but my daughter, who is already fast asleep when I exit her bedroom door.

NUMBERS

Beezus and Corona

THE BOOK OF NUMBERS NARRATES THE LONG AND PRO-tracted period in which the Israelites wandered in the wilderness between the Exodus from Egypt and their arrival at the threshold of the Promised Land. Coping with tremendous doubt and uncertainty, the Israelites complained frequently to and about their leaders and had difficulty maintaining faith in God's promise. I thought often about the wilderness wanderers during the Covid pandemic, which our family spent in lockdown in our home in Jerusalem. We navigated the pandemic with as much anxiety and complaining as they—albeit allayed, to some extent, by reading together. Through reading, we ultimately learned how to sit with uncertainty and inhabit a narrative without knowing where it was leading or how it would end.

1

𝒞

Panic, Plunder, Pandemic

WE WERE FORTUNATE TO GO INTO LOCKDOWN IN A house full of books. During the first few months of the Covid pandemic, all the schools, synagogues, and libraries in Israel were shuttered. It happened quite suddenly—one day there was school as usual, and the next day all the teachers and school-children were instructed to stay home for the indefinite future. One Shabbat we went to synagogue, and the next week, everyone prayed on their porches, trying to join in with singing neighbors. One afternoon the library was open, and the very next afternoon, I received a text message informing me that the library would be closing at 3 P.M. and would remain closed for the rest of the week. At the time I didn't know that the "rest of the week" would actually be several months. I looked down at my watch. It was 2 P.M. I grabbed my coat and ran out the door.

At the library, I was one of only a few patrons. The library staff looked tense and distracted—the man behind the circulation desk kept eyeing the clock nervously. As I searched for books for each of my children, I asked if the regular rule of eight books per patron applied. "You can borrow as many books as you want," the librarian urged me. "Just hurry, hurry, we're closing soon, it's dangerous to be out."

A few days before the Israelites left Egypt for the wilderness, the Torah teaches that God instructed them to "borrow" clothing and jewelry from the Egyptians (Exodus 3:22), thereby fulfilling the prophecy to Abraham that they would leave Egypt "with great wealth" (Genesis 15:14). Amid the rush of fleeing from bondage before Pharaoh changed his mind again, the Israelites grabbed what they could, ensuring that they did not leave Egypt empty-handed. The Egyptians, worried that "we shall all be dead," urged the Israelites to take whatever they wanted and leave as soon as possible (Exodus 12:33).[49] As my tower of books rose even higher, I felt a bit like the Israelites on the eve of the Exodus, stocking up for the period to follow. I had no idea what lay ahead, just as the Israelites still did not know that God would provide for them in the wilderness, ensuring that they had enough food, that their feet never swelled, and that their clothes never wore thin.

As I scanned the shelves, I tried to choose judiciously, aware that I was limited by what I could carry. I took only a few picture books, focusing instead on chapter books that would occupy the kids for longer stretches. The Bible teaches that when the Israelites entered the wilderness, they were accompanied by a "mixed multitude" (Exodus 12:38) who tagged along during the Exodus and the desert journey. At the time I did not know that we would make our way through the wilderness of a pandemic trailed by such a mixed multitude—including Beverly Cleary's Beezus and Ramona, the sisters who rarely get along, and Peggy Parish's Amelia Bedelia, the housekeeper who never seems to get it right.

※

The book of Numbers is known in Hebrew as Bemidbar, which literally means "in the wilderness." But it is in fact the vast majority of the Torah—from the middle of Exodus to the end of Deuteronomy—that is set in the wilderness, with its flat sands stretching endlessly in all directions. Moses herds the Israelites as he herded his father-in-law's sheep in Midian, passing some of the same landmarks. At first God leads them "roundabout, by way of the wilderness" (Exodus 13:18) to avoid the Philistines, who might attack them and cause them to turn tail. The Israelites are deliberately led along a longer path, with no clear sense of when they will arrive at the Promised Land.

When the Covid pandemic began, we had little sense of what to expect and how long it would last. How many people would get sick? When would it end? Everything took so much longer when we could not leave the house. We learned to bake our own bread, shop for groceries online, and log in to virtual classrooms. Nearly everything had to be accomplished in an alternative, creative, roundabout way. Surely these were all just temporary measures, we thought wishfully. Surely this could not last more than a few months.

Perhaps the newly freed Israelites thought it would take just a few months to travel through the Sinai Desert to the Jordan River by God's circuitous route. Maybe a year at most. But then during their second year of wandering, they send out twelve spies to scout out their destination, and ten of them return with a negative report, throwing the whole enterprise into question. "It is a land that devours its inhabitants," the spies warn an increasingly terrified congregation. "The people who live there are giants!" (Numbers 13:32). The Israelites break out in loud cries of panic, and no amount of reassurance from Joshua and Caleb—the two spies who have a more optimistic perspective—can assuage their sense of doom.

At the start of the pandemic, some prognostications were more optimistic than others. But it was the dire predictions that caught the public's attention, just as it was the negative reports of the majority of the spies that captured the Israelites' imaginations. People everywhere were panicked, alternating between hand-washing and hand-wringing.

Following the report of the spies, God punishes the Israelites for failing to have faith in the divine promise to give them the land of Israel. "How long will the people spurn Me, and how long will they have no faith in Me?" God asks Moses in frustration and fury. "As I live," swears God, "none of the men who have seen My Presence and the signs that I have performed in Egypt and in the wilderness . . . shall see the land that I promised on oath to their fathers" (Numbers 14:11, 21–22). As punishment for the forty days the spies spent in the land of Israel, the Israelites have to wander for forty years in the wilderness, and an entire generation dies out. By the time the Israelites enter the Promised Land, no one who had been an adult in Egypt will still be alive, with the notable exceptions of Joshua and Caleb. The rabbis teach that every year, on the ninth of Av—the anniversary of God's decree of death—the Israelites would dig graves and sleep in them, in case they died in their sleep. The next morning, an announcer would go around the camp proclaiming, "Let the living separate themselves from the dead." And only those still alive would rise from their graves.[50]

Throughout those early weeks of the pandemic, I woke each morning to messages on my phone bearing grim statistics: the number of Covid fatalities, the number of critically ill patients, the rate of virus transmission. Who had not risen from their beds that morning? Who would not rise tomorrow? When summer came, the billboards outside continued to advertise plays, concerts, and movie screenings scheduled for dates that had long ago elapsed. The month of March seemed like a perpetual present, as if we had sunk into the desert sands.

2

Revealing the End

A HALLMARK OF THE WILDERNESS EXPERIENCE WAS uncertainty. The people had to trust in Moses's leadership and have faith that God would provide for them. They had to pack their belongings and prepare to travel every time they saw the pillar of cloud rise above the Tabernacle, without knowing where they would camp next. They had to believe that even as they arrived at a clearing with a large imposing rock and no fresh water in sight, somehow they would find enough to drink. They had to live from day to day, with no ability to plan ahead.

I have always been an obsessive planner. For as long as I can remember, I've kept a "daily planner" notebook, jotting down meetings, appointments, and to-do lists. I carried this notebook wherever I went—until suddenly I stopped going anywhere. When the country went into lockdown, my planner lay untouched in my bag, and every penciled-in commitment faded into irrelevance. Should I even bother to cancel my son's haircut? My annual dentist appointment? Would anyone remember that this was supposed to be the week of the school play? Or that my daughter had a book report due at the end of the month?

I wasn't reading the same way either. I found myself flipping to the end of each novel to peek at the final chapter long before I got to it. The uncertainty in literature compounded the uncertainty in life, and my anxiety became too much to bear. I needed to know how the story would end.

Jewish tradition looks unfavorably upon "revealing the end," a reference to the Messianic age in which the dead will be revived and the world will be redeemed. The rabbis teach that Jacob, on his deathbed, tried to "reveal the end" to his sons, but at that moment, the divine presence departed from him, and he lost access to that vision.[51] "Cursed are those who try to calculate the end," the Talmud declares, warning that those who think they know when the Messiah will arrive end up losing faith that the Messiah will come at all.[52] I spoiled quite a few books for myself by "revealing the end"—I knew that Caro would lose her husband and fall for the man who had always loved her in Shirley Hazzard's *The Transit of Venus*, a book whose artistry lies in the careful scattering of the seeds of the ending in the soil of the beginning. The final chapter was not as satisfying as it otherwise would have been; I had lost my share in the World to Come.

Our children, too, pleaded with us to reveal the end, unable or unwilling to accept that we were as much in the dark as they were. "When can we see our friends again? When will we go back to school?" They had no classmates to play with and no school to fill their days, so I began reading Beverly Cleary's novels about Ramona Quimby's school days aloud to them. I sat on the living room floor with my back against the bottom of the couch and the kids sprawled all around me—on the floor across from me, where Matan built towers of blocks while he listened; on the couch above me, where Liav and Tagel could see the occasional illustrations; at the coffee table, where Shalvi didn't really follow the story but drew pictures of rainbows while keeping us company. It was easiest to read when Yitzvi was napping—he turned one and then two during the pandemic, and learned to sit, but not to sit still. When he was awake, he was a welcome distraction for whichever kid had stormed off in anger—and it seemed there was always one, running off to play with their one sibling who still couldn't talk back. The price of storming off was missing out on the story. I would not read the same chapter twice.

In Israel the pandemic was referred to as "Corona," which my children liked to confuse playfully with Ramona. "It's Corona, read Ramona," they would chant, bringing me the next book in the series. In the absence of any external routine during lockdown, it was reading that gave shape to our days. We ate when we finished the chapter, and we shut off the light at bedtime when we turned the final page. "How many pages left?" Daniel would holler down the hall from Yitzvi's room, where he was changing a diaper. When the kids awoke, they didn't ask me what day it was, or even what time it was. "Wait, is Ramona's mom going to make her a sheep costume for the Christmas carol program?" my daughter asked woolly-headed when I woke her and inquired what she wanted for breakfast. We always ate breakfast before we read, but beyond that, there were very few rules.

It would be several weeks before school reopened on Zoom and the kids would have more structure. "I wish we could go to school," my daughters continued to lament. "It was so fun to play in the playground at recess." It was as if they forgot all the reasons they used to dread the start of the school week—the homework, the tests, the strict gym teacher, the dirty bathrooms. "We remember the fish that we used to eat free in Egypt, the cucumbers, the melons, the leeks, the onions, and the garlic," the Israelites complained to Moses (Numbers 11:5). The Israelites were quick to forget the backbreaking labor they'd endured as slaves, insisting that "it would be better for us to go back!" (14:3).

The Israelites did not go back to Egypt, and my kids did not go back to school—at least not initially. For a while it felt like they'd merely transferred from their elementary school in Jerusalem to the Glenwood School in Portland, Oregon, where they sat alongside Ramona. They peered over her shoulder during "seat work," and when everyone was supposed to be absorbed in their workbooks, they tried to overcome the temptation to pull the hair of the girl sitting in front of them. They listened as the children presented their dolls and stuffed bunny for show-and-tell. They stood up for "The Star-Spangled Banner," even though they had never heard of "that American song," as they came to refer to it. But even Ramona was initially unfamiliar with the words of the national anthem, as we discovered together.

On Ramona's first day of kindergarten, her teacher, Miss Binney, teaches the class the words to "The Star-Spangled Banner" without explaining what they mean. Ramona, unable to parse the words properly, finds the song puzzling: "O say can you see by the dawnzer lee light." She decides that a "dawnzer" must be some kind of lamp. A few chapters later, when Mrs. Quimby admonishes Beezus for reading in poor light, Ramona comments that she ought to turn on the dawnzer. "What's a dawnzer?" Beezus asks, and Ramona is proud to show off her new kindergarten vocabulary. "It's a lamp that gives lee light," she tells Beezus knowingly. Beezus realizes her sister's misconception and bursts out laughing, embarrassing and infuriating Ramona. From that point on, my kids never let me start reading without first reminding me to turn on the dawnzer. Already Ramona was filling the dark days of the pandemic with lightheartedness and lee light.

My school-age children refused to touch their pencil cases or their workbooks, but they dutifully accompanied Ramona to school every morning. When Mrs. Griggs taught the class how to add by imagining the various kids in the class exchanging apples, my attentive listeners chimed in with sums before Ramona could even lift her hand in the air. When Ramona discovered that curly-haired Susan had copied her drawing of an owl for Parents' Night, they shared in Ramona's outrage. By the time my children came back from Glenwood School each day, they were exhausted, even though they'd never left home.

Anything good enough for Ramona was good enough for my kids. "What's a fad?" they asked, when we came to a chapter titled "The Egg Fad," in which all the students in Ramona's class begin bringing hard-boiled eggs for lunch and cracking the shells against their foreheads. One day Mrs. Quimby accidentally packed Ramona an uncooked egg, and an unsuspecting Ramona smashed it on her forehead, with consequences as messy as they were mortifying. At the start of the pandemic, there was a severe egg shortage in Israel. Matan enjoyed the look of horror on my face each time he took one of our precious few raw eggs out of the refrigerator and pretended he was about to smack it against his forehead.

My kids knew that I had read the Ramona books when I was a child, and they frequently interrupted with questions about what would happen next. "Is Ramona's father going to find a new job?" Liav asked concernedly, after he'd been unemployed for several weeks. "Will Ramona get punished for squeezing all the toothpaste into the sink?" Tagel wanted to know. I thought about God's pledge to bring the Israelites to a land "flowing with milk and honey" (Numbers 14:8), and realized that every divine promise is a spoiler of sorts. With so much uncertainty around us, I was relieved that I could promise my children that at least in the book we were reading, it would all turn out OK.

3

⁊

The Quimby Crock-Pot and the Egyptian Meat Pots

AT THE START OF THE PANDEMIC, WE HAD NO ENERGY to argue with the kids over food, so we ate pasta for dinner most nights. I felt embarrassed by the proper meals Mrs. Quimby served to her family—meat and baked potatoes and broccoli, all neatly plated. Even when Ramona's mother went to work as a receptionist at a doctor's office and her father continued to work long hours at the checkout counter at Shop-Rite, the family ate wholesome dinners, thanks to their trusty Crock-Pot. But one evening, after the Quimbys have been out all day at work and school, they come home hungry and tired only to discover the house cold and musty, without the welcome smell of simmering meat. Who neglected to turn on the Crock-Pot that morning? Ramona's parents blame each other, and the sisters can only look on in worry as their parents hurl nasty insults back and forth.

From the moment the Israelites left Egypt, food was a subject of tension. At one of their first encampments, they complain about the shortage of water and lament how they miss the abundant meat and bread in Egypt: "If only we had died by the hand of God in the land of Egypt, when we sat by the meat pots, when we ate our fill of bread!" (Exodus 16:3). They neglect to mention that presumably they were responsible for filling those meat pots and lighting the fire beneath them before setting out to build the pyramids each morning. Again and again they insist that God brought them out of Egypt to starve in the wilderness. "Why did you make us leave Egypt to die in the wilderness? There is no bread and no water, and we are sick of this miserable food" (Numbers 21:5).

The Quimbys decide to make pancakes for dinner, but the bickering continues. Dinner is eaten mostly in silence, in spite of Ramona's attempts to distract her parents by reporting on her least favorite aspect of school—the dreaded weekly spelling test. Although Ramona's parents assure the children the next morning that they are no longer quarreling, food remains an issue, especially when Mr. Quimby loses his job and goes back to school. One night Ramona finds herself confronted with a plate of roasted meat and broccoli as she sits dreaming of corn bread; then she realizes that the meat on her plate is tongue. She pushes it away, pronouncing that tongue is disgusting. In Hebrew, the term for speaking ill of someone or something else is *lashon hara*, which literally means "evil tongue." Ramona slanders the tongue, and her parents are none too pleased.

When the Israelites complain about the lack of food in the wilderness, God rains down manna for them to gather in the mornings. At first the Israelites hoard the manna, anxious that new manna will not fall the next day, even though God warns them that any leftovers will spoil. Faced with uncertainty, the instinct to stockpile supplies is hard to resist, as the pandemic reminded us. God then sweeps up quail from the sea and strews it all over the camp, and while the meat is still between their teeth, God strikes the people with a severe plague, and the place becomes known as "the Graves of Craving" (Numbers 11:34).

Even the meat the Israelites desired proves ultimately unsatisfying, like so many aspects of the wilderness experience. Fed up after years of wandering, the Israelites speak ill of their leaders, and their leaders even speak ill of one another: The book of Numbers describes how Aaron and Miriam criticize Moses behind his back for his choice of wife, and 250 men led by a dissatisfied Levite named Korach rebel against Moses's leadership. Perhaps it is the intensity of sharing a makeshift camp in the desert for so many years, each family confined to a small tent with little privacy, but the Israelites are quick to provoke and perturb one another.

Does living in close quarters through a period of uncertainty bring out the worst in us? During our lockdowns, it was just the seven of us under one roof. We tried not to get too irritated by the dirty dishes left on the counter or the cookie crumbs trailing along the kitchen floor, though these minor infractions loomed much larger when our whole world seemed to have contracted to the space of the kitchen. Sometimes the kids looked for excuses to quarrel merely as a way of amusing themselves, and Daniel and I could only exchange exasperated glances.

I warned the kids that arguing often resulted in someone getting hurt, even inside the house. In the final book in the series, Ramona gets into an argument with her new friend Daisy. They are playing dress-up when Daisy, dressed as the wicked witch, shuts Ramona the beautiful princess in a dungeon. But the dungeon is actually a small door leading to the unfinished part of Daisy's family's attic, where the floor is covered in lath and plaster. Ramona hears an ominous cracking sound beneath her feet as the lath snaps and the plaster gives way. Thankfully she is rescued by Daisy's older brother, who pulls her out of the hole.

When Korach and his 250 followers rebel against Moses in the book of Numbers, God punishes them by creating a hole in the earth to swallow them up: "The ground under them burst asunder, and the earth opened its mouth and swallowed them up" (Numbers 16:31–32). When the ground implodes, they sink into the underworld shrieking, and no one comes to their rescue. Given all the arguing in our home, it was a cautionary tale.

Desperate for a way forward, I took my cue from Mrs. Whaley, Ramona's third-grade teacher, who introduces the class to Sustained Silent Reading. She instructs the students that every day after lunch, they are to sit silently at their desks and read a book they have chosen from the library. But then on second thought, Mrs. Whaley decides that Sustained Silent Reading sounds rather dull, so she renames it DEAR—Drop Everything and Read. If my kids could drop everything and read silently to themselves, perhaps we'd have some quiet at last.

Daniel and I agreed it was only fair for us to take part in silent reading as well, and so each day, during Yitzvi's nap, we took turns sitting with the kids as everyone read to themselves. Even Shalvi was willing to flip through a large stack of Curious George or George and Martha, examining the pictures and occasionally trying to sound out a few words. The twins picked up early readers, finally warming to the Amelia Bedelia paperbacks. They laughed at the antics of the well-intentioned but featherbrained housekeeper who misinterprets all the instructions she receives but then invariably redeems herself by baking one of her irresistibly delicious confections. Occasionally I had to explain the puns and idioms that were the source of Amelia

Bedelia's misapprehensions. My kids had been camping before, but they didn't understand why Amelia Bedelia was not supposed to whack the pavement with a stick when she was told to "hit the road," or why instead of "pitching" the tent, she threw it into the bushes.

When I was the parent overseeing Drop Everything and Read, I never told the kids how long it would last. Sometimes they got bored or restless. "How many more minutes?" they'd ask, eyeing the oven clock. But I refused to reveal the end. Sometimes we lasted all through Yitzvi's nap, the cries from his bedroom playing the same role as the pillar of cloud rising above the Tabernacle to signal to the Israelites that it was time to pack up their tents and hit the road.

🌿

When we weren't arguing or reading, we were baking, like so much of the world. We learned to make crusty peasant bread in a cast-iron pot, thin focaccia with fresh rosemary, and sugar cookies dipped in cinnamon. The twins took inspiration from Beezus and Ramona, whose parents insisted they make dinner for the family on the night after the infamous tongue. When Ramona contends that she only knows how to make French toast and Jell-O, her mother tells her this is "nonsense," because she is in third grade and knows how to read, and "anyone who can read can cook." I've thought about this statement quite a bit—I'm a voracious reader, but as my kids will attest, my culinary skills leave much to be desired.

In the end Beezus and Ramona work together and pull off a successful dinner, though my kids were rather disgusted by the main course: chicken thighs dipped in banana yogurt and seasoned with chili powder. The kids were relieved that we couldn't try to replicate their recipe in our kosher kitchen—it's forbidden to mix dairy and meat products. But they were inspired to try their hand at making dinner. "We can do it on our own," they assured me. Matan, noticing our empty pretzel jar, suggested they make pretzels. The girls shared his enthusiasm. "Pretzels aren't dinner," I objected, but the kids agreed to eat them with cottage cheese so they would have some protein. We looked up a recipe for soft pretzels, made the dough together, and then I let the kids shape them into twisted knots before I dipped them in a pot of boiling water and baking soda.

That night, I sang the twins the prayer Jews recite just before bed: "Hear, O Israel, the Lord is our God, the Lord is One." While waiting for them to fall asleep, I absentmindedly turned on my phone to read in the dark. I googled the term "pretzel" and was astonished to discover that pretzels are widely thought to have originated in Italy fifteen hundred years ago as prizes given to Christian children for learning their prayers well; the term "pretzel," it is held, comes from *pretiola*, Italian for "little rewards." The three empty sections of the pretzel represent the three parts of the trinity, and the dough is folded over to resemble arms crossed in prayer. Was that really true? Had I sung the Shema to my children just hours after ingesting the catechism?

The kids were calm in bed, but I was not. I shared with them what I had learned. Tagel wanted to know if that meant they couldn't eat pretzels as a snack in synagogue. "I'm not sure we can eat pretzels at all," I responded. I told the kids about the Talmud's prohibition on following "the ways of the Amorites," an idolatrous people living near the land of Israel who refused to let the Israelites pass through their borders in the book of Numbers (21:23).[53] The Talmud makes no mention of pretzels, of course, but even so, the twins and I were in agreement. Next time we made pretzels, we would shape them into rods instead.

⚜

Many of the scenes in the Ramona books take place in the kitchen, and the series is full of cakes. Beverly Clearly writes in her memoir that during her senior year of high school in Portland, her mother's cousin Verna invited her to California to live in their home and attend a junior college there. Verna proposed that Cleary receive free room and board in exchange for keeping her room clean and baking two cakes a week for the family. Cleary was thrilled by the prospect of leaving home. But first she needed to learn how to bake.

That summer, her mother taught her how to make all sorts of cakes I'd never heard of: Arabian spice cake, potato caramel cake, Lady Baltimore cake, prize devil's food cake. "Always sift the flour before measuring it, otherwise your cake will be heavy," her mother instructed, referring to their baking sessions as "Beverly's college preparatory course."[54]

Cleary never tells us whether she enjoyed baking with her mother, but it is clear they had a fraught relationship. She writes that her mother, whose life was circumscribed by narrow middle-class Portland during the Depression, had no job and no hobbies and lived vicariously through her only child. She took greater interest in Cleary's insufferable long-term boyfriend than Cleary herself, and she was probably the reason the couple stayed together as long as they did. Perhaps most disturbing, as Clearly discovered one day when she came home from high school, her mother kept a diary of her daughter's life as if it were her own. I imagine Cleary and her mother baking side by side in a culinary rite of passage, the air between them as heavy as a cake made from unsifted flour.

For Ramona and her mother, too, there is much tension surrounding the baking of cakes. When Ramona is four, she ruins Beezus's tenth birthday cake twice over, first by dropping all the eggs into the batter with their shells. Ramona's exasperated mother pleads with Beezus to distract her sister while she starts working on a new cake, so Beezus reads Ramona the story of Hansel and Gretel. Ramona, inspired by the story's happily-ever-after ending in which Gretel pushes the witch into the oven, decides to push her favorite rubber doll into the oven when no one is looking. Suddenly Beezus smells something rubbery. She runs to the oven to check on her cake, only to discover Ramona's doll melted into the batter. Perhaps anyone who can read can bake, but sometimes too much literacy can ruin a cake.

Eight books later, when Ramona turns ten, her mother organizes a party in the park for all her friends, including Susan, the prissy girl with irresistibly springy curls. Susan tells Ramona that her mother read in a book that blowing out candles is unsanitary. "There might be spit on the cake from blowing on the candles."

After the other girls run off to play, while Ramona is helping to clear off the picnic table, her mother tells her that Susan's mother is not the only one who learned something from a book. "The book I read said ten is the nicest age of growing up," she says, kissing Ramona on her hair. I looked over at my girls. I was tempted to kiss them on their hair, too, except that apparently eight is not such a nice age for being kissed. They squirmed away squeamishly. "Ew, Ima, don't kiss us, we're going to get your germs."

※

Shortly after we read about Ramona's party, the twins surprised me by asking me to bake a cake. It was a few days before my birthday, and I had my suspicions.

"Ima, please make us a plain cake. A cake with nothing on it. We can't tell you why, but we need it. OK?" they said.

"OK," I agreed. "A sheet cake, right?"

My kids looked puzzled. "Not a sheet cake," said Liav. "A bed cake." I had no idea what she meant, so I made a plain chocolate cake, hoping it would not disappoint.

On the morning of my birthday, they presented me with the cake I had baked for them, decorated with whipped cream, sprinkles, and two marshmallows on one end. "These are the two pillows, yours and Abba's." I asked them why the cake needed pillows, and Liav shrugged her shoulders matter-of-factly. "Because it's a bed cake," she told me. I still wasn't quite sure what she meant. The cake was accompanied by a card—only now, on my forty-second birthday, had I finally merited to receive a handwritten card from my semiliterate children: "To Ymo yor a grate mothor from the cids," they wrote. I knew I was an Ima and sometimes an Ema—as it's often spelled. But Ymo was a first. I wondered if Ramona, who was terrible at spelling, would have done any better. "What difference does spelling make if people know what you mean?" Ramona asks her fourth-grade teacher petulantly.

The kids added a line at the bottom of the card that read, "fancyue Ymo for macen a kcece." For a moment I thought I was being called fancy. Then I realized this was just their phonetic rendering of "thank you Ima for making a cake." Under the word "a" I could see there was a crossed-out "the," and I asked Liav about the rough draft. "First I wrote thank you for making THE cake, but then I realized you would know that the cake you made was for you, so I changed it to A cake. So it would be a surprise."

Only several days later did I realize that the whole idea for this bed-sheet cake came from *Amelia Bedelia Bakes a Cake*, in which the exasperating but earnest housekeeper wins a baking contest for her bed-shaped sheet cake after a similar misunderstanding. As an Ymo, I had underestimated my children. The cake they had made me was, in fact, a literary allusion. What better gift could I want?

4

⁊

The Unreliable Narrator

IT WAS A LONG TIME BEFORE ANYONE HELD BIRTHDAY parties again, even without blowing out the candles. But after two months of lockdown, the Israeli educational system reopened and our children prepared to go back to school. As they tried on their masks and stuffed their bags with "alcogel" and sanitizing wipes, I felt uneasy. I trusted the school to keep the kids safe, but it seemed unfair to be sending my children out into the brave new world of the pandemic before we had braved it ourselves. For two months, Daniel and I had hardly left the house, aside from the occasional pharmacy or grocery run. When the kids went back to school, we'd continue to sit at our desks, maskless in sweatpants in the comfort of home. Why were we asking so much more of our kids?

Since an entire generation of Israelites died out in the wilderness, it was only their children who conquered and settled the Promised Land. What was it like to wander through the wilderness knowing that you would not be around when your children finally crossed the Jordan River? Did the generation of liberated slaves share my trepidation about sending their children out into a new and unfamiliar reality? I stood at the door as my kids headed out that first morning, in awe of their courage.

That was when I began kissing the mezuzah by our front door whenever I left home. The mezuzah, a piece of parchment containing specific biblical passages rolled up inside a decorative case, is positioned at an angle on the doorpost. One side of the parchment contains the word *Shaddai*, a name for God and an acronym for a Hebrew phrase meaning "one who protects the doorposts of the people of Israel." The mezuzah is sometimes believed to serve as an amulet protecting the home and its inhabitants. I am not a superstitious person, but during the pandemic, I felt the need for that protection.

⚸

Our amulets are not just the texts we read but the stories we tell ourselves to guard against our deepest fears and anxieties. One afternoon during the second week after the return to school, my kids came home with a dramatic story. Before they had even made it to the sink to wash their hands with soap for the requisite two minutes, it was already spilling out of them. "Ima, Ima, you won't believe it," Liav told me breathlessly.

Her twin sister took the words right out of her mouth. "There were *ganavim* in school today! Real *ganavim*! And Ronen caught them and now they are in *beit keleh*!" Sad to say, despite all my reading aloud, this is really how our kids speak when they return from the Hebrew-speaking environment of school to our English-speaking home.

Liav would not stand for it. "No, Tagel, it's my story, be quiet. I'm telling Ima." The problem of who gets to narrate what has been an issue in our family for years, and is particularly acute for the twins, who have many of the same stories to tell.

I thought of the spies who returned from scouting out the land of Israel to report on their findings. At first ten of the spies

rushed breathlessly to Moses and Aaron to report on the forti-
fied cities they would never be able to conquer and the giants
who inhabited them. Only once they finished did Joshua and
Caleb offer their own account: "The land that we traversed
and scouted is an exceedingly good land. . . . Have no fear"
(Numbers 14:7, 9). I assumed my girls didn't have such wildly
divergent accounts of whatever it was that had happened in
school, and yet each was determined to tell her version.

Liav speaks faster and with greater fluency than Tagel, but
Tagel is physically stronger and more agile; often in these situa-
tions, Liav gets the words out first and then Tagel turns a cart-
wheel or breaks out in a choreographed dance and "accidentally"
kicks Liav in the face. I tried to avert this catastrophe.

"Girls, whose class did this happen in?"

"Mine, it's my story," said Liav. Tagel stormed off.

"OK, so there were thieves in school and now they're in
jail?" I repeated back in English.

"Yes, you won't believe it," said Liav. I was already a bit skeptical, but Matan, who was waiting for me to make him lunch, piped
up to alert me that "they need a better *shomer* at school. It's very
dangerous. Every time Shilon goes inside for a break, *ganavim*
can climb right over the fence."

"I'm sure Shilon is an excellent guard," I assured Matan,
washing a cucumber and dicing it for a salad. "You don't need
to worry."

"Not true," insisted Liav. "That's what I'm trying to tell you.
Today when Ronen was passing the principal's office on the way
to the bathroom, he overheard the *menahelet* telling the *sgan
menahelet* that *ganavim* were trying to steal *machshevim* from
the *chadar machshevim*."

"The principal told the assistant principal that the thieves

were trying to steal computers from the computer room?" I
translated, now on to the peppers.

"And they said that the *ganavim* weren't wearing masks!"
Liav exclaimed indignantly.

This one had me puzzled, but only for a moment. I was picturing bank robbers in comic books. Don't thieves usually wear
masks? But now, during the pandemic, when everyone is supposed to be masked, anyone who isn't is immediately suspect.

"Did they catch the thieves?" I asked, still somewhat in-
credulous.

"No!" Matan chimed in. "They hid in the school office and
then ran out the door when Shilon was taking a break. It's not
safe. They shouldn't just let anyone go into the office like that!"

I knew from the Ramona books that the school office was
a site of intrigue. Ramona had to sit there after she'd cracked
the raw egg against her forehead. The secretary forgot she was
there, and Ramona overheard her teacher come into the office
and complain that she was such a nuisance in class. Ramona was
insulted and outraged. Apparently, it could be quite dangerous
to listen in on conversations in the school office.

Tagel, who had been listening in on Liav and Matan's account, came into the kitchen because she was too hungry to sulk
in her room any longer. She sat down before her bowl of diced
vegetables. When it comes to salad, the kids each have their
own versions of the same basic story: peeled cucumbers, red
peppers, yellow peppers—Liav. Peeled cucumbers, tomatoes—
Tagel. Unpeeled cucumbers, red peppers, tomatoes—Matan.
Everyone felt better once they began eating. They crunched
their vegetables heartily, each kid determined to impress upon
me what seemed the most critical takeaway. For Liav, it was
Ronen's heroism when confronted with real-life criminals in

his school. For Matan, it was the security breach. Tagel just wanted to tell the entire story again herself, which she did, with some embellishment. I tried to make sense of it all, not sure how much to believe.

That night, I happened to be texting Ronen's mother, a policewoman, about a homework assignment. After we exchanged a few messages, I added a postscript: "Oh, and by the way, you must be so proud of Ronen. I heard all about the thieves." She wrote back with a bewildered emoji: "What are you talking about? For real?"

"If your son is not a policeman, then my daughter is a creative writer," I responded with a smiley face.

"Liav," I said to her the next morning when she was the first to climb into our bed. "I spoke to Ronen's Ima last night and she hadn't heard anything about the thieves in school. Did that really happen?"

"Well," she said, "like I told you, it was mostly true."

"Mostly true?" I wondered if it was as true as the negative report of the ten spies, who felt reduced to the size of grasshoppers by the giants living in Canaan.

I still don't know what really happened that day in school. Presumably there was some suspicious activity, which Ronen interpreted as an attempted theft. My children, already on high alert after so many months of staying closed off from the outside world, readily believed anything that confirmed their general sense of danger—even if it was really just a visit from a couple of computer technicians who stopped by the school office. I never bothered to ask the principal about it, because I was sure she had her hands full. Besides, as a parent, I was less concerned with what actually happened than with how my kids felt about it.

For my kids, as for the spies, the dominant emotion was

fear. The return to school after such a long lockdown was fearsome and fraught. On one of the first days back, the girls reported that the classroom next door had been vacated after the class was quarantined—even the tables and chairs had been removed for sanitizing. I imagine it felt haunting each time they passed by. Liav wanted to believe that there was a superhero who would rescue her from danger, even if that superhero was three feet tall and carried a SpongeBob backpack. Matan wanted to make sure that someone was always standing guard to keep the bad guys out—whether they were germs or thieves.

Should I have responded more skeptically to their story? Skepticism, according to a midrash, was the sin of the spies. They refused to believe God, who assured them that the land was good. The midrash compares the episode of the spies to the case of a king who secured for his son a beautiful wife, but whose son insisted on seeing her first because he did not trust his father. The people needed to see the land for themselves, unaware that even their own eyes could deceive them.[55]

The spies spoke about conquering the land. But the biblical story teaches that the spies, like my kids, were really struggling to conquer their own fears. If we can train ourselves to listen closely, sometimes unreliable narrators are the most reliable of all.

5

Sit Here for the Present

I FINISHED READING ALOUD THE ENTIRE *BEEZUS AND RAMONA* series during the very same week that we completed the book of Numbers in the Torah reading cycle, nearly five months after the pandemic had begun. When I came to the final paragraph of the last book, Liav pronounced, *"Chazak, chazak v'nitchazek"*—"strong, strong, may we be strengthened," a phrase typically recited upon completing a book of the Bible. It felt appropriate. The Ramona series, like the book of Numbers, had accompanied us through the first phase of the pandemic: As Ramona grew from an exasperating preschooler to a spunky, self-aware fourth grader, the Israelites made their way through their desert wanderings, her four-plus years corresponding to their forty.

The Ramona books are about growing up, which is also what the Israelites had to do in transitioning from slaves entirely dependent on their masters to free people beholden to God. "Growing up is hard work," Mr. Quimby tells Ramona. We were all there as it happened, Daniel, the kids, and I—doing our own hard work of growing up alongside Ramona and the desert wanderers.

There is no age at which we stop doing the hard work of

growing up. Toward the middle of the book of Numbers, still during the early years of the Israelites' decades of wandering, Moses grows exasperated with the people and wants nothing to do with them. He cries out to God in frustration, seeking to renounce his responsibility as caregiver for the Israelites: "Was I pregnant with these people? Did I birth them, that You should say to me, 'Carry them in your bosom, as a nursemaid carries an infant?'" (11:12). Moses invokes the metaphor of a mother to describe how burdened he feels by the children of Israel. Even Moses became frustrated and wanted time on his own. Now, in lockdown, I thought back to that Shabbat afternoon walk when I had tried to convince Tagel not to come with me. Had I really told my daughter not to talk to me because I wanted to read? Was I really such an ogre? If only we could go for long walks now—instead of being shut in—I would take each of my kids to walk and chat, I told myself. I'd take them to the library. To the park. I would wander with them wherever they wished and talk to them the whole way.

I imagine that at some point, Moses regretted his outburst of frustration. I surely regretted so many of mine.

ⵊ

We still had all the Ramona books checked out from the library, and I left them on the living room table for the kids to peruse at their leisure. While reading the series aloud, I hadn't always stopped to show them the pictures that appeared every few pages. Sometimes pausing to pass around the book would just lead to more arguing, so I simply read on. But now the kids wanted to go back and review all the pictures in order, from the first book to the last. It was almost like a *siyum*, the ceremony Jews conduct when completing a significant unit of Torah study.

"Remember when Ramona ate one bite from each apple?" Liav asked me, prompted by a picture in the very first book. How could I forget? Ramona had disappeared to the cellar with a box of apples when her sister, Beezus, was supposed to be watching her, and there she had defiantly taken one bite out of every apple in the box. Beverly Cleary recounts in her memoir that as an only child growing up on a farm, she had hours of freedom and self-amusement; on Sunday afternoons, she would sit under an apple tree "among the windfalls" and take one bite out of each apple, throwing the rest away: "The first bite of an apple tastes best," she writes.[56]

We spent quite a while leafing through the paperbacks, pausing each time we came to a picture to recall the scene it captured. It reminded me of the last portion in the book of Numbers, *Masei*, which means "journeys." The text reads like a detailed itinerary of the Israelites' wanderings: "They set out from Rameses and encamped at Sukkot. They set out from Sukkot and encamped at Etham, which is on the edge of the wilderness. They set out from Etham and turned toward Pi-Hahiroth . . ." (33:5–7). Rashi asks why the Torah takes pains to record all these stations in the wilderness, answering by means of a parable: "This is like a king whose son was sick so he took him to a distant place to heal him. On their way back, his father began to enumerate all the separate stages of the journey. He told him: Here we slept, here we caught cold, here you had a headache, etc."[57]

Like this review of all the stages of the journey in which the king cared for his son, the Torah reviews all the stages in the wilderness in which God cared for the people of Israel. There were sickness and death throughout the wilderness journey, but also many moments of intimacy and closeness, and many lessons learned.

On her first day of kindergarten, Ramona's teacher shows her to her seat. "Sit here for the present," she tells Ramona, meaning that it isn't necessarily the seat she will ultimately be assigned. But Ramona, who has an element of Amelia Bedelia's literal-mindedness, misunderstands. She thinks Miss Binney is telling her that as long as she sits still, she will receive a present. When the class is dismissed for recess, she refuses to budge, lest she forfeit the gift she's been promised. When Ramona eventually realizes her mistake, she is crestfallen. But with time she comes to love Miss Binney and to enjoy going to school, and the present—or lack thereof—becomes more bearable.

One of the many stages in the Israelites' itinerary was the journey from a place called Midbar to a place called Matanah. The term *matanah* means "gift" in Hebrew, and the Talmud explains that this place name is also a reference to Torah—the gift given to the Jewish people in the *midbar*, the wilderness.[58] Our pandemic experience was reminiscent of the Israelites' long and tiresome wilderness wanderings, but it was also filled with surprising gifts, including the gift of time to read together and enjoy—or at least tolerate—one another's close company, without ever knowing how long it would last and how it would end. We learned to stop asking questions we couldn't answer and to sit here, instead, for the present.

DEUTERONOMY

Moses's Memoir

IN THE FIFTH AND FINAL BOOK OF THE BIBLE, MOSES NAR-
*rates his own version of the wilderness journey from the Exodus
from Egypt until the arrival at the threshold of the Promised
Land. Moses's account differs from the version of events we have
previously encountered because it is colored by his disappointment,
resentment, and aspirations. We might think of the book of Deuteronomy as a memoir, in which Moses tells the story of his leadership
career from his perspective, focusing on and prioritizing what matters most to him. As my children became more competent readers,
I encouraged them to keep journals to document their experiences
and, more importantly, their reactions to those experiences. I read
them novels by authors who were writing about their own lives,
hoping that they would come to appreciate the value of telling their
own stories. Perhaps not surprisingly, my kids did not always want
to share their writing with me, nor did they always want me to
read the books they were reading. Ultimately, like Moses, who had
to part from the Israelites before they entered the Promised Land,
I have had to learn how to let go as my children venture into stories
and settings without me, leaving me to look on from afar.*

1

An Incandescent Mind

TOWARD THE END OF OUR FIRST CORONAVIRUS LOCK-down, Daniel and I decided to set aside journal time for the family. Each of us was supposed to sit quietly at the table with a notebook and pencil, but that was the only requirement. The kids didn't have to write; they were free to sketch if they preferred, or even sit there idly. Our hope was that they would begin to fill their notebooks with a recounting of their days, so that this period would not go by unrecorded.

I had high hopes that the kids would come to enjoy our writing sessions. It sounded so idyllic: We'd sit around the table together, and everyone would be silent, focused on the page before them. In my fantasy, the kids would have so much they'd want to write, and they'd interrupt us only on occasion to ask how to spell a word. Then when they finished writing about their days, they would start filling the pages with poems and plays, until they produced their own juvenilia, like the Brontë sisters, or founded a Pickwick Club, like Jo March. They loved hearing stories about other children who wrote; surely, we thought, they would be excited to become writers themselves? Alas, as the kids made abundantly clear, they wanted to live their lives, not write about them.

Daniel and I tried to model how to sit quietly and write for a sustained period of time. Each of us scribbled in spiral-bound notebooks and pressed a finger to our lips whenever anyone tried to interrupt. It had been a long time since I'd translated my thoughts into longhand rather than typing them up, and I wrote quickly and sloppily, trying to keep pace with my ideas. At one point, Tagel peered over my shoulder. "Ima, I thought you're supposed to be a good writer," she told me. "But your letters are all crooked, and you're not even staying between the lines. Your writing is terrible!"

Each time we told the kids to take out their journals, they groaned. Matan spent his journal time making pencil drawings of elaborate machines featuring pulleys, levers, and wheels, with arrows showing the moving parts. Liav dropped her pencil angrily, climbed under the table, and kicked her feet against the floor like Judy Blume's Fudge throwing a toddler tantrum. I wondered if she felt threatened by her twin sister, who seemed to fill the pages as freely as Harold with his purple crayon, so that even I envied her. Tagel, the only one who enjoyed journal time, wrote in large Hebrew letters on every other line, her spelling entirely phonetic and her printing only occasionally legible. She couldn't be bothered to date her entries; I'm not sure she even knew how to write the date. But she headed each page, as she'd been taught in school, with the Hebrew letters Bet Samekh Dalet, an acronym for the phrase "With God's help"—a reminder that everything human beings write and do is made possible by God.

When Matan and Liav went back to school, they converted their journals into school notebooks, ripping out the first few pages, which were all they had managed to fill. Only Tagel continued to write most evenings, documenting each moment of her day, so that a considerable part of her entries was fixed and unvarying: "With God's help. Today I woke up and ate corn-flakes and went to school," she always began, followed by a re-counting of any drama at school that day, each clause strung to the next by the repeated phrase "and then." Though mostly re-portorial, her entries—which she was eager to share with me—occasionally offered a window into her inner life: "Today Matan went to the park with a friend and then Liav had a friend over and then only I was left, but then Ima took me to the bakery to get pita and then I felt better." She continued writing after the end of the school year, filling every page in her notebook until she asked me for another, which I purchased for her the very same midsummer week we started reading the book of Deuter-onomy in the weekly Torah reading cycle.

Although there are Five Books of Moses, it is really only Deuteronomy that is Moses's book. "Deuteronomy" is Greek for "second law," and the book refers to itself as a "second To-rah" (17:18), since it is Moses's retelling of the events of the previous biblical books. Moses, addressing the people of Israel, provides his own version of the wilderness journey. He reviews the various encampments, recording how long the Israelites stopped each time, the rivers they crossed, and the nations they battled along the way. But even these mundane details are laced with his anger, frustration, and resentment.

Moses begins by reminding the people about how they be-came such a burden that he could not bear to care for them on his own and had to appoint tribal leaders to assist him: "Thereupon I said to you: I cannot bear the burden of you myself" (1:9). He retells the story of the revelation at Sinai from his own perspec-tive, focusing on his intervention to save the people from God's wrath: "I threw myself down before the Lord, eating no bread and drinking no water for forty days and forty nights, because of the great wrong you had committed" (9:18). And he blames the people for the greatest tragedy of his life—his inability to enter the Promised Land to which he has been leading them for forty years: "Because of you, the Lord was incensed with me, too, and He said: You shall not enter it either" (1:37). Moses, initially enlisted by God at the burning bush, never wanted to liberate and lead the people, and his ongoing ambivalence about the task with which he was charged colors his personal account.

Perhaps Moses originally set out in the book of Deuteronomy to recount the history of the Israelites in the wilderness. But he cannot tell this story in a straightforward manner, because he is so consumed by his anger and frustration with the people that his historical account is repeatedly interrupted by his own accusations. "God got angry with me on your account!" he cries in the middle of his chronicle of the revelation at Sinai (4:21). Virginia Woolf writes in *A Room of One's Own* that women have not written fiction as well as men because "the mind of an artist, in order to achieve the prodigious effort of freeing whole and entire the work that is in him, must be incandescent, like Shakespeare's mind. . . . There must be no obstacle in it, no foreign matter unconsumed." But, Woolf contends, women have been so consumed by their frustration at the injustices leveled against them throughout human history that they cannot write fiction that is unadulterated by their grievances. Women in the era of Woolf, like Moses in the book of Deuteronomy, are so "harassed and distracted with hates and grievance" that nothing they write can be truly incandescent.[59]

And yet perhaps the book of Deuteronomy is richer because it is not merely a historical chronicle; it also offers us a window into Moses's sensibility at the end of his life, after he has borne the Israelites through the wilderness for forty years "as a nursemaid carries an infant" (Numbers 11:12). Moses recounts in the book of Deuteronomy that even though he has been so furious with the people at times, he nonetheless has always stood up for them and advocated on their behalf. Even when God offered to destroy the Israelites and make Moses the head of a new nation, Moses refused to abandon the people. Moses, like the classic ambivalent mother, resents the tremendous toll that the people have taken on him, but he also cannot imagine life without them. Deuteronomy is his chance to share this ambivalence with the people, and to narrate the wilderness experience from his perspective.

Like Moses, we all need and want to tell our stories our own way. "But you can't say that! It's not true!" Tagel protested one afternoon, interrupting the silence—we were all sitting at the table writing in our journals while Yitzvi napped. I looked up at Tagel, who was leaning over her sister's shoulder. "Ima, Liav lied. She made something up in her journal. She's writing about third grade, and who her teacher is, and what art projects she'll do in school. But we're not even in third grade yet!"

"I'm writing about what I think is going to happen in third grade," Liav said in her defense, elbowing Tagel away. "I'm bored in second grade. We're not even in school this year. Next year is going to be so much more interesting, so I'm writing about that."

"Isn't that lying?" Tagel asked me.

I looked at Tagel, knowing I needed to choose my words carefully. I thought about the scene in *A Tree Grows in Brooklyn* where Francie learns the relationship between writing and truth-telling. After a classroom Thanksgiving celebration, her teacher asks if anyone wants to take home the small five-cent pumpkin pie used as a prop in the class performance. Francie's mouth waters. She is poor and hungry, and she has never tasted pumpkin pie; but she is also too proud to accept charity. So she tells the teacher that she would like to take the pie to give to a poor family. The next day, when the teacher asks her about her act of charity, Francie spins an even more elaborate fabrication about destitute twins named Pamela and Camilla who would have starved to death if not for the gift of her pie. But ultimately, Francie cannot bear her own dishonesty. She confesses to her teacher, who gently suggests a distinction between "lies" and "stories." The teacher instructs Francie that she must always tell the truth, but she is free to write her story down the way she thinks it should have happened.

"That's why you have your own journal," I explained to Tagel. "In your journal, you can write whatever you want. But you can't tell Liav what to write. Everyone gets to tell their own story." Tagel was not happy, but she didn't protest. She wrote Liav's name in her journal and made a big X through it. It was as close as she could come to undermining her sister's narrative, and I let it be.

🕊

When Moses narrates the wilderness journey, he tells it in his own way, offering an account that is sometimes at odds with what we, as readers of the Bible, have previously been told. One of the first incidents he recounts is the story of the spies sent to scout out the land of Israel. In reminding the people about this difficult episode in their history, he tells a different story from the account that appeared earlier in the Bible, in the book of Numbers. There it was clear that the spy mission was

God's idea; it was God who commanded Moses, "Send men to scout out the land of Canaan, which I am giving to the Israelite people" (13:1). Yet in the book of Deuteronomy, Moses presents the spy mission as the Israelites' initiative. Moses tells the people, "Then all of you came to me and said, 'Let us send men ahead to reconnoiter the land for us'" (1:22). Presumably Moses wants the people to take responsibility for their inability to trust in God's promise.

Like the spy mission, nearly all the events in the book of Deuteronomy are narrated in Moses's voice alone. The people who complained and cried throughout the previous three books of the Bible seem to listen silently, accepting and internalizing Moses's version of events. In Deuteronomy, Moses is not just a main character but also the narrator, and perhaps the author as well.

My children, who have studied the Five Books of Moses in school, are fascinated by the question of biblical authorship. In school they are taught the traditional understanding—that all Five Books were dictated by God on Mount Sinai, and not just the Ten Commandments. "But if Moses wrote down the entire Torah when he went up to Mount Sinai, didn't he know what was going to happen?" Matan persists. "Didn't he know that he was going to hit the rock, and that when he did, God was going to be angry and tell him he couldn't enter the land of Israel? And since he knew that, why didn't he stop himself from hitting it?"

I try my best to respond. "Matan, you know that's not how it works," I begin. "When you get angry at Tagel, you know you're not supposed to hit her, right? You know that if you hit her, you're going to get punished. And you don't want to get punished. So why do you hit her?"

"Well, I'm angry, so I hit her anyway. But if I knew I wasn't going to get what I want most in the entire world—if I knew you would never buy me a dog—I think I would stop myself. I don't understand how Moshe could know what was going to happen to him and do the wrong thing anyway."

I try to explain to Matan that it's not clear, even to the rabbis, that Moses wrote the entire Torah. Although the first books of the Bible are referred to as the Five Books of Moses, the Talmud states that Moses wrote "his own book," generally understood as a reference to Deuteronomy.[60] But Matan is still unsatisfied because even if Moses wrote only the book of Deuteronomy, he still would have had to foresee the future. After all, as Matan notes correctly, not all of Deuteronomy is Moses's recounting of the Israelites' history. At the very end of the book, Moses ascends Mount Nevo and dies. He is buried by God in the valley of Moab, and the people mourn him for thirty days. Matan points to these verses triumphantly: How could Moses describe his own death? How could he know in advance exactly when he was going to die, and how he would be mourned? Surely, declares Matan, this is proof that Moses did not in fact write the Torah, or even the book of Deuteronomy.

I tell Matan that he is not the first to grapple with this question. The Talmudic sages are also puzzled by how Moses could dictate his own death, and they propose two solutions. According to the first, Moses wrote the entire Torah except for the final eight verses, which were written by Joshua after Moses's death. According to the second, Moses did indeed write the entire Torah, but he wrote these final eight verses somewhat differently. When it came to the rest of the Torah, God dictated the words to Moses and Moses then repeated them back to ensure he got them right, before writing them down. But the last eight verses were dictated by God and not repeated by Moses, who was too overcome by grief to repeat what he had heard. Moses wrote these words in tears, heartbreakingly sealing his fate.[61]

I wonder if Matan can feel the anguish and pathos of Moses's final moments, but he's still focused on the injustice of it all. "If Moshe's writing the book, he should be able to end it the way he wants," he insists. "Why didn't Moshe just write that he went into Israel with the people? Then God would have to let him go, because it's the Torah—it has to be true." Perhaps Matan is not really speaking about Moses but about himself. Matan, at age ten, wants to be the author of his own story. He has little interest in the narrative he feels that we, his parents, are forcing him to write—a narrative of school, homework, and a good night's sleep so that he can wake up on time the next morning.

In her essay "The Little Virtues," Natalia Ginzburg writes about the mistakes parents make when it comes to the education of their children. She argues that parents should not ascribe undue importance to their children's academic performance, nor should they get overly involved in their children's studies. Children have no obligation to succeed in school, certainly not for the sake of satisfying their parents. Rather, she insists, the purpose of education is to instill in children a love of life and a love of learning, which may develop independently of school. Sometimes it may seem to us, as parents, that our children are wasting their time—they are lying in bed with headphones on for hours on end, or programming their computers to send notifications to their parents' cell phones. "We cannot know," writes Ginzburg, "whether this is really a waste of energy and skill or whether tomorrow this too will bear fruit in some way that we have not yet suspected. Because there are an infinite number of possibilities open to the spirit."[62]

Sometimes, when Matan chafes against our imposition of

authority, it feels like he's writing his story in tears—dragging himself out of bed after we wake him for the third time, lifting his heavy backpack onto his shoulders, and trudging off to school. When are we going to let him write the story of his life himself?

2

⌇

The Bus Driver Who Wanted to Be God

IN THE BOOK OF DEUTERONOMY, IT IS NOT JUST MOSES who must write the Torah. Among the laws that the Israelites are commanded to observe once they enter the Promised Land, God tells them that they may wish to appoint a king to govern them. The Torah explains that the king is subject to certain restrictions—he may not marry too many women or amass too much gold and silver and horses. Moreover, the king must have a copy of the Torah written out for him on a scroll, and he must carry it with him everywhere and read from it always. Presumably the purpose of this commandment is to ensure that the king conducts himself in accordance with the Torah's laws, but the rabbis of the Talmud explain that this commandment is not specific to the king. Rather, every person must write a Torah scroll. As the Talmud teaches, "Even if a person inherits a Torah scroll from his ancestors, it is a commandment to write one for himself."[63]

We all inherit parts of our story. Life is not a blank page for us to fill; that page is speckled and dotted by factors beyond our control, such as our parents, our birth order, and our health and resources. But ultimately it is up to us to decide how we will connect those dots. There are an infinite number of ways to draw those connections, but every constellation is unique. How will we choose to tell the story in which we star?

As Jews, we are part of a people as numerous as the stars in the sky (Deuteronomy 1:10), and the story we are commanded to write is not just our own story but the Torah. We are charged to make our story part of the larger Jewish story, and to read the Torah and the texts of our tradition in light of our own questions and aspirations. When do I hear the call of the transcendent, and how do I respond to that call? When have I felt bound and oppressed, and how have I been liberated? What is the promised land toward which I am setting my steps, and what obstacles stand in my way? When answering these questions, we map our story onto the story of our biblical forebears, such that their story provides us with the images and metaphors to narrate our own.

ℵ

My children know about telling their own stories not just from Jewish tradition but also from Laura Ingalls Wilder, whose Little House books accompanied us for over a year of reading aloud. When I started reading them the first book, they asked me what a prairie was. "A large open area without trees, stretching on and on for as far as you can see," I told them, and immediately they asked, "Like a desert?" I knew they were picturing the Israelites' wilderness encampment in their illustrated Bible books, confusing the Great Plains with the Sinai Desert. "Not exactly," I said. "The prairie is covered in grass, and there are rivers and streams that cut through it." At the time, none of us had ever been west of the Mississippi. But neither had Laura when the series begins in the Big Woods of Wisconsin, where her family lived in the only log house, surrounded by a rail fence to keep the bears and deer away. All around them were trees, miles and miles of trees so similar that it was easy to get lost in the Big Woods. "There were many other children at the time who traveled out west with their families in covered wagons," I told my kids, thinking about our journal-writing sessions. "But we know about Laura Ingalls Wilder because she wrote and published the story of her life."

When we read the first book in the series, my children learn about collecting sap, churning butter, and whittling wood. But they are most fascinated by the dialogue. "How did Laura remember every single word that everyone said? Did she write it all down?" Tagel asks. When I was a child reading the Little House books, I had the same question. Now, of course, I know that's not how it works. Ann Patchett writes in her memoir, *This Is the Story of a Happy Marriage*, that sometimes one has to make things up to tell a true story. Patchett explains that when she includes dialogue in her memoir, she is not writing what her characters actually said, but what she believes they would have said. I could explain to Tagel that the same was true for Laura Ingalls Wilder, who might not have remembered exactly what her family members said but who knew them so well that she could imagine what they would have said. Yet I know that Tagel, who insists on accuracy, would be disappointed by this answer.

As I try to answer Tagel's question, I'm conscious that I'm conflating Laura the character with Laura Ingalls Wilder the author, but at this point, I'm still trying to keep it simple. I tell Tagel that Laura did extensive research: She went back to visit the towns where her family had lived, interviewed her younger sisters, Grace and Carrie, consulted family letters, and copied song lyrics from old hymnbooks so as to put words to the melodies Pa played on his honey-brown fiddle as Laura and her older sister, Mary, fell asleep in their trundle beds and Ma's knitting needles flashed in the moonlight. I kneel next to Tagel's bed as I answer her question, the moonlight streaming through her window and illuminating her earnest eyes and her still-unfurrowed brow. Tagel believes earnestly in Laura's story. I can't bear to be the one to ruin it for her.

And yet already Daniel is ruining it for me. One Shabbat afternoon I sit on the couch reading *Little House on the Prairie* to Liav and Tagel, who have just spent an hour building a fort out of blocks, sheets, and couch cushions. They tell Matan that he is not allowed to enter their fort—he didn't help them build it, and so he can't go inside without them. But Matan, eager to provoke his sisters, crawls under the sheet and declares, "It's my house now!"

I lose my reading audience. Liav and Tagel rush to defend their fort, leaving me alone on the couch with Laura and Mary, who are huddled outside their house in fear. In the chapter we are reading, "Indians in the House," Pa has gone off hunting, leaving Ma and baby Carrie home alone. Laura and Mary are outside the house when they see two Indians approaching, a knife and hatchet attached to the skunk skins they wear around their waists. Laura slips into the house and hides behind a slab of wood, terrified as she watches her mother accede to the Indians' demands that she hand over all of Pa's tobacco.

"See," I tell the kids, "Pa and Ma can't leave their home because then the Indians will come in and take everything they have."

"Matan, you're an Indian!" Tagel hollers, the parallel not lost on her. "It's our house. Just because we left for a few minutes doesn't mean you can take over."

But Daniel is disturbed by the scenario the kids are enacting. He is a professor of literature, and in the circles in which he travels, no one mentions the Little House books anymore without raising eyebrows. "Do you really want the kids to think of 'Indian' as a derogatory term?" We recently read the scene in which the Ingallses' neighbor, Mr. Scott, pronounces that the only good Indian is a dead Indian. "Would you read a book that says that the only good Jew is a dead Jew?" He worries about what our kids will think when Indians are referred to as wild, terrible, and savage—let alone as "Indians," a term I have only just begun to try to unpack for my Israeli children, who have never learned in school about the European exploration of America or its implications for the indigenous populations.

I tell him that I am trying to teach our children that books reflect the prejudices of the time in which they are written, and we have to take note of that context when we read them today. Daniel is not confident in my ability to regard the books I remember so fondly through a critical lens. Eventually we strike a deal: I will read the kids the Laura Ingalls Wilder books, but at the same time, I will read to myself a critical assessment of Wilder's life and writing, Caroline Fraser's *Prairie Fires*.

I learn as much from Fraser as my children learn from Wilder. When Wilder's books were originally published, their pale-yellow covers were emblazoned with the words "The True Story of an American Pioneer Family." But the story Wilder tells in her novels is more "folk art" than truth, as Fraser demonstrates. It is the story of her life, but only insofar as she wanted it to be remembered.

Throughout the series, Wilder elides much of the pain, sadness, and hardship of her childhood, portraying her family members as she would want others to come to know them. This is particularly evident in her depiction of Pa. As Fraser notes, Wilder emphasizes her father's successes as a breadwinner, downplaying his repeated failures to sustain a farm that could support his wife and four daughters. She does not tell us that he lied under oath when finalizing the application for his homestead land, or that he once snuck his family out of town to avoid paying rent. She depicts her father as a hardworking, self-reliant hero driven west by his pioneering spirit. In reality, though, his many mistakes and miscalculations left the family in such penury that he had no choice but to repeatedly sell their land and relocate, which explains why the family moved so frequently—from the Big Woods to the banks of Plum Creek to the shores of Silver Lake.

My children, like young readers of the Little House novels everywhere, assume that Laura's childhood was idyllic, spent wading in creeks, picking wildflowers, and chasing jackrabbits through tall grass. They do not know the truth about Pa's economic hardships, nor would I want them to know it. Not yet. There comes a time when all of us realize our parents are flawed human beings. Some children come to this realization at a very young age, and others are spared until significantly later. It can be a great gift to believe that one has been blessed with good parents. I would like my children to hold on to this gift for as long as possible.

I am selective about what I share with my children from my reading of Fraser's critical assessment. But to Tagel, who is so fixated on accuracy, I want to explain that there are many reasons for telling our stories, and accurate documentation is only one of them. Before writing the series for children that made her famous, Wilder penned a memoir about her childhood, *Pioneer Girl*. It was 1929, the stock market had just crashed, and Wilder, then sixty-two, was thousands of dollars in debt. She had spent a lifetime weathering booms and busts, and she knew the only way forward was through hard work. But what did hard work mean when the banks were collapsing and investors were jumping to their deaths?

Wilder, in need of cash, began to write *Pioneer Girl*, summoning her memories of the Big Woods, the open prairie, the covered wagons, and the claim shanties in the hope that she might recoup her losses by publishing her story. She filled six handwritten tablets with many of the details that she would later leave out of the books she went on to publish—her father's crushing debt, her sister Mary's battle with scarlet fever, her infant brother Freddie's death at nine months. When she was finished, she sent the manuscript to her daughter, Rose Wilder Lane, to edit and type up. She noted which details were intended for her daughter's eyes alone, like the terrible lice that she and her sisters contracted when living in town. From the very beginning, Wilder was selective about which parts of her story she saw fit to share. But then again, aren't we all?

"Ima, can you read to me from one of your journals?" Tagel asks me one day after stumbling upon the pile of colorful notebooks in the back of our attic closet.

"I'm not sure," I tell her, worried about what I'll find if I crack open the spines of those hardbound volumes that I haven't touched in years but can't quite bring myself to throw away.

Tagel looks into my eyes, as if trying to gauge whether I am in the right mood to hear what she wants to tell me next. "Actually, I started reading the pink notebook with the jewel on the cover. I thought it would be OK. I read the first page, where you say that you decided to start writing in a new journal because now you were a mother. You wrote that the day Matan was born was the best day of your life. But what about the day I was born? You had two babies that day, not just one!"

I am more amused than disconcerted to hear that Tagel has been reading through my journals, and I wonder what else she has stumbled upon in those pages. No doubt the memories I've shared with her are very different from the version she'd find in those volumes. There is a reason I have not looked at them since.

Wilder's daughter, who was also a writer, had no luck when she tried to submit her mother's manuscript for publication. But at the suggestion of an encouraging editor, she began working with her mother to revise the memoir into a series of novels for school-age children, unfolding primarily from young Laura's perspective. Mother and daughter went on to collaborate for decades, in a relationship that was both fruitful and fraught. Wilder's books made her rich in her lifetime—she received several literary awards and honors as well as fan mail from children all over the world. Settling the frontier had led to repeated frustration, but writing about the frontier proved enormously lucrative. "It turned out there was indeed gold on the farm—but in books, not crops," Fraser notes.[64]

I explain to Tagel that the Little House books were a sort of second draft, written after Wilder had already completed a memoir. "She already had her journals, but then she made them into stories." Tagel proposes that maybe she should start keeping two notebooks—one to write down everything she remembers, and one to make up stories. One day, she says, she will publish all her stories, but she'll keep her journal for herself. "I'll be better at hiding it from my kids than you are," she tells me, looking up cautiously to see if I smile.

✻

I am wary of the degree of control I exert when reading aloud to my children. The kids usually want to read more—one more story, one more chapter—and so it falls to me to decide how many pages we will read, and whether we will stop on a sad note or continue on to a more hopeful point in the story. "I'm not going to read until everyone has brushed their teeth," I might pronounce one evening, with the arbitrariness of a tyrannical despot. And the kids, who want to hear the story, have no choice but to comply.

In his short story "The Bus Driver Who Wanted to Be God," the Israeli author Etgar Keret compares the power of a bus driver—who can decide arbitrarily when to keep the door open for a passenger arriving at the bus stop just a few seconds late and when to drive off—to the power of God, who can seemingly arbitrarily treat human beings with justice or mercy. Sometimes when reading aloud, I worry that I am like the bus driver who wanted to be God. Although the kids may choose which books we read, I am the one who determines what exactly it is that they are hearing. Sometimes I will change around the details of a story or add explanatory background without indicating that it's my own gloss. I can get a sense, from the kids' questions and expressions, of what they understand and what they misconstrue, and I can clarify and correct when necessary. I'm also free to add my own moralizing comments, hoping each time that I manage to pull it off undetected. I know it's not quite fair to marshal literature in service of teaching my children how I want them to behave. But I can't always stop myself.

In his final address to the people of Israel in the book of

Deuteronomy, Moses implores the people to follow God's word, neither adding nor subtracting from it: "You shall not add anything to what I command you or take anything away from it, but keep the commandments of your God that I enjoin upon you" (4:2). I wonder, when I add or change words to the books I read to my children, whether I am guilty of violating this commandment. What is the relationship between the written Torah—the Five Books of Moses—and the Oral Torah, the countless commentaries and interpretations that have resulted from centuries of engagement with that written text? Where does the text end and the commentary begin?

In reading aloud from the Little House books, I become the storyteller, channeling Wilder's voice. But when Wilder expresses sentiments that I find troubling, I try to interject my own explanations. At one point Laura asks Pa whether it will make the Indians mad that the government keeps forcing them to move west, and Pa cuts her off. He tells her not to ask any more questions, because it's time to go to sleep. Even though it is late for us, too, I encourage my children to ask these questions. As a citizen of the Jewish State, I am acutely conscious that we live in a land that is highly contested and that belongs, rightfully, to more than one nation. I want to think with my children about who has the right to a land, and what happens when two nations are unable to live side by side in peace. I do not offer answers, because I don't have them. But I know that I cannot simply close the book and turn off the light at the end of the chapter. In sharing the Little House books with my children, it is not just Wilder's story I am telling, but ours.

In the penultimate book in the Little House series, *These Happy Golden Years*—a volume we come to several months later, when we return to Wilder after a long hiatus—Laura takes a job teaching at a small school of five pupils in the Brewster settlement, twelve miles from her home. Laura boards with her employer, Mr. Brewster, and his sullen, resentful wife. Laura is miserable. Each week she cannot wait for the moment when Almanzo Wilder—whom she will eventually marry—pulls up in his cutter, the sleigh bells ringing merrily, to drive her home through the snow for the weekend.

We soon learn the reason for Mrs. Brewster's discontent. It is not just that she resents Laura's presence in her home. She is also unhappy living so far away, in a flat country beset by wind and cold. She wants to return East, but Mr. Brewster will not give up his land claim. One night we come to a chapter titled "A Knife in the Dark." I do not need to look at the picture of a woman in a long nightgown wielding a butcher knife at her angry husband lying before her, with Laura sitting upright and startled in bed, peering through the thin curtain that separates her bed from theirs. Even without the illustration, I remember how this chapter terrified me when I first read it as a child. It should not be the last chapter I read the girls before bed. "The next chapter is scary, so we are going to read it tomorrow," I tell them, grinding the bus to a halt.

As I sit there in their dark room waiting for them to fall asleep, my back propped against Liav's bed, I wonder if I should skip over that next chapter, or tone it down so it's not so terrifying. To what extent am I authorized to change the story? It's a question I ask not just when I am reading but also when I am writing. Am I bound to narrate the events of our lives as I best remember them? Whenever I am tempted to pull out that proverbial knife and cut and trim a story about our family, I think about Daniel, who reads everything I write. "You can tell it that way, but that's not how it happened," he'll sometimes comment when I show him a draft.

As Daniel often notes, many of the arguments in our marriage are about inconsistencies in the stories I tell. I am forever narrating our story as we are living it, sometimes even writing the ending before it has had time to unfold. There are costs to living inside my own head, as Daniel reminds me. Ann Patchett titled her memoir *This Is the Story of a Happy Marriage*, though it's as much about writing as it is about marriage. A happy marriage to Daniel makes me a better writer, but being a writer does not always make for a happy marriage.

The relationship between truth, journal, and memoir poses complicated ethical questions. My account of our family's reading life is certainly not the only way to tell our story; no doubt my children would each remember and record this period in their lives quite differently. Mary Karr—who has not only written several award-winning memoirs but is also the author of *The Art of Memoir*—writes about a truth contract between the writer and the reader. She argues that if a writer of memoir makes up events, it not only violates this contract but also prevents the memoirist from accessing the deeper truths that would only surface after working through that truth in successive drafts. But when I write about my life, I am less focused on uncovering truth than on making meaning.

When I learn about the discrepancies between Laura Ingalls Wilder's lived life and the story she tells in her Little House novels, I marvel at Wilder's ability to convert her life into art. How do we create meaning and beauty out of our lives before we and everything we hold most dear crumble to dust?

We start with the introspection necessary to identify our hopes and dreams. Only then can we find a way to tell our story that seems true not just to who we are but to what we most fervently desire. We trace that fine line where recollection meets aspiration—where the arc of our lives becomes the art of the story we wish to tell.

3

The Kind Family

MOSES'S LENGTHY ADDRESS TO THE PEOPLE IN THE book of Deuteronomy unfolds not chronologically but episodically. Moses narrates the journey away from Mount Sinai in chapter one, but then in chapters nine and ten he returns to tell about the revelation that took place on the mountain. This is Moses's version of events; he is free to tell it as he sees fit, piecing together the episodes into a narrative whose internal logic may make sense to him alone. We might think of Deuteronomy as Moses's patchwork of the past, a metaphor that makes even more sense to me when we finish the Little House books and move on to *All-of-a-Kind-Family* by Sydney Taylor.

In the *All-of-a-Kind Family* novels, the father works in a junk shop. Papa's job is to patch the rags and mold the scraps collected by peddlers, repurposing them for resale. In her biography of Taylor, *From Sarah to Sydney*, June Cummins observes that Taylor, like her father—on whom the character of Papa was based—was also in the business of recycling old materials, though in her case it was not junk but stories. Using her childhood recollections as her raw material, she wrote a series of five novels that set the imaginative stage on which the Jewish immigrant experience in America would be enacted for generations of readers.

Taylor, like Wilder, chronicled her childhood in a historical time and place that would forever be associated with her literary legacy. Taylor grew up three decades after Wilder's long winter and thousands of miles east of the Dakota Territory, on the pre–World War I Lower East Side, where the weather was considerably milder, yet Mama insisted on thick stockings for her five daughters, all dressed alike in stiffly starched white pinafores over dark woolen dresses. Taylor was one of five sisters, all of whom had the same names as their fictional counterparts: Ella, Henny, Sarah, Charlotte, and Gertie; middle sister Sarah changed her name to Sydney, and then married Ralph Taylor. The real-life Charlotte explained in her memoir that she and her sisters all attended the same public school, where they were once called into the principal's office to greet a group of Chinese women visitors. "They're all of a kind—an all-of-a-kind family," Charlotte remembered one of the visitors remarking, unwittingly furnishing Taylor's series with its title.[65]

The All-of-a-Kind Family novels are episodic, with each chapter featuring a self-contained narrative: The sisters shop for the Sabbath with their mother, prepare a giant pancake to serve to a visiting neighbor, and go on a family outing to Coney Island. In the final chapter of the first book in the series, Mama gives birth to a boy, to Papa's delight. The sisters—ranging in age from twelve to four—are excited about the new baby, but Ella points out that now that they have a brother, they're not really all-of-a-kind anymore. "In a way we are," Mama assures them, telling them that they are all close and loving and loyal to one another. As Charlie grows from a toddler to a young boy over the course of the next four books, my girls laughed at his misadventures and compared him to our increasingly rambunctious Yitzvi. Charlie climbs into the dumbwaiter—a kitchen cabinet in a shaft attached to a pulley—and giggles as his sister pulls him up and down, just like Yitzvi, who developed such a fascination with the elevator in our building that his sisters had to take turns riding up and down with him. We live in a four-story building; Yitzvi learned to recognize all the numbers from 0 to 3 before his second birthday.

The All-of-a-Kind family observes the Jewish holidays, but the children attend public school and are fully steeped in American culture. And so when I read the books to my Israeli children, I had to do a fair amount of explaining to familiarize them with those aspects of the American terrain we hadn't already traversed by horse and buggy. Thanks to Wilder, my kids knew about Santa Claus—whom little Charlie mistakes for the boogeyman—but they had not heard of the boogeyman. "What's so special about the Fourth of July?" they asked when Papa's best friend arrived with firecrackers and took the children out at night. American Independence Day was foreign to them, but the Pesach Seder and Purim play were not. I realized the irony of trying to translate the unfamiliar aspects of American culture to my Jewish children, given that Sydney Taylor wrote the All-of-a-Kind Family books in part to normalize Jewish culture for American children. As Cummins wrote in her biography of Taylor, "It was impossible to find books about Jewish children at bookstores or public libraries before *All-of-a-Kind Family*," published between 1951 and 1978 as a series of five books for young readers.[66]

Cummins hails Taylor as a "pioneer in ethnic literature for children."[67] As a child, I had not known how groundbreaking she was. By the time I became an independent reader in the late 1980s, there were plenty of Jewish heroines in the chapter books I found in my local public library—from Marilyn Sachs's

Call Me Ruth, about the child of Jewish immigrant parents, to Johanna Hurwitz's *The Rabbi's Girls*, about growing up in small-town America in the 1920s. Still, it was the All-of-a-Kind Family books that I read again and again.

Taylor, like Wilder, began writing novels romanticizing her childhood only later in life—she published the first All-of-a-Kind Family book when she was in her late forties. Upon hearing the news that her manuscript was accepted for publication, she called her mother in Florida, where her parents were wintering, and announced: "Mama, you're going to live forever."[68] But the Mama she immortalized in her stories—a serene, sensible bedrock of stability who always knew just what to do and say, much like Laura's Ma—was very different from her actual mother, the depressed, dissatisfied Cilly Brenner, who never felt at home in America and longed to return to the comforts she had enjoyed in Germany. The real-life Ella—the eldest sister—later recalled their mother's attempts to induce a miscarriage when pregnant with Gertie by jumping on and off tables and washtubs, to no avail. Cilly tried to kill herself twice, and ultimately ended her life at eighty-two, leaving behind a suicide note that read, "I am too sick and old to run a household. . . . It's time for me to go."[69] Wilder once said that "there were some stories I wanted to tell but would not be responsible for putting them in a book for children, even though I knew them as a child."[70] Presumably Taylor felt the same way.

As I read Taylor's stories to Matan, Liav, and Tagel, there was much they could identify with from their own experiences over a century later and halfway around the world. They, too, are resistant to helping around the house before the Sabbath— though unlike Mama, I don't hide buttons around the house for them to search for as they dust. In our home, too, the older

kids dote on their younger brother and have been known to argue about who gets to bathe him—though unlike Henny, they
have yet to hoodwink their friends into paying for the privilege
of witnessing the baby's bath. To my surprise, the drab, poky
tenement exerted as much of a hold on my kids' imagination as
the vast open prairie. They referred to the series as "The Kind
Family," and sometimes it really seemed that, inspired by the
five sisters, they were kinder to one another.

🙌

There are only five books in the All-of-a-Kind Family series,
and at the rate of a chapter a night, we finished the first four
books in less than two months. I thought we would be wise to
stop there. I wasn't sure whether the kids were ready for the final book, about Ella's romance with her boyfriend, Jules, and
her career on the vaudeville stage. The book is set just after the
end of World War I, when Jules returns from the battlefields in
Europe and is eager to resume courting Ella, if only they can
find some privacy from her nosy siblings. But Ella is not ready
to settle down. After years of directing Sunday school holiday
plays, she has begun taking professional singing lessons, and
soon after she is recruited by a theatrical agent who wants her
to participate in his traveling vaudeville show. Ella finds herself
drifting apart from Jules even as she continues to love him. She
wonders if it is selfish to desire a career of her own, or whether
it is selfish of Jules to expect that his life will become hers. These
are weighty considerations, and Liav and Tagel were only eight.
I thought perhaps they would appreciate the novel more when
they were a bit older.

   I ought to have known better. The moment I told the kids
that perhaps they weren't quite ready for *Ella of All-of-a-Kind*

Family, Liav ran off with the book—featuring an image of Ella and Jules embracing on a garden path—and began reading it on her own. I am sure there was much she did not understand, because anytime I happened to be within earshot while she was reading, she would ask me to explain the words she had trouble sounding out: What is vaudeville? Where is Broadway? What's a headliner? When she came to the last chapter—in which Ella decides to leave the traveling vaudeville company and join a choral group so that she can continue to live at home, close to Jules—I offered to read it aloud to her. Matan and Tagel, who had not read the previous chapters but were familiar with the characters from the earlier books, climbed atop the bed to listen in as well.

In the final scene, Ella and Jules sit down on a park bench near a small pond to have the conversation that will determine their future. Just moments after I begin reading, I can already hear my voice beginning to tremble; I always cry at romantic scenes, to my children's embarrassment and exasperation. "Ima, whatever happens, don't cry," Tagel groans. "It's so annoying when you cry so much that you can't even finish the sentence." I sigh. How can I explain to her that reading about romance at my age is so different from reading about romance at hers? When I read about Ella and Jules, one romantic scene summons countless others like beaus on a string, and suddenly it is not just Ella and Jules who are sitting on that park bench but also Anne of Green Gables and Gilbert Blythe, and Elizabeth Bennet and Mr. Darcy—and a much younger Daniel and I, too.

Fortunately, we have Matan to provide comic relief when I read the next line. "A penny for your thoughts," Jules tells Ella, eager to hear what will become of their romance. Surely the kids, who have not read the story before, are feeling as tense with anticipation? But it's clear that Matan, at least, has his mind elsewhere.

"A penny is like a shekel?" he asks me.

I look at him with eyebrows raised. "Huh?" I ask.

"Jules said he would give Ella a penny. How much is that worth?"

Is he for real? Is he really thinking about currency conversion at a time like this? I know that Matan will not let me continue reading until I respond.

"A penny is not worth very much. You can't buy anything for a penny. At least not now. Back then it was worth more."

Matan's eyes light up. "Is all money worth less now than it was then?" he asks, trying to wrap his mind around the concept of inflation.

"Yes," I say curtly, eager to get back to the book. But I can see the wheels turning fast and furiously in Matan's head. "That's amazing," he says. "So if I traveled back in time and brought my money with me, I could be a millionaire?"

I sigh. "Matan," I plead with him. "Ella and Jules are falling in love. Can we go back to the story?"

Ella tells Jules that she's quitting the vaudeville troupe, but she's going to continue taking singing lessons as part of a local choir. She explains that even though she won't earn a living on the stage, she'll continue to be devoted to music. Someday, she tells him, she'll sing to her children.

"*Our* children, Ella," Jules corrects her, and in the book's final line, he seals his declaration of love with a kiss. At this point I am tearing up again, Tagel is rolling her eyes at her overwrought mother, and Matan is still working on his get-rich-quick time travel scheme. Only Liav is beaming with happiness for the young couple, perhaps because she feels more invested in Ella and Jules's future, having read the final book on her own.

When I look at Liav's face, I realize I was wrong about what my children could handle. Liav understands that Ella's decision has not been easy, and that it's hard to choose between two things you really want. Though she's never heard the term "feminism" before, she has witnessed me rush home from teaching and burst in the door five minutes after she and her siblings got home from school, even though I promised I'd be home when they arrived. She has heard me negotiate with Daniel about who gets to work when, and who needs to stay home to pick up the younger kids at the end of the day. She understands that having a job is not always perfectly compatible with having a family, and that parents have to make choices and compromises.

Tagel, on the other hand, seems embarrassed by Ella and Jules, as if we have just walked past two people kissing on a park bench, which in a sense we have. She wants to stop and watch, but not if I'm there alongside her. Already she is venturing into territory she would rather traverse on her own, without her mother looking over her shoulder or reading to her aloud. One day after school I find Tagel on the couch reading a book called *Boy-Crazy Stacey*—she'd borrowed it from an English-speaking friend at school. When she sees me, she puts her finger inside the book to mark her place and takes it with her to her room, where she closes the door.

As my children begin reading books without me, including books that they don't even want me to know they are reading, I think about the end of Moses's life. At the conclusion of the book of Numbers, God tells Moses, "Ascend these heights of Avarim" (27:12). From this summit, Moses will be able to view the land that he will not be permitted to enter. The term "Avarim" comes from the same Hebrew root as the word for transitions and for crossing over. It is a variant of the term Moses uses when he pleads with God in the book of Deuteronomy to "let me cross over" into the Promised Land with the people (3:25). But God has a different transition planned for him: "When you have seen it, you shall be gathered to your kin" (Numbers 27:13).

Moses does not go gentle into that good night—at least not in the midrashic account. The rabbis imagine Moses pleading with God to let him enter the land. He asks God to rise from the throne of divine justice and sit instead on the throne of divine mercy, so that he might be spared the clutches of the Angel of Death. When God refuses, Moses entreats the various aspects of the created world to intercede with God on his behalf, but to no avail. There is to be no divine intercessor for Moses, the only human being to speak to God face-to-face.[71]

Does Moses ever fully resign himself to his fate? At the end of his life, he ascends Mount Nevo and God tells him, once again, that he will not be allowed to go any farther: "This is the land. . . . I will assign it to your offspring. I have let you see it with your own eyes, but you shall not cross there" (Deuteronomy 34:4). Moses still has the energy to keep going, if only God would let him: "Moses was a hundred and twenty years old when he died; his eyes were undimmed and his vigor unabated" (34:7). No wonder he writes the account of his death in tears. His eyes, undimmed, are bright from weeping.

4

The Sense of an Ending

MOSES CRIES WHEN HE COMES TO THE END OF HIS
story, and I can relate, given my propensity to grow teary-eyed
when I come to the end of a novel. Sometimes I cry because
the endings are truly sad—Uncle Morris dies when Maggie is
sent away from the house with the dolls behind the attic wall,
and Jess loses his best friend when Leslie crosses the bridge to
Terabithia for the final time, swinging perilously on a rope hung
from a crab apple tree over the flooded creek bed. But even if a
book doesn't end in the death of a beloved character, the ending
of the book means that it is time for us, as readers, to take our
leave.

When we come to the end of a book, sometimes it seems as
if the author is pulling the curtain closed before we are ready. At
the end of Edith Nesbit's *The Railway Children*, the father, who
was falsely imprisoned for espionage, finally returns, to the delight of his wife and three children, who have been sojourning in
a large white country house near a railway station, far from their
London home. In the book's final scene, Father steps off the train
into the arms of his oldest daughter, Bobbie. Bobbie calls Father
into the house, and the door is shut behind him. As readers,
we are eager to be privy to their long-awaited reunion, but just

at that moment Edith Nesbit steps in. "I think we will not open the door to follow him. I think that just now we are not wanted there," she writes, her use of "I think" jarringly reminding us that we are entirely at her mercy.

I cried when I came to the end of each of these books—*Behind the Attic Wall, Bridge to Terabithia, The Railway Children*, and of course *All-of-a-Kind Family*. I cried even though I was reading these books aloud to my children, who find it unsettling and embarrassing to witness my tears. But when I think about my favorite mothers in the novels I read to my children, so many of them cry, if not in front of their children, then certainly in front of their young readers. Nesbit's railway children know that their mother cries when she thinks about their missing father; her eyes are bright red when she comes to tuck the children into bed at night. In *Little Women*, Mrs. March makes no effort to hide her tears when speaking to Jo about their father, who is away at war. And in yet another book about an absent and much-longed-for father, *A Wrinkle in Time*, the oldest child, Meg, sees her mother's unhappiness through a crystal ball when traveling intergalactically to bring her father home.

I am fortunate that when I weep in front of my children, it is usually merely on account of something I am reading. This was true, too, for the rabbis of the Talmud, who describe being moved to tears by particular biblical passages. Each rabbi had a different verse that he was unable to recite without falling apart. Some of these verses were simply about terrible moments in the history of the Jewish people. But other rabbis wept over poignant moments of narrative drama—Rabbi Elazar, for instance, would cry whenever he came to the verse in which Joseph, who has been unable to hold back his own tears, reveals his identity to his brothers. Still other rabbis confess that they are moved to tears by verses that allude to the death of the righteous and to standing before God in judgment.[72]

The rabbis of the Talmud teach that "anyone who cries over a dead person too much is really crying over another dead person," suggesting that when we cry excessively, we are not always crying about what we think we are.[73] Sometimes when I weep while reading to my children, I suspect that I'm not just crying for the characters; I'm also mourning for something unresolved or unhealed in myself. I hope my children will learn this lesson, if not now, then someday: Literature can illuminate vast oceanic depths, like a lantern we carry down that treacherous spiral staircase into the unexplored chambers of our hearts.

⚜

One winter afternoon when it's already dark even though it's not yet time for dinner, Liav comes into the kitchen and asks me for a new book to read in English. I leap at her request—my kids are not always interested in my recommendations. We head to the closet where I keep all the books I am saving to read with them one day, many of which I salvaged from my childhood bedroom. Liav reaches for *Mandy*, the story of an orphan girl who discovers a deserted cottage with an overgrown garden, which she adopts and tends to as if it were her own, unaware that she is not as alone as she thinks. The illustration on the cover depicts a girl of about Liav's age kneeling to prune flowers along the stone pathway leading to the cottage, a pensive look on her face. "Who is this girl? Is this her garden?" Liav asks me, and before I can answer, she pulls the book close to her chest proprietarily. "This is the one I want to read."

I'm not sure about her choice. I always assumed this was a book I would read aloud to the kids, not a book they'd read to themselves. I've saved this novel since I was the same age as quiet, introverted Mandy, who would rather be on her own, reading and dreaming, than spending time with her friends. I remember how excited I was to learn that the author, Julie Edwards, is in fact Julie (Andrews) Edwards, the star of *The Sound of Music* and *Mary Poppins*. Mandy represented a part of my childhood that I was excited to share with my children, an old friend I wanted to introduce them to someday—and yet here was Liav, eager to go off and meet her without me.

Liav reads the brief description on the back of the book. "So Mandy is an orphan, like Sara in *A Little Princess*," she muses. "And she finds a secret garden and takes care of it, just like *The Secret Garden* you read us, Ima." I hadn't realized, until that moment, that *Mandy* is essentially a recombination of these two novels by Frances Hodgson Burnett, both of which I'd read aloud to the twins. But Liav is right.

"Can I read you the first chapter?" I ask her, flipping through the dog-eared pages as the story comes back to me, along with the stories it echoes: Mandy's attic bedroom with the small skylight recalls the garret of the little princess, and the sparrow Mandy befriends is like the robin that leads the way to the secret garden. It is as if the novel we are reading is a palimpsest, and I can still make out the traces of the stories that came before.

There are critics who argue that there are only a few plots—that all stories follow seven basic plots, or sometimes it's nine, or just three. Maybe it's true. Maybe there are just a few stories we keep telling. Perhaps Mandy is the little princess in the secret garden. But I don't think it's so simple. A lifetime of reading the Bible and its many centuries of midrash and commentary has taught me that later stories rework and expand upon earlier stories, combining them and reading them in a new light. When, in the book of Samuel, David is married off to Merav even though he loves her sister Michal, he is also Jacob in the book of Genesis who is married off to Leah even though he loves Rachel. When, in the book of Judges, Gideon resists God's call to deliver his people and insists that God show him a sign, he is also a reluctant Moses at the burning bush in the book of Exodus. The later stories are informed by the earlier ones, and the earlier stories, in turn, are part of the later ones. If we have read the stories that came before, we can more deeply appreciate their later reworkings.

I do not end up reading much of *Mandy* to Liav. When I am two pages into the first chapter, Yitzvi falls off a stool in the kitchen and I have to run to help him. By the time I return to the couch, Liav is absorbed in the story and Matan has announced he is hungry for dinner. As I stand in the kitchen chopping vegetables for a salad, looking over at Liav as she ventures forth in the book without me, I know, of course, that I am not Moses. And yet I cannot help thinking that part of his story is mine.

5

❧

Weaning My Children All Over Again

SO MUCH OF BEING A PARENT IS ABOUT LEARNING TO let go. There is joy in watching my children become more in-dependent and self-sufficient, but there is also the melancholy and poignance of knowing that they will never again need me in quite the same way. From the moment they are born, they are already weaning.

I cried for several weeks each time I weaned my children, conscious that the time had come for them to move on. Breast-feeding was one of my greatest pleasures as a mother. When I breastfed, the baby's head nestled in the crook of my elbow and a soft tiny hand reaching behind to caress my back, I nearly al-ways held a book in my other hand. I was able to be at once fully present for my child and fully immersed in the novel I was reading or the Torah I was chanting to them.

When Moses addresses the people at the end of his life in the book of Deuteronomy, he reminds them of the manna that rained down from the heavens in the mornings and covered the earth in a fine flaky layer like frost. In the Torah, the taste of manna is described as *shad hashamen*, a sort of rich cream. The Hebrew word *shad* is also the word for "breast," which leads the Talmud to comment that "just as a baby tastes different flavors from the breast, so too with the manna, every time the Jewish people ate it, they found in it many flavors."[74] Throughout the wilderness journey, when the Jewish people were still in their infancy, they nursed on manna from heaven as Moses distilled the Torah for them.

Of course, no child nurses forever. The manna stops falling for the Israelites when they enter the land of Canaan. As Moses tells the people in Deuteronomy, "For the Lord your God is bringing you into a good land . . . a land where you may eat food without stint, where you will lack for nothing" (8:7–9). Moses, who earlier in the Torah compares himself to the nursemaid of the Israelites, will no longer be present to bring down God's word from heaven. The Israelites will have to find their own sources of physical and spiritual sustenance.

Of all my children, the youngest, Yitzvi, was the hardest to wean—not because he wanted to continue breastfeeding but because I wasn't ready to stop. One morning, when he was about eight months, he woke from his morning nap just as I was sitting down to breakfast, and I decided to eat before I fed him. His siblings were all in school, the house was quiet, and I let him sit on my lap as I peeled off the foil-backed cover on my container of yogurt. The sun streamed through the window as I dipped the spoon in, breaking the smooth surface like a shovel breaking through a field of newly fallen snow. As I lifted my hand to my mouth, drawing it over my baby's head, he stopped me, seized hold of my wrist, and directed the spoon to his mouth. I was too astonished to do anything other than surrender control and sit back as my breakfast was hijacked by my baby, to whom I proceeded to feed the entire yogurt. Afterward, when I offered him the breast, he refused, and I was devastated.

As my children become increasingly independent readers,

it is as if I am weaning them all over again. Now, when I come into my older children's rooms to read to them at night, it is usually only after they have read to themselves for a while. Increasingly they are reading books I never read, or books I fear I'll never have the chance to reread. They go to the library themselves, or they borrow from friends, or they ask me to buy them books their friends have recommended. Not long ago Tagel came home from a friend's house insistent that I buy her a graphic novel called *Tzipor Lavan*, Hebrew for "white bird." I looked up the title on the internet, only to discover that the book—a Holocaust story about a Jewish girl hidden by a school friend in a barn in Nazi-occupied France—had been translated from English.

When R. J. Palacio's *White Bird* arrives, the twins can't stop fighting over it. For a while the girls pass our copy back and forth. But when they can't agree whose turn it is to read next, they arrange themselves on the couch so that they can read simultaneously, their fingers holding the book open to mark their places. It looks like Tagel is at the beginning and Liav is about to finish—hence Tagel is sitting to Liav's left—but in fact, Tagel has already finished the book and has returned to the beginning to read it all over again.

At night in bed—after they have already each read the book twice since its arrival just a day earlier—they insist that they must read it aloud to me. Liav makes room on her bed for me to lie down, and Tagel wants to hear, too, so she kneels on the floor next to Liav's bed, following along with her eyes until Liav comes to the end of the chapter, and it's her turn to read aloud. The arrangement suits me perfectly—I can focus on the images and listen to the words. Every so often I interrupt to point out a line that speaks to me; I am particularly excited about the epigraphs from Muriel Rukeyser, since it's as close as my children will let me come to reading poetry with them. But for the most part I just listen.

I marvel that, for the first time, my twins are reading to me not because they require my assistance but because they are so deeply in love with a book that they feel compelled to share it with me. I understand the impulse. It is the same impulse that motivates much of my reading aloud to them—when I love a book, I want to read it aloud, as if I had originally spoken those words myself. It is also the same impulse that led me to work as a translator—if I'm reading something powerful and affecting in Hebrew, I want to share it with everyone I know, including those who don't speak the language. I also want to imagine what it would be like to write it myself, which is what I do when I translate—I rewrite for myself, but in English. Both when I read aloud and when I translate, I am sharing a text I love with others, and making it my own.

Liav and Tagel continue to read to me late into the night, even though it is the same night we "spring ahead" into daylight saving time, which means we'll lose an hour of sleep. The parent in me knows that I ought to turn off the light and let my girls fall asleep. But the reader in me keeps acceding to their pleas for "just one more chapter"—because we can't stop now, with the bats flying about the barn; and we can't stop now, in the field of bluebells; and we can't stop now, with the war almost over. I wonder if we are moving into the next stage of our reading relationship, in which my children and I recommend books to one another. It used to be that I supplied all the books, just as I cooked and provided the food they ate. Now every so often the twins will make dinner for the family, boiling the pasta themselves and experimenting with a sauce in the blender. The tables are turning.

I suspect that my kids are becoming good cooks because I am so hopeless in the kitchen. My limitations leave space for them to cultivate new interests and skills. According to the Kabbalistic tradition, God had to withdraw and contract to allow for the creation of the world. The Torah begins with God's withdrawal, and it ends with Moses's withdrawal from the historical stage to allow the people to enter the land independently. As a parent, I may feel as if I am letting go, but perhaps I am just pulling back, enabling my children to grow and explore and create new worlds of their own.

CONCLUSION

The Promised Land

SOMETIMES AT NIGHT, AFTER THE YOUNGER KIDS ARE in bed, I bring the novel I am reading into the twins' room and read on the floor, by the light of their small bedside lamp. It is a different kind of reading together: Tagel is soaring across the Pacific with *The Twenty-One Balloons*, Liav is in Vienna with *Lisa and Lottie*, and I'm in a paradise lost and regained. I miss snuggling together in bed, being part of the same story. But there is the rediscovered pleasure of sustained time to read to myself, instead of just stealing a glance at my poetry book while the soup simmers. At some point, I hope, even my younger children will all read to themselves at night. Is that not paradise, or at least the promised land?

From paradise to the promised land, the story of my family's reading life has unfolded against the backdrop of the Bible's narratives. It is a story about beginnings—the first books we read as parents, the books that create our world. It is a story about an exodus and a journey to freedom that our kids undertake when they learn to read on their own. It is a story about the sacred spaces we create when we connect with our children over what is most important to us. It is a story about traveling through the wilderness, going through periods when we navigate our ambivalence and uncertainty as we try to forge a way forward. It is a story about taking our children as far as we can until we recognize that the time has come for us to let go, and for them to move ahead—and read onward—independently.

In Jewish tradition it is customary to finish reading from the Torah and then immediately return to the beginning. On Simchat Torah—a festival that takes place at the conclusion of the autumn harvest holiday of Sukkot—Jews read the final Torah portion, which recounts the death of Moses, who ascends Mount Nevo and looks out over the land he is forbidden to enter. Just moments later, another Torah scroll is brought before the congregation and rolled all the way to the beginning, to the story of the creation of the world and the first human beings.

The story of the first human beings concludes with Adam and Eve banished from the Garden of Eden, their entry barred by a fiery ever-turning sword. There is no going back to Eden. At some point all my children will decide they have graduated from the board books and picture books that line the shelves in their bedrooms, no matter how many times I might want to read them again. Having eaten from the Tree of Knowledge, they cannot go back to the simplicity of many of the stories that once brought them such joy. Not much happens in *The Snowy Day*, as my younger daughter points out when I ask if she'd like to hear it one cold winter evening. "The snowball melts in Peter's pocket. I already know that book," she tells me.

"Yes, but then when he wakes up in the morning, new snow has fallen. There will always be new snow."

Shalvi shakes her head. To her mind, *The Snowy Day* is over. And while it's still hard to imagine a time when no one in my house will want me to read *The Very Hungry Caterpillar* over and over, eventually even my youngest child will crawl into his own cocoon, curling up under the covers to read to himself.

Now that we have no more babies and even our toddler is growing up, there are books I suspect I shall not return to for a very long time. We've always kept the board books on the bottom shelves of our bookcase so that little toddler hands can easily access them; often at night I would stumble over a series of small square board books strewn across our hallway like stones on a footpath. These days no one reaches for those books anymore, and I wonder if we should use that space instead for the heavy Eyewitness reference books my kids enjoy leafing through, about painting and world history and wildflowers. As I rearrange the books on the shelf to correspond to my children's shifting reading preferences, I think about which books they are no longer interested in, and which books they never would have considered reading just one year earlier.

As a parent, it is difficult to remain oblivious to time's passage. Often our kids could not do yesterday what they can do today: The child who couldn't crawl six months ago is soon walking from one end of the apartment to the other. And yet I so rarely take the time to document these strides. When we visit friends and cousins, my children are dazzled by the photo albums—not just by the carefully selected images showcasing every family member's development but also by the notion that someone would take the time to memorialize in this manner. "Why don't we have photo albums like that?" they ask me, and I am hard-pressed to answer.

I used to feel bad about the photo albums, just like I felt bad that my kids didn't come home to freshly cooked meals every afternoon, and that I've never been interested in fancy accessories. But the older my kids get, the more I have learned to let go of the mother I am not, and to embrace the mother I am. I'll never be fancy like Nancy, no matter how many lessons my daughters give me. And anytime I try to cook anything at all complicated, I'm likely to make silly mistakes worthy of Amelia Bedelia. I'm grateful my kids can laugh alongside me.

Instead of lamenting our lack of photo albums, I look up and down the many bookcases that line our walls and realize that the books we have read serve as our memory keepers. The plethora of books about cars and trucks reminds me of my son's vehicle phase, when the hero of every story we read had to have four wheels. The Angelina Ballerina books transport me back to my daughter's early ballet lessons, when I used to pick her up from school and watch her dance through the keyhole because the teacher was strict about keeping the studio door closed. *The Penderwicks*, about the adventures of four sisters vacationing in a summer home, is a memento of the summer when I read the book to my children by flashlight in the dark basement of my parents' beach house rental. "Remember the summer of *The Long Winter*?" my daughter will ask me, and I know she's referring to the August we read Laura Ingalls Wilder on the beach together, shielding ourselves from the blazing sun under an umbrella while Laura's hands were so numb from cold that she could barely grasp the horse's reins.

I wonder what will happen to those shared memories now that my children prefer to read to themselves. When my kids are reading their own books—especially books that I have never read—we might as well be in different countries, even if we are all reading in the same room. These days Matan is reading a series about spies and criminals on his e-reader. Every so often he'll announce to me that he's finished another book in the series, but when I ask him what it is about, he is too busy

searching for the next volume in the "library," which is also online. Liav and Tagel, who now have completely separate social
circles, have begun sharing books, but they are no longer interested in my recommendations. The books I've saved for them
feel dated, too American, too far removed from their world.
They reject a novel I show them about a Jewish girl on roller
skates on the Lower East Side; instead, they return home from
school with a series of graphic novels about teenagers who surf.
I leaf through the pages when they are not around, and it is as
if I am listening in on their conversations late at night, after I've
closed their door and they've promised to whisper only a little
bit more.

Nowadays when the older kids and I read together at bedtime, we are often studying Torah. In the world of Jewish text
study, the term "Torah" is interpreted broadly as referring to any
sacred literature. Tagel and I are studying the book of Judges,
from the prophetic books of the Hebrew Bible. Matan and I
are learning Mishnah, a collection of rabbinic teachings from
the early centuries of the Common Era. Liav and I are studying
the Talmudic discussion about the laws of the Purim holiday.
Each evening I read to them a chapter or a section, and they
respond with questions and comments that offer a window into
what they are thinking and how they are feeling. Tagel wants to
know what Jephthe's daughter did when she ran off to the hills
after learning that her father had inadvertently vowed to take
her life; if I had made such a terrible vow, she asks, what would
I do? Matan asks whether it is really OK to recite one's prayers
while riding a donkey, and whether that means he can go late to
school and recite his morning prayers en route. Their questions
lead me to invoke other texts, which in turn connect with other
aspects of their experience, and once again I find that I'm not

just teaching my children how to read texts; I'm also teaching myself how to read my children.

If I survey the long arc of our family's reading life, in a sense we have come full circle. When my children were infants, I used to chant to them from the weekly Torah portion while they nursed. Now I study Torah with them at bedtime. Our minds are in the same place like they were in the beginning, at the very beginning of their lives.

It all comes back to the beginning. The Torah is the source of the stories that Jews have been telling for millennia: Genesis, Exodus, Leviticus, Numbers, Deuteronomy. We read our stories—the developments in our lives, and the books we share—against the backdrop of the Torah's narrative, in the hope that our children will continue this story. They are the next chapter, growing so quickly that I can barely remember what it was once like. It is hard to believe that we are already here, at this stage in our family's journey, with children who read to themselves and write their own stories in the pages of their journals—what happened, what is happening, and what they can only imagine is yet to come. I look forward, wistfully, to reading on.

Acknowledgments

GENESIS. BEFORE EVERY BOOK IS WRITTEN, THERE IS nothingness. The blank page, a formless void. I am grateful to those who coaxed this book forth: my agent, Deborah Harris, a dear friend and mentor; and my editor, Elisabeth Dyssegaard, who never stopped believing in me. Thanks, too, to the dedicated staff at The Deborah Harris Agency and at St. Martin's Press.

Exodus. Writing a book is not backbreaking, but it also isn't always a labor of love. I am thankful for the support, compassion, and kindness of so many dear friends and neighbors: Elisa Albert, Gila Ashkenazy, Anaelle Attias Nowotny, Sally Berkovic, Galit and Alon Bezalel, Yisrael Campbell, Naomi Danis, Galya Diller-Sacks, Ruti Ebenstein, Nina Fischer, Shira Fischer, Rachel Furst, Rabbi Daniel Goldfarb, Miriam Goldstein, Izzy and Abby Gordan-Uhrman, Stu Halpern, Josh Kulp, Shana Schick, and Susan Weidman Schneider. I am deeply indebted to the talented and dedicated Tammy Hepps, publicist and confidante extraordinaire. Tremendous thanks to my parents and to my siblings—Naamit Gerber, Ariella Kurshan, and Eytan Kurshan—for being my pillar of fire on the other end of the line at all hours of the night.

Every book may be read, on some level, as a commentary on

the Torah received on Mount Sinai. This book drew inspiration from the Torah I have been privileged to learn from my teacher Avivah Zornberg, my regular study partners Yavni Bar-Yam and Yedida Lubin, and the faculty and students at the Conservative Yeshiva and Beit Midrash Harel. Thanks, too, to Jason Rogoff and the Hakhel Hashkamah minyan, for ensuring that words of Torah are always on my lips.

Leviticus. I am so grateful to the family members who provided me with the sacred space and quiet in which to work by caring lovingly for our children on many occasions: Alisa and Neil Kurshan, Rella Feldman and Curtiss Pulitzer, Estie and Elizur Agus and family, Michael and Nira Feldman, Joe Feldman and Dana Septimus, Mindy and Eric Hecht, Keren and Effi Warshavsky, and all our other siblings, nieces, and nephews.

Numbers. For helping me navigate the uncertain wilderness of the writing process, I am so appreciative of the wise counsel and incisive edits of all who commented on early chapters and drafts: Ilana Blumberg, George Eltman, Ruth Franklin, Naamit Gerber, Jessica Kasmer-Jacobs, Erin Leib, Anna Squires Levine, Ayelet Libson, and Elisheva Urbas, as well as my parents and siblings. My deepest debt of gratitude to Paola Tartakoff, who read the entire manuscript multiple times and taught me that a corollary of "Love your neighbor as yourself" is to treat your best friend's writing as if it is your own.

Deuteronomy. My heart overflows with love and gratitude for my husband, Daniel Feldman, who always insisted it was my story to tell, and for our children, to whom this book is dedicated, the inspiration for it all.

Reading Recommendations

A partial list of the titles discussed in these pages:

Picture Books
Miss Nelson Is Missing / Harry Allard, illus. James Marshall
The Steadfast Tin Soldier / Hans Christian Andersen
Otto: The Story of a Mirror / Ali Bahrampour
Hello Lighthouse / Sophie Blackall
Birthday Monsters / Sandra Boynton
But Not the Hippopotamus / Sandra Boynton
The Going to Bed Book / Sandra Boynton
Mike Mulligan and His Steam Shovel / Virginia Lee Burton
The Very Hungry Caterpillar / Eric Carle
Princess Smartypants / Babette Cole
Freight Train / Donald Crews
Chirri & Chirra (series)/ Kaya Doi
Ella Kazoo Will Not Brush Her Hair / Lee Fox
The Seven Silly Eaters / Mary Ann Hoberman
Angelina Ballerina / Katharine Holabird
Peter's Chair / Ezra Jack Keats
The Snowy Day / Ezra Jack Keats
The Philharmonic Gets Dressed / Karla Kuskin
George and Martha (series) / James Marshall
The Paper Bag Princess / Robert Munsch
Five Minutes' Peace / Jill Murphy
The Watermelon Seed / Greg Pizzoli
Before You Were Born / Howard Schwartz
Tell Me a Mitzi / Lore Segal
The Cat in the Hat / Dr. Seuss
One Fish, Two Fish, Red Fish, Blue Fish / Dr. Seuss
Gregory, the Terrible Eater / Mitchell Sharmat
Wild About Books / Judy Sierra
The Giving Tree / Shel Silverstein
Caps for Sale / Esphyr Slobodkina
Brave Irene / William Steig
Doctor De Soto / William Steig
Pete's a Pizza / William Steig
Spinky Sulks / William Steig
Yellow & Pink / William Steig

The Library / Sarah Stewart
The Blueberry Pie Elf / Jane Thayer
Alexander and the Terrible, Horrible, No Good, Very Bad Day / Judith Viorst
Cherries and Cherry Pits / Vera B. Williams
The Queen Who Couldn't Bake Gingerbread / Dorothy Van Woerkom
A New Coat for Anna / Harriet Ziefert
Harry the Dirty Dog / Gene Zion
The Passover Parrot / Evelyn Zusman

Series for Early Readers
Ivy & Bean / Annie Barrows
Danny and the Dinosaur / Syd Hoff
My Happy Life / Rose Lagercrantz
Frog and Toad / Arnold Lobel
Fancy Nancy / Jane O'Connor
Amelia Bedelia / Peggy Parish
Clementine / Sara Pennypacker
Morris Goes to School / B. Wiseman

Chapter Books
Little Women / Louisa May Alcott
Fudge / Judy Blume
A Little Princess / Frances Hodgson Burnett
The Secret Garden / Frances Hodgson Burnett
Behind the Attic Wall / Sylvia Cassedy
Beezus and Ramona (series) / Beverly Cleary
Matilda / Roald Dahl
The Twenty-One Balloons / William Pène du Bois
Mandy / Julie Andrews Edwards
The Hundred Dresses / Eleanor Estes
Harriet the Spy / Louise Fitzhugh
The Rabbi's Girls / Joanna Hurwitz
The Phantom Tollbooth / Norton Juster
Lisa and Lottie / Erich Kästner
A Wrinkle in Time (series) / Madeleine L'Engle
The Railway Children / E. Nesbit
Mrs. Frisby and the Rats of NIMH / Robert C. O'Brien
White Bird / R. J. Palacio
Bridge to Terabithia / Katherine Paterson
Call Me Ruth / Marilyn Sachs
The Little Prince / Antoine de Saint-Exupéry
Five Little Peppers and How They Grew / Margaret Sidney
A Tree Grows in Brooklyn / Betty Smith
All-of-a-Kind Family (series) / Sydney Taylor
Charlotte's Web / E. B. White
Little House on the Prairie (series) / Laura Ingalls Wilder

Notes

1. Genesis Rabbah 1:1, 1:4; Song of Songs Rabbah 5:11.
2. M. Berachot 5:1.
3. Berachot 26b.
4. Hullin 60b.
5. Genesis Rabbah 8:4.
6. Genesis Rabbah 8:10.
7. Hagigah 15b.
8. Ecclesiastes Rabbah 7:13.
9. Taanit 5b.
10. Andrew Solomon, *Far from the Tree: Parents, Children, and the Search for Identity* (New York: Scribner, 2012).
11. Eruvin 100b.
12. Avodah Zarah 8a.
13. Genesis Rabbah 17:4.
14. Tanchuma Noah 9.
15. Pirkei d'Rabbi Eliezer 24.
16. See, for instance, Sotah 8b.
17. Tanchuma Vayera 23:5.
18. Pirkei d'Rabbi Eliezer 38.
19. Mekhilta d'Rabbi Yishmael, Nezikin 1:2.
20. Tanchuma Pekudei 3; see also Niddah 30b.
21. Sotah 12a.
22. Tanchuma Pekudei 9.
23. Beitzah 16a.
24. Gittin 43a.
25. M. Avot 3:6.
26. M. Berachot 9:3.
27. Shabbat 88b.
28. Tanchuma Vaera 6.
29. See Rashi on Exodus 4:13, based on Pirkei d'Rabbi Eliezer 40.
30. M. Rosh Hashanah 3:8.
31. Hagigah 2a.
32. M. Avot 1:1.
33. M. Avot 5:21.
34. M. Avot 2:8.
35. Y. Peah 1:1.
36. M. Avot 2:16.
37. Eruvin 22a.

38. Natalia Ginzburg, *Family Lexicon,* trans. Jenny McPhee (London: Daunt Books, 2018), xv.
39. Megillah 25b.
40. Menachot 29a; Tanchuma Buber Shmini 11; Bemidbar Rabbah 12:8. I am indebted to Avivah Zornberg for first bringing these midrashim to my attention.
41. Avivah Zornberg, *The Hidden Order of Intimacy: Reflections on the Book of Leviticus* (New York: Schocken, 2022), 47–48.
42. Menachot 99b.
43. Bava Batra 99a.
44. Yoma 54a.
45. M. Yadayim chapter 3; Megillah 7a.
46. Megillah 29a.
47. Y. Berakhot 1:2 [3b].
48. Numbers Rabbah 18:21.
49. Also see Rashi on Exodus 12:36, based on Mekhilta d'Rabbi Yishmael 12:35.
50. Rashi on Taanit 30b.
51. Genesis Rabbah 98:2. Also see Rashi on Genesis 49:1.
52. Sanhedrin 97b.
53. Shabbat 67a.
54. Beverly Cleary, *A Girl from Yamhill: A Memoir* (New York: Avon, 1988), 339.
55. Numbers Rabbah 16:7.
56. Cleary, *A Girl from Yamhill,* 24.
57. Rashi on Numbers 33:1.
58. Eruvin 54a.
59. Virginia Woolf, *A Room of One's Own* (London: Hogarth Press, 1929), 58, 62.
60. Bava Batra 14b.
61. Bava Batra 15a.
62. Natalia Ginzburg, *The Little Virtues,* trans. Dick Davis (New York: Arcade Publishing, 1989), 107.
63. Sanhedrin 21b.
64. Caroline Fraser, *Prairie Fires: The American Dreams of Laura Ingalls Wilder* (New York: Picador, 2017), 489.
65. June Cummins, *From Sarah to Sydney: The Woman Behind All-of-a-Kind-Family* (New Haven, CT: Yale University Press, 2021), 34.
66. Cummins, *From Sarah to Sydney,* 232.
67. Cummins, *From Sarah to Sydney,* 322.
68. Cummins, *From Sarah to Sydney,* 221.
69. Cummins, *From Sarah to Sydney,* 261.
70. Fraser, *Prairie Fires,* 396.
71. Tanchuma Buber Vaetchanan 2.
72. Hagigah 4b.
73. Moed Katan 27b.
74. Yoma 75a.

About the Author

Sharon Gabay

Ilana Kurshan is a graduate of Harvard University and the University of Cambridge. She has worked in literary publishing both in New York and in Jerusalem, serving as a translator, a foreign rights agent, and the book reviews editor of *Lilith* magazine. Kurshan is the author of *If All the Seas Were Ink*, winner of the Sami Rohr Prize for Jewish Literature.